FROM
CANTON
TO
CALIFORNIA

FROM
CANTON
TO
CALIFORNIA

The Epic of
Chinese Immigration

Corinne K. Hoexter

Four Winds Press   New York

TO HERBERT AND VIRGINIA,
WHO STARTED IT ALL

Library of Congress Cataloging in Publication Data
Hoexter, Corinne K   From Canton to California.
Bibliography: p.   Includes index.
Summary: A history of the Chinese in the United
States from their early days in California to the present,
including the biography of Dr. Ng Poon Chew, who, as
editor of the first Chinese language newspaper in the
United States became a leader of all Chinese Americans.
1.   Chinese Americans—California—History—Juvenile
literature.   2.   Ng Poon Chew, 1866–1931—Juvenile
literature.   3.   Chinese Americans—California—Biography
—Juvenile literature.   4.   Journalists—California—
Biography—Juvenile literature.   [1.   Chinese Americans—
History.   2.   Ng Poon Chew, 1866–1931.   3.   Journalists.
4.   Chinese Americans—Biography]   I.   Title.
F855.2.C5H63   979.4'004'951   [92]   76–14504
ISBN 0-590-07344-3

Published by Four Winds Press
A Division of Scholastic Magazines, Inc., New York, N.Y.
Copyright © 1976 by Corinne Hoexter
All rights reserved
Printed in the United States of America
Library of Congress Catalog Card Number: 76–14504

Book design by Kathleen F. Westray

1 2 3 4 5 80 79 78 77 76

CONTENTS

NOTE ON ROMANIZATION OF CHINESE NAMES

Most Mandarin names are romanized according to the Wade-Giles system, the one in most common use among scholars, except for those well known in English such as Tzu-hsi, Chiang Kai-shek and Sun Yat-sen.

In the case of Cantonese names, words and expressions, because there are several dialects with different pronunciations, I have had to choose the one most often used in my sources, i.e., *gum shan, fan qui* and Ng Poon Chew.

ACKNOWLEDGMENTS

WHEN I was working on a biography of Frederick Douglass, my old friend Virginia Kee, for many years a teacher in social studies and bilingual programs at a junior high school in the heart of Chinatown, New York, said to me, only half in jest, "I wish you could find a Chinese Frederick Douglass. The students I teach have no idea that any Chinese were involved in American history." Her husband, Dr. Herbert Kee, himself a fifth-generation American, nodded agreement. All the time I was finishing the Douglass book, her words rang in my ears. They had touched a sympathetic chord; from my childhood I can remember being fascinated by stories about China. Many Chinese friends and much reading about China had extended and deepened that interest. As a researcher and writer about the role of minorities and immigrants in American history, I was being offered a chance to combine two of my strongest interests. It was a challenge I could not—and did not—resist.

What followed my decision was a five-year quest through crumbling letters, nineteenth-century newspapers, old travel books and reminiscences and finally to the doorstep of some of the sons and daughters of the early Chinese pioneers. Through the help of their memories and the pages of a Chinese-language newspaper ably translated by my research assistant, Mr. Joseph C. K. Ng, I began to sense the dimensions and fit together some of the pieces for the story I was seeking. It is a story which is just beginning to receive the attention it deserves. In the past the Chinese in America have been, for reasons of tradition as well as self-protection, understandably reticent about revealing too much of their past. The record will soon make the reasons clear.

Fortunately, the recently growing interest of young Americans of Chinese descent in their roots has begun to part this veil. The pioneer study in the sociology of the Chinese in America by the late Prof. Rose Hum Lee has been fleshed out by new and more graphic work by Prof. Betty Lee Sung and Victor and Bret de Bary Nee on the real life of a modern Chinatown. Tremendous research by Prof. Stanford M. Lyman and his associates on the structure of Chinese society in nineteenth-century America has carried the story back to its origins. However, the only scholarly history of the early immigrants relied heavily on nineteenth-century American newspapers and unfortunately adopted their racist tone, its thesis being that the Chinese were responsible for their own persecution. Since then the work of Prof. Stewart Creighton Miller, showing the causes and pervasive nature of racism and stereotypes from the beginning of China's contact with America, has helped set the record straight.

Still, the actual people who inhabited this nineteenth-century world—the real pioneers from China—have remained shadowy. What one would not give to know more about such merchant leaders as Norman As-sing and Tong K. Achick, who make brief, tantalizing appearances in these pages, or Lee Kan, the classic marginal man between the Chinese and American worlds. In the case of Dr. Chew, luck and much legwork unearthed the missing links. The end of my search was the actual house where he had lived for the last twenty-five years of his life. Through the kind assistance and cooperation of Miss Mansie Condit Chew, still living there, I was able to read and copy her collection of unpublished speeches, letters, souvenirs from the Chautauqua circuit and clippings by and about her father. Her brother, Mr. Edward Chapin Chew, supplied additional facts. The daughter of Dr. Chew's early mentor and later colleague the Reverend Soo Hoo Nam Art—Mrs. William L. Z. Sung (Lillie Soo Hoo)—supplied a number of interesting vignettes. The son of another younger colleague of Dr. Chew's—Mr. Ira Lee—did important spadework in helping bring to light a vital period of Dr. Chew's life. Useful reminiscences came from the noted scholar Dr. Clifford Drury and Donaldina Cameron's lawyer, Mr. Hilary Crawford. A number of people at Donaldina Cameron House in San Francisco were immensely helpful and encouraging—the Reverend F. S. Dick Wichman, Mr. Lambert Choy, Miss Lorna Logan and especially Mrs. Enid Lim.

So many people helped that it is hard to do justice to them all. My attendance at the first National Conference on "The Life, Influence and the Role of the Chinese in the United States, 1776–1960" gave me an opportunity to share my knowledge of Dr. Chew with new friends and gain new insight. My special thanks go to Mr. Thomas W. Chinn, Chairman of the Conference and President for many years of the Chinese Historical Society of America, as well as one of its founders. Indeed, he has been a spiritual father to most students in the field of Chinese-American history. Other helpful members of the staff of the Society were Mrs. Daisy W. Chinn, Ms. Edna Chinn, Mrs. Eva Lim and Mrs. Annie Soo. Mr. Him Mark Lai helped lead me to the world of Chinese-language newspapers. Most of all, I benefited from the friendship and knowledge of a brilliant young scholar, Ms. Eve Armentrout-Ma, who specializes in early twentieth-century politics in the Chinese communities of the Americas.

Apart from the Kees, my most constant mentor and source of both material and intellectual aid was Prof. Conrad Schirokauer, Professor of Chinese History at The City College, New York. He supplied me with many useful leads and also read and clarified the sections of the book dealing with Chinese history.

An important guide to the early period was the archives of the Presbyterian Historical Society in Philadelphia, where Mr. Gerald W. Gillette, the Reverend William Miller and the whole staff were extremely helpful in finding me letters from the early missionaries to the Chinese in San Francisco. In fact, it was the Reverend Miller who first set me on the path that led to finding Dr. Chew's surviving descendants.

Librarians, whether Ms. Irene Moran of the Bancroft Library at the University of California at Berkeley, Mr. Jay Williar at the California Historical Society, Ms. Gladys Hansen of the San Francisco Public Library or those at the Library of Congress and the New York Historical Society, proved as always a researcher's best friend. Above all, the great resources and staff of the New York Public Library have been the indispensable cornerstone of my research—though beleaguered by a continuing and worsening budget crisis, they have struggled to maintain the integrity of their priceless collections and their services to the scholars who need them. I found special assistance from the people in the Central Reading Room, Oriental Collection, Print Room, Rare Book Room, American History Room, Map Room, Local History and Genealogy Room, Microfilm Room and Annex. The Missionary Library at the Union Theological Seminary yielded some rare periodicals, and Ms. Mary Tepper, Librarian at the San Francisco *Chronicle*, supplied me with some important clippings of Dr. Chew's speeches and writings after 1906. Finally, Mr. William M. Robertson, News Editor for the Public Relations Department of the Southern Pacific Transportation Company, sent me useful information and early photographs of Chinese workers on the transcontinental railroad.

The encouragement of my husband Rolf provided the atmosphere essential to the completion of the book. And his logical mind and perceptive reading sometimes extracted the main point from a paragraph or chapter with which I had been struggling all day. My children, Vivien and Michael, often helped to finish the stew so I could finish a paragraph, or cooked the hamburgers when I returned late from a day's research in Philadelphia or Washington. Happily, they seem quite at home in the multiethnic, multiracial society that America is struggling to become.

*I*N 1866 two boys who were later to have great influence on their countrymen were born in Kwangtung Province, China, in villages not seventy miles apart. One of the boys was Ng Poon Chew, a native of Sinning, a district near Canton, the provincial capital. The other, Sun Yat-sen, lived out his childhood in the Hiangshan delta village of Choyhung (Fragrant Hills). Though Ng never achieved the world renown of Sun, he greatly influenced the lives of the Chinese in America. And though the two men never met as youths, their lives intertwined in America after they were grown and had set out on their life's work. Their

story is the story of the Chinese immigration to the United States—
and an expression of the hopes and aspirations of a people, in this
country and in China.

To understand their story, and Ng Poon Chew's in particular,
one must know that Kwangtung Province in the nineteenth century
was the most populous in China, and one of the poorest. It lacked
sufficient arable soil to support its population, and it was often
devastated by revolts and rebellions. As a result, the Kwangtung
Chinese were overseas-minded. They sometimes left their poverty-
stricken villages in the hills around Canton and crossed the oceans
in hopes of earning a living, even a small fortune. The wives would
stay at home in China to care for the children and aging parents
while the travelers were away; and bound to home by ties of family
obligations, the husbands would send back money for their support.
Then, their fortune made, the sojourners would return to their
native villages to pass a peaceful old age in the bosoms of their
families.

In this the people of Kwangtung were both similar to, and
yet vastly different from, other Chinese. Tradition discouraged
emigration from China. And the law of the Manchu emperor
stated that "all officers of the government, soldiers and private
citizens who clandestinely proceed to sea to trade . . . shall be
punished according to the law against communications with rebels
and enemies and consequently suffer death by being beheaded."
Only a strong promise of speedy riches or the stern demands of
family survival could cause a people so wedded to its homeland to
go abroad.

Even a people who have reason to go must also have the
opportunity. The Kwangtung peasants were different from the
other Chinese in this respect as well. For Canton was the sole
Chinese port open to foreign merchants in the early nineteenth
century. The Portuguese, the French and the British, who had
opened China to trade, could sail their vessels to China, but until
the 1840s the destination was either Canton or Macao—and both
were in Kwangtung. Americans, too, sailed to Canton. Thus, when

word of the *Gum Shan*, the "Mountain of Gold," reached China, Kwangtung was most affected. News of the discovery of gold spread quickly through the impoverished countryside.

Thus it was that the Chinese and the Americans met at Canton and on the Pacific Coast of America. Out of these meetings grew the tangled history of Chinese-American relations on both sides of the Pacific, in which, in differing ways, both Ng Poon Chew and Sun Yat-sen played a part.

Though the history of America's official China policy has been endlessly studied and analyzed, the story of the Chinese experience in America has been largely obscured behind a few lines in the history books about "coolie" laborers and exclusion laws and in popular books by allusions to slave girls, tong wars, opium dens, and hatchet men.

Yet the Chinese lived through a great adventure and a great ordeal on American soil. Their history here has been both bloody and shameful, glorious and triumphant. The Chinese were deeply involved in the building of the American West. And they played a role in such complex problems as the rise of labor unions and the regulation of immigration. The "Chinese question" was as controversial and significant an issue in its day as the "Negro problem" in the South after the Civil War. It was discussed nationwide. The reasons for the violent confrontation that occurred between white and Chinese labor in California and the cause and results of the exclusion laws are little better understood in San Francisco and New York today. The irony by which the Chinese, who were needed to labor in the mines and fields, in construction and industry, became hated and persecuted, and then were almost forgotten, is perhaps no stranger than any other in the long uneasy history of racial tension in America. But it is less well known.

The aim here is to sweep away the cobwebs that cover the dusty archives, crumbling letters and early Chinese-language newspapers. For that is where the facts of the Chinese experience in America lie buried. Since the Chinese who came to America had not expected to stay, they settled their own colonies, formed their own organizations and, in the midst of a hostile population, tried to retain their identity as Chinese, the customs and manners that were peculiarly their own, to which they would return in China.

Still, there were a few, the young or the daring, who attempted to integrate themselves into this new world. And there were others who, discouraged by this effort, gave up hope for success and returned to China.

This, then, is the story of why the Chinese came to America, where they came from, how they lived in this country and how they tried to accommodate themselves to the difficult and dangerous conditions that surrounded them on the rugged frontiers of the old West.

It is also the story of Ng Poon Chew—Ng in Chinese, but Chew to us—one of the Chinese sojourners who came to America by the classic route of the Kwangtung peasant. He lived through the crucial phases of Chinese-American history, from his arrival in 1880 to his death more than fifty years later. He played an active role in improving the position of Chinese in America and in explaining China to Americans, and he deserves to be remembered for it.

FROM
CANTON
TO
CALIFORNIA

THE
GOLDEN
MAGNET

CHAPTER *1*

CELESTIAL PIONEERS

It may not be many years before the Honorable Ching Chang will be found making a proposition in the halls of Congress or of our state legislature to unite the Chinese wall and the Golden Gate by a sub-marine telegraph.
                                    Daily Alta, JULY 8, 1851

*A*NY San Franciscan in search of drama at the midpoint of the nineteenth century was sure to find it on the bustling natural stage that was the city's heart—Portsmouth Plaza. Here the vacationing miner, the born loafer, the street urchin, the business-man on his way to the wharfs or warehouses, could pause to watch a feverish activity. Or on special occasions he might be diverted by a political rally, a parade or a hanging. But the event promised for the afternoon of August 28, 1850, was to be unique, a sure proof of the growing importance of San Francisco in the world.

A stir at the southeast corner where Kearney Street entered the plaza announced a procession more exotic than any yet seen in America. It made its stately way across the mud and cobblestones toward a hastily erected platform. There a party of silk-hatted gentlemen and a couple of bonneted ladies were seated. One hundred sober-faced Chinese in long robes of a rich dark silk "with their pigtails nicely braided . . . presented a perfectly neat and singularly picturesque appearance" as they mounted the platform and took their seats.

The audience, as colorful as the participants in this drama, ranged over the entire spectrum of the races of man, from the pale-faced Scandinavian to the blackest African. They had plenty to stare at—the large, beautifully painted fans carried by most of the Chinese merchants, the exceptionally tall old man with over-sized spectacles and a fur mantle—clearly a mandarin—or the "sallow, dried, cadaverous" man of uncertain age to whom the others kept turning for advice. This man—Norman As-sing, already the best-known Chinese in San Francisco and therefore in America—had eyes so keen, so piercing, that those who were tempted to stare at him soon dropped their gaze.

Prominent among the Americans were clergymen, city officials and businessmen, including the merchant Selim Woodworth, recently chosen "Mandarin of the Celestial Empire and China Consul" by the local Chinese community. The Reverend Albert Williams of the First Presbyterian Church delivered the first greetings to the "citizens of the celestial empire." As he explained, years later, "Several speakers united in expressing . . . the hope that more of their people would follow their example in crossing the ocean to our shore and finally charging them with a message to their friends in China, that in coming to this country, they would find welcome and protection."

Norman As-sing stood at the side of each speaker and translated his words into the mysterious chantlike tones of Cantonese. Next the Reverend Timothy Dwight Hunt approached the main purpose of the meeting:

Though you come from a celestial country, there is another one above, much better, much larger than your own. Here and in your country, you are sometimes taken sick and suffer and even die, and are seen no more, and your fathers and mothers and brothers and sisters all die, but in the other heavenly country, all the good China boys* live. They will meet there and never die![1]

After a moment's hesitation, Norman As-sing recast the words into the fluting pitch of his native tongue. Scarcely had the last syllable echoed through the plaza than a new, more abrasive sound erased it. The perfect gravity of all those seemingly expressionless faces had cracked, and most of them were laughing heartily. The Chinese found his words incredible because in Chinese tradition there is no afterlife in the Christian sense. The irreverent miners added their guffaws to this cultural misunderstanding until Dr. Hunt held up his hand for silence. He and the other ministers, quite unperturbed by the laughter, proceeded to hand out tracts and Bibles in Chinese, printed and sent from Canton.

Finally Mayor John Geary rose to deliver the closing remarks. "Tomorrow," he explained, "our city, the Queen of the Pacific, will march in tribute to the memory of our late departed President Zachary Taylor. We invite the 'China boys' to join the procession to honor our leader 'all the same like your Emperor.' " He paused and looked hopefully at the Chinese as if he had finally pierced the language barrier. "This will mark the first time that China and America join hands in such a demonstration of respect."

Accompanied by cheers, the Chinese marched back to "little China," the silk-hatted gentlemen to their countinghouses and parishes. The spectators dispersed to the gambling "hells" that occupied the most substantial buildings around the plaza, or, if too broke to gamble, watched luckier men hurry into El Dorado

---

* The Chinese were so called, condescendingly, because of their small size.

or one of the other "hells." Those left out in the cold hoped that a
duel over gambling losses might yet erupt onto the plaza and
enliven the rest of the afternoon.

To most Americans it will come as a surprise to learn that
there was a small but well-organized community of Chinese living
and working in San Francisco at this early date. The population
of the city in 1850 was only about 34,000 and though reliable
figures are lacking, the number of Chinese may have been as many
as 5,000, but possibly considerably less. These Chinese, including
the dignified merchants who set up shop in gold-rush California,
had crossed the treacherous seas, despite the prohibitions of Chinese
law, in search of wealth.

The discovery of gold in California in 1848 offered such a
promise—and not to the Chinese alone, of course. By the time the
news of the new El Dorado had circled the globe by sailing ship,
most of the year had worn away. The epic migration of adventurers
from every land to the goldfields of the Sierras came in 1849. Then,
through messages sent home by the handful of Chinese merchants
and workers who had reached California in 1848, word filtered back
to the hills around Canton of the great wealth awaiting those who
dared to join this international treasure hunt. The Chinese responded by making an epic journey requiring the courage of a
true pioneer.

Chinese and Americans met in San Francisco in 1850 in a
state of mutual and almost total ignorance of each other's civiliza-
tions. The Americans were only slightly better informed about the
Chinese than the Chinese were about them. Each had gone to the
other's country for the same basic reason—gold. American seamen
had followed the lead of European merchants in seeking the
treasure of the East—tea, spices, silks and porcelain. The Chinese
had come to California for the same purpose as the other forty-
niners—to find the gold nuggets hidden in western streams and
hillsides.

Like most treasure-seekers, the Chinese in America and the

At the Customs House in San Francisco in 1877 inspectors searched a group of newly arrived Chinese immigrants (a rare woman in the foreground) before releasing them to go by wagon to their company house (inset, top right), as a merchant in mandarin dress looked over a cargo list in a Harper's Weekly drawing. (GENERAL RESEARCH AND HUMANITIES DIVISION, THE NEW YORK PUBLIC LIBRARY, ASTOR, LENOX AND TILDEN FOUNDATIONS)

Americans in China did not intend to become immigrants. The Chinese considered their land the Middle Kingdom, the center of the earth, and always expected to return home. Americans were just as ethnocentric. They considered the United States the New World, the last, best hope of earth, which should attract the best men from the tired Old World.

Rooted in their own soil, indifferent to other nations, the Chinese expected other peoples to be just as rooted in theirs. So they welcomed rather than resented the American desire to trade in China and then go home. Americans, however, belonging to a nation of immigrants, thought all men should want to come to the United States as permanent settlers. Therefore, they were prejudiced against the Chinese because they came to America first as sojourners, or temporary settlers. But many other people, such as the French, had the same attitude at the time of the gold rush.

Norman As-sing, the leader of his community in its first meetings and celebrations with the white world of San Francisco, must have been a Chinese attracted to California by the lure of gold. As early as December 10, 1849, he had made his mark on the California scene, when three hundred of the Chinese then in San Francisco elected him a leader of the Chew Yick Kung Shaw (Luminous Unity Public Office), the first Chinese mutual-aid society in America. By the end of 1850 As-sing had fully grasped California's promise of incredibly speedy fortune to the quick-witted, the lucky and the ruthless. Frank Soulé, in his 1854 chronicle, *Annals of San Francisco*, has vividly recaptured the breathless excitement and amoral confusion of those days of easy money:

> *The great sums, forming the total of such wages, salaries and profits, were always rapidly passing from hand to hand, and came and went, and finally disappeared in the gambling saloons and billiard rooms, at bars and in brothels, in land-jobbing, building and mercantile speculations, in every kind of personal profusion, extravagance and debauchery. . . .*

In this atmosphere of freewheeling capitalism, Norman As-sing could amass the kind of fortune which would have been impossible for him at home. In China the merchant was far down in the Confucian social scale, below not only the scholar-officials but also, in theory, the peasants who owned and worked the land, the source of China's wealth. Far from being a leader in China, the merchant was hemmed in by all sorts of restrictions and regulations in carrying on his business. In California, on the other hand (as in the United States generally), the businessman was king. Freed of most restraints on his trade, As-sing could rise quickly to the top. An old settler, James O'Meara, recalled thirty years later how As-sing's "candy store and bakery" made him rich.

Norman As-sing always claimed to be an American citizen, naturalized in Charleston, South Carolina, and converted to Christianity. Though there is no historical evidence for his claims to citizenship, which would have been unusual for one of his race at that time, he certainly possessed greater knowledge of American ways and language than most of his countrymen. At his Macao and Woosung Restaurant on the corner of Kearney and Commercial streets, about a block from Portsmouth Plaza, he gave banquets at which he entertained local politicians and policemen. In the early 1850s he invariably turned up at the head of the Chinese contingent in any procession—whether to celebrate California Day, marking the admission of the state to the Union, or the Fourth of July.

The average Cantonese peasant arriving in San Francisco was a striking contrast to Norman As-sing and the other emerging merchants. This sojourner was male, young, frightened of the rough frontier society that awaited him, lonely and usually illiterate in Chinese. He neither spoke nor understood English. These factors, combined with his small stature, made him an easy prey to violence and exploitation. It was natural that he should turn to men like Norman As-sing. Such leaders could protect him from the *fan qui* ("foreign devils"), assure his cultural survival in an alien land and help him earn the money he required to return home.

The glamour of gold outweighed the dangers in the first few years. In the winter of 1850–51 the sloop *Race Horse* had carried back to Hong Kong three or four lucky Chinese miners with fortunes of $3,000 or $4,000 each. As they showed the gold dust to friends and relatives at homecoming banquets, reports of the fabulous *Gum Shan*, the "Mountain of Gold," across the water spread like flames through dry underbrush. The news traveled from Canton into the districts bordering the Pearl River delta where the city stands. By May 9, 1851, the bark *Magnolia*, with thirty Chinese aboard, had docked in San Francisco, and the ship's captain told reporters that the gold excitement was still growing in Kwangtung Province. The *Magnolia* was being closely followed by five or six more ships with far heavier loads of prospective Chinese miners.

In 1851 the Customs House in San Francisco recorded 2,716 Chinese immigrants. In 1852 the number leaped to 20,000. In the first rough census of the Chinese community in California, taken that year, 25,000 Chinese were counted in the state. In the beginning most of the Chinese hurried to the mining country as soon as they could procure the necessary tools and American boots. For years boots were the only item of American dress added to their loose blue blouses and trousers and wide straw hats. Not more than one in ten remained in San Francisco. Indeed, in those days an overwhelming majority of all arrivals in the state went directly to the mines.

In the beginning the Chinese were not so rigidly segregated as they later became. Their houses and businesses were to be found in all sections of the city. Still, partly from preference for the company of their own people and partly from the demands of security, they began to form a "little China" in San Francisco and Chinese camps in the mines. "Little China" in San Francisco spread out along upper Sacramento Street and the length of Dupont Street (now Grant Avenue). Here, as well as in the larger Chinese settlements of the mining region, Chinese restaurants and stores selling food, clothing, mining tools and medicinal herbs sprang up.

The bustling life of San Francisco's Chinatown was captured by an artist for the Illustrated London News *in 1875.*

The need for entertainment felt by lonely men, especially when in sudden possession of money, was supplied by gambling dens, brothels and theaters.

The treatment of the Chinese in America was conditioned by several important factors. They were strangers in a strange land, clearly set apart by physical characteristics and customs, though at first these distinctive customs seemed to make little difference in the tolerant atmosphere of cosmopolitan San Francisco. The democratic feeling of the early gold rush also helped promote a friendly atmosphere. Reporters like the one from the *Daily Alta* who covered the Portsmouth Plaza meeting found them a constant source of wonder and amusement. Beyond an appreciation of their quaintness, early leaders in California foresaw the benefits that the Chinese could bring to the state because of their ability to work hard and well. Yet even at this time the Chinese were exposed to dangers because easy identification made them a target for ruffians.

Another factor was the writings about China by Americans who had visited there. With few exceptions, these accounts were condescending or even contemptuous. They began to filter into the minds of Americans who were the most literate and thoughtful. By the time Californians came to regard the Chinese with a less friendly eye, these books had given them reasons for their attacks. Unfortunately, these visiting Americans had arrived in China at a moment when the empire was experiencing corruption and decay. They wondered what had become of the golden Cathay of Marco Polo and the peaceful, benevolent monarchy described by early Jesuit missionaries.

The third factor which conditioned American response to the Chinese was the particular historical and social setting of gold-rush California. Side by side with the natural democracy of the period was the potential violence which was bound to erupt when the wildest adventurers came together in search of quick and easy wealth. An early participant in the gold rush has described the character of the first miners thus: "The aspect of personal neglect and discomfort, filth, rags and squalor, combined with uneasiness, avidity and recklessness of manner—an all-absorbing selfishness as if each man were striving against his fellow-man—were characteristic of the gold-fever, at once repulsive and pitiable."[2] Such men will think nothing of shooting each other down over a gambling loss, a woman or a jumped claim. The famous historian H. H. Bancroft estimated that 4,200 murders and 1,200 suicides had occurred in California up to 1854. There was almost no legal check to this violence; only vigilante law occasionally brought some kind of order in the mines.

For many miners the early equality of opportunity applied only to *white* men. Gangs of black workers and Chinese, Malays and Mexicans (not white enough for Anglo-Saxons), early attracted hostility. Even in 1849 there were already moves to eject the Chinese from some mining camps. "These conflicts were often serious in their results," wrote William Shaw, a British forty-niner. "Retaliations were made, and where might makes right, retributions upon unoffending individuals often took place, which were nigh producing a war of race against race."

The movement to organize and civilize this wide-open society first began in San Francisco in 1851. In the spring of that year the hoodlums known as "hounds," who preyed on successful miners and other prosperous citizens, deliberately set a series of fires to facilitate robbery. Many blocks of the insubstantial frame buildings that then composed the city were destroyed. Community leaders, soon disgusted by the slow pace of justice and the general corruption of judges, formed the first Committee of Vigilance, led by William N. Coleman and including "Chinese mandarin" Selim Woodworth. Though extralegal in its authority, the committee was careful to follow the forms of law.

The peaceful, industrious Chinese, who were rarely seen in law courts in those days, naturally received no attention from the committee at first. Then Norman As-sing, like many an entrepreneur before and since, saw a chance to make use of the legal confusion. Wanting control of the brothel run by the "strangely alluring" Atoy with her "slender body and laughing eyes," he and John Lipscomb, a local labor importer, asked the committee to deport her and several of her friends back to China because of her "free and easy style of living." Since living in this fashion was contrary to the Confucian code of conduct, other Chinese doubtless approved of As-sing's actions, but Americans, who chiefly visited Atoy, saw the matter in a different light.

Fortunately for Atoy, Selim Woodworth suspected As-sing's motives and alerted the committee to the scheme. He also pointed out to the other members that it would be difficult to deport Atoy for living in exactly the same manner as the thousand other women of assorted nationalities who entertained the international army of miners. As-sing was enjoined by the Recorder's Court from interfering with Atoy's liberty again.

Though there was nothing specifically Chinese about the kind of blackmail and intimidation that As-sing had tried on Atoy, it helped to plant in American minds the idea that the Chinese had their own laws and ignored those of the state. Other examples of attempted coercion of Chinese workers by leaders like As-sing came to light in the next few years. Such incidents began to tie in with the uncomplimentary things that some Americans had read in books about China.

By this time most of the Chinese living in San Francisco were divided into companies (known as *wui kun*). These were not businesses but mutual-aid societies. Though all immigrants have needed such organizations to help them adapt to alien soil, some Americans associated the companies with a "secret government" among the Chinese. Rumors of secret societies with mysterious rites also added to the confusion.

These negative impressions were the first signs of the distant storm gathering about the Chinese. At the same time, several more hopeful signs appeared. There arrived in San Francisco the first Chinese who had learned English and something of American ways at mission schools in China itself. The friends of the Chinese, notably the kind-hearted Reverend Albert Williams of the Portsmouth Plaza meeting, welcomed them eagerly and even started a Bible class for them in the winter of 1851. One of the Bible students, Tong K. Achick, was instrumental in founding one of the companies. It was the Yeong Wo Wui Kun (Masculine Concord Company) for sojourners from his native district of Hiangshan, home of the Pearl River delta farmers. With his greater grasp of American ideas and ideals, Tong K. Achick began to challenge the amoral leadership of Norman As-sing.

This pioneer missionary effort in California also encouraged the Board of Foreign Missions of the Presbyterian Church to send to California their first missionary to have served in Canton, the Reverend William Speer. The board thought he would have a much easier job converting the Chinese in California than in China itself. Speer was an ideal candidate for this post. He had worked on Chinese soil for four years and gained great sympathy and respect for China and his Chinese students. Moreover, he had the ability, unusual for an American, to speak the Cantonese dialect spoken by most California Chinese. He was to be one of the staunchest and most articulate American defenders they were ever to have.

Speer reached San Francisco in the fall of 1852. By June 1854, helped by friends of many denominations, he had opened a new chapel at the corner of Sacramento and Stockton streets in the heart of the Chinese quarter. Only thirty Chinese were present along with one hundred white well-wishers.

Despite many Chinese friends, even Dr. Speer ran up against an impenetrable wall of indifference from most Chinese he met. A tightly knit web of family, clan and district obligations and loyalties kept the average Chinese sojourner from finding any place in his life for Christianity. Unlike most missionaries, Speer did not make the mistake of rejecting the venerable Chinese culture as "deader than that of ancient Egypt." He sensed its vitality, its awesome inner consistency.

All the Chinese sojourners, whatever their interest in American ways and Christian teaching, had been formed by this distinctive civilization. Only by following these complex strands of loyalty and obligation back to the Pearl River delta where they originated can we hope to understand the difficulties faced by both Americans and Chinese in their first meeting on American soil.

CHAPTER *2*

THE SOURCE

*After all, the Chinese are, at least were, until treaty days, a
happy and contented people, of exemplary industry, sober
and of simple frugal tastes, passing through the ordeal of
existence as sensibly and as successfully in view of their
resources as the inhabitants of any other land.*

W. C. HUNTER, *Bits of Old China*

THE China first visited by Western merchants and missionaries and the China from which most sojourners
came were the same—the Pearl River delta which contains the city
of Canton and nearby districts in the mountains and along the
seacoast. Kwangtung Province, of which Canton is capital, is far
distant from the heart of the Chinese Empire. Peking with its
forbidden city sheltering the emperor, the Son of Heaven, lies
twelve hundred miles to the north, near the border of Manchuria.

On the whole, the Chinese are not a migratory people. They
are too attached to their villages. For most of them, anything beyond

the borders of China is outer darkness. Yet the people of the south have always been different. Early contact with the West, the availability of ships, the arduous struggle for existence in an over-populated, land-poor region, all contributed to their willingness to accept the risks of emigration. With a fatalistic shrug, they would say, "To starve and to be buried in the sea are the same."

For centuries, even before they crossed the Pacific in the gold rush, the Cantonese had been sailors and fishermen. For over two centuries, they had emigrated into the *nan yang* ("overseas") in southeast Asia to earn their bread in the plantations and mines. An authority on Chinese immigration has noted that "a marked characteristic of the people of Kwangtung and Fukien is their independent and unbending spirit." The more placid northerners spoke disparagingly of "southern savages." Kwangtung was slow in rendering allegiance to the emperor at Peking.

One continual cause of unrest in the Pearl River delta was the coexistence of three ethnic strains in the area. The Punti were the native Cantonese. Their traditional rivals, the Hakka, or "guest families," had originally pushed down from the north and settled in separate villages. And the Tanka were the boat people whose floating homes made Canton Harbor one of the great sights of the East. The Tanka, considered outcasts and scorned by everyone else, were condemned to be ferrymen, smugglers, pirates or prostitutes.

Even among the Punti there were divisions by district, each having its own dialect and distinctive character. Canton and its suburbs comprised three districts (or Sam Yap): Nanhai, Pwanyü and Shunto. These city merchants and artisans with their sophisticated speech and manner were rather scornful of the rustic speech and ways of the peasants from the hill regions of Sze Yap ("four districts"). Sze Yap, extending southwest of the city to the South China Sea, included Sinhwui, Anping, Haiping and, most important, Sinning (now Toi Shan). Perched on mountains just above the shore, Sinning, with its steep stony soil, offered such a low level of subsistence to its farmers that many became fishermen and

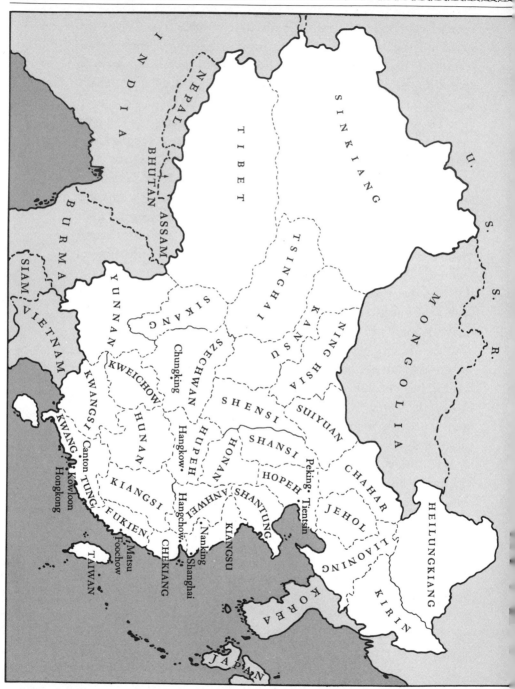

peddlers. From Sze Yap came over 70 percent of the immigrants to America, and their descendants dominate Chinese-American communities to this day. And from Sinning came two-thirds of the Sze Yap immigrants. Still another important group were the rice-growing farmers from Hiangshan, an island in the center of the delta.

Beyond these divisions by district and racial subgroup, every Chinese in Kwangtung Province had more fundamental loyalties—to his village, often the home of one clan, and to his immediate family, which defined his existence to a degree incomprehensible to Americans. The stable, enduring pattern of life practiced in these villages and common to all China had evolved over three thousand years ago when the Shang dynasty emerged from prehistoric obscurity amid the yellow dust of the North China plain. Almost twenty-four hundred years before, Confucius had developed the fundamental beliefs and principles that had governed Chinese society ever since.

Living at a time of anarchy, Confucius had made human harmony in family and state the center of his system. There were three basic bonds in society—those between ruler and subject, father and son, and husband and wife. All stressed the domination of age over youth and male over female. In the family the sons were trained in filial piety and obedience to become loyal subjects of the emperor. At the same time, the emperor, husband, father was obligated to assume responsibility for his subject, wife, son.

The strength of this pattern of life enabled the peasant farmer in his country village to survive through dynastic convulsions for thirty centuries:

> To an American with his higher material standard of living the amazing thing about the Chinese peasantry is their ability to maintain life in these poor conditions. The answer lies in their social institutions which have carried the individuals of each family through the phases and vicissitudes of human existence according to deeply ingrained patterns of

behavior. . . . China has been the stronghold of the family system and has derived both strength and inertia from it.[3]

Each village of seventy-five households at most was one of twelve to eighteen surrounding a market town, which was no more than a day's journey distant from the farthest village. Here marriages were arranged and holidays celebrated. Here the local gentry informally judged and settled the cases of personal injury and property damage that in America led to lawsuits. They also shielded the peasants, at least in peaceful, prosperous times, from too many and abrasive contacts with government officials such as tax collectors and magistrates. In time of war the gentry were responsible for raising a militia to defend the country.

Self-sufficient in her resources, the vast, conservative Chinese Empire had rarely sought trade with the outside world or encouraged the outside world to trade with her. At various times in China's past, the Son of Heaven had graciously allowed foreign traders to visit certain ports in order to buy such goods as tea, silk and spices which they seemed so desperately to desire. The Chinese, however, showed little interest in buying Western goods in exchange.

The Renaissance and the Age of Exploration and Discovery brought a new wave of Europeans to the Far East. The Portuguese, Dutch and Spanish explorers and merchants who reached the gates of the Chinese Empire aroused suspicion by their aggressive behavior. So in the sixteenth century, the Ming emperors restricted them to the tiny colony that is still nominally held by the Portuguese near Canton—Macao.

The Ming dynasty was the last ruled by emperors of Chinese blood. In 1644, as had happened so often before in Chinese history, conquerors from the north, called the Manchus, swept into Peking. Within twenty years they had driven the last Ming princes and generals to the south and then into exile or defeat. The alien Manchus had meanwhile ascended the dragon throne at Peking under the name of the Ch'ing dynasty. Only the Mongols before them had conquered the whole of China in this way.

The Ch'ing ruled as Chinese emperors, adopting practically the whole system of government and laws practiced by their predecessors. The bureaucracy of Chinese officials, filled by competitive examination, continued to control the government, but with a Manchu as well as a Chinese head for each department. During their long reign the Manchus managed to stay in control by attempting to enforce absolute obedience. For example, as a sign of loyalty, each Chinese male had to shave his forehead in Manchu fashion and wear the queue. The Ch'ing also produced two exceptional rulers whose reigns spanned more than a century.

During the early years of the Ch'ing dynasty, the inevitable rebellions against the new regime cut down on commerce, but by the eighteenth century it was on the rise again. Under the second great Ch'ing emperor, who went under the name of his sixty-year reign—Ch'ien-lung—the increasing power of European traders, especially the British, caused the officials much concern. As a result, after 1760, foreign merchants were confined in Canton to thirteen factories (business firm, named after "factor," or agent). The factories were a combination of office-dock-warehouse-residence on a narrow strip of land, just a thousand feet long, facing Canton Harbor. This enclave was the only piece of Chinese soil on which foreigners might legally live and trade before the Treaty of Nanking in 1842.

Next to the foreign factories stood the Hongs (Chinese for *factories*) of the Chinese merchants of the Co-hong, who had been granted a monopoly on foreign trade. Originally, they were thirteen in number, and every foreign ship entering Canton Harbor was the responsibility of one of them.

In theory, the foreign trade monopoly should have opened the door to immense wealth for the Chinese Hong merchants. For some, like the famous Howqua (*qua* means "sir"), the wealth was realized. (Howqua was the honorary name of Wu Ping-chien.) A great favorite of Americans, Howqua became in his day (1769–1843) one of the richest men in the world, his fortune estimated at $26 million. Yet many found the cost of obtaining such wealth to be too high. The insatiable greed of the mandarin officials at Canton drove many Hong merchants into bankruptcy.

Indeed, as the historian Chang Hsin-pao has aptly stated, "the whole Canton system was built on a central theme of contempt for foreigners and disdain for merchants." The most ambitious young men in China did not sail the seas looking for new markets to exploit—they studied for years to master a literary language so difficult that it became the exclusive property of an elite. If they succeeded, they passed progressively more difficult examinations to win a place in the imperial civil service. These best minds and greatest statesmen of China were rarely sent to deal with the *fan qui* ("foreign devils") at Canton, and so learned little about them. The post of hoppo, or revenue agent, at Canton was considered a road to quick riches and was naturally sought by corrupt officials.

Nothing better illustrates the Chinese attitude toward foreigners and merchants than the detailed regulations that hemmed in

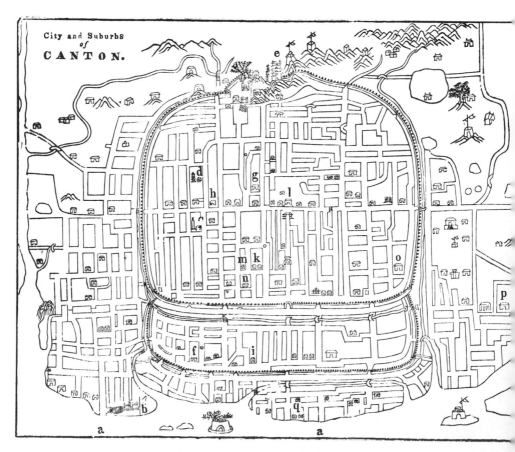

the daily lives and business dealings of foreigners in China. Warships, personal arms of any kind and foreign women were forbidden to enter the Pearl River and go up to Canton, and the movement of trading ships up and down the river was carefully regulated. The only Chinese who might have any dealings with foreigners, or even talk to them, were officially licensed business agents (compradors), river pilots, linguists, the Hong merchants themselves and a limited number of servants. Significantly, it was the Chinese merchants or linguists and not the foreigners who were punished if the foreigners did not abide by the rules. Many of the regulations were intended to prevent smuggling. Unfortunately, they neither controlled the aggressive and ill-bred foreigners nor prevented the Chinese from conniving at smuggling.

By the early nineteenth century the industrial revolution in the West had created pressure for a vast expansion of overseas trade. As a result, American and British traders began to chafe at their confinement to the factories and the antiquated regulations of the Canton system. This growing sense of exasperation foreshadowed a clash between Chinese officials and the Western traders, especially the British.

Western irritation was aggravated by the Chinese refusal to establish normal diplomatic relations with the West. The Chinese emperor simply refused to recognize any country as the equal of the Middle Kingdom. All must approach him as satellite countries bearing tribute. Several British diplomatic missions were turned back because they refused to perform the three kneelings and nine knockings of the kowtow ceremony required in the presence of the emperor.

Another frequent source of confrontation between Chinese

A copy of an old Chinese map (circa 1830) of the city of Canton. The added roman letters indicated the important landmarks for foreign traders in the days before the Opium War: (a) the Pearl River and harbor, (b) the foreign factories, (d) and (e) two important pagodas. Most of the others were public buildings or houses of major officials such as those of the governor (f) and the hoppo or collector of revenues (i). The larger serrated line represented the wall of the old city, the smaller one that of the new city to the south. (CHINESE REPOSITORY) officials and foreigners at Canton was their differing codes of justice. The Chinese insisted on trying and even executing foreigners for crimes, such as involuntary manslaughter, that would have brought a lesser penalty in their own countries. Moreover, torture was still an official feature of Chinese court and police procedure when its use had died out in Western Europe. Small wonder that the Chinese themselves avoided the courts and settled their disputes through the arbitration of village elders.

Last, but not least, as a source of frustration to Western traders was the unfavorable balance of trade with China. The frugal, nonconsuming Chinese wanted little or nothing offered by the foreign traders in exchange for the luxury goods of China. Yankee ship captains touched exotic Pacific islands in search of betel nuts, ginseng, sandalwood, fish maws and sharks' fins for the groceries and apothecaries of China. Before the War of 1812 furs from the Pacific Northwest formed the chief medium of American trade with China till Americans almost drove the sea otter to extinction.

Until the British began to import cotton from India and the mills of Manchester, they usually had to pay in silver for their tea and silk. Then they hit upon a commodity for which there was a great demand among the Chinese because it was forbidden by law— opium. Americans did not neglect this new source of profit, finding their opium in Turkey rather than in India. Most of the Yankee drug traders defended themselves as merchants supplying a need. William C. Hunter, a nostalgic celebrator of the old Canton system, expressed the sentiments of most Americans in the trade: "The smoking of opium was a habit as the use of wine was with us, in moderation." And if some Chinese passed from occasional smoking to addiction, what concern was that of the merchant's?

Despite the illegality of the opium trade and the dire penalties threatened by Chinese officials, the Chinese participated in every phase of distribution once the cargo reached their shores.

Outside the mouth of the Pearl River was the island of Lintin, or Solitary Nail. There, in a snug harbor, the junks called by the

The idyllic enclosed world of the foreign factories before the Opium War was immortalized in this painting by George Chinnery. The large building at left was the Customs House, the American factory was marked by the flag furthest to the left while the East India Company stood second from the right.
(NEW YORK HISTORICAL SOCIETY)

Chinese "scrambling dragons" or "fast crabs" lay at anchor waiting for an American or British schooner. These ships lacked the insignia that a commercial house displayed when the brassbound chests were meant to contain tea, for these chests contained opium. The skippers of the fast crabs would maneuver up to the rail of the foreign schooners and barter for the chests. By the 1830s the price had risen as high as $800 for a chest. As soon as the chests were loaded, the junks would disappear upriver. Thus, despite the law, the "foreign mud" always reached someone who was willing to pay for it. Occasionally, a newly appointed official would arrest a drug dealer or two and issue threatening proclamations against the "foreign ships loitering about in unauthorized places." But all would shortly be arranged by the right bribe in the right place.

While a potentially dangerous situation was building up between foreign merchants and Chinese officials, still another disturbing Western influence came knocking at the closed door of the Chinese Empire. That influence was Christianity as preached by the first Protestant missionaries to reach Canton in the early nineteenth century. (Previously, missionaries had been Roman Catholic, especially Jesuits.) The most famous was the pioneering Englishman, Robert Morrison, author of the first Chinese-English dictionaries and grammars.

These men were carried East on the waves of religious revival that grew out of the various "Great Awakenings" in eighteenth- and nineteenth-century Protestant churches in both Britain and America. This movement was by its nature missionary, not only in religion but in social reform. And what better subject could there have been for both conversion and reform than the vast, unawakened Chinese Empire?

Both the missionaries and the merchants wished to make direct contact with the Chinese people. While the missionaries watched from the shelter of the factories, the opium smugglers, growing increasingly aggressive, pushed up the coast as far as Shantung. But in the north the mandarins were more active and less corruptible than those around Canton. Sometimes they fired on the smugglers; lives and ships were lost on both sides.

At last, news of these exchanges reached the emperor, Tao kuang. He chose Lin Tse-hsü, a rising official who had suppressed opium smoking in the interior, to go to Canton and do the same. To the amazement of the foreigners, the strong-minded and incorruptible Lin seized and burned twenty thousand chests of opium valued at $6 million.

The British responded by sending for the navy. This precipitated the so-called Opium War, or First Anglo-Chinese War. Fought between 1839 and 1842, the war consisted primarily of a series of engagements between the British navy and the Chinese fleet. These sea battles irrevocably demonstrated the skill and firepower of modern warships over the lumbering, antiquated junks of the Chinese.

The emperor, believing in his own superiority, failed to grasp the extent of the debacle till the British pushed determinedly up the coast and threatened the supply route to Peking. Under British guns Tao-kuang agreed to the Treaty of Nanking. It exacted $21 million in indemnities, ceded Hong Kong to the British, ended the Co-hong, and provided for the setting of fair and regular tariffs and opened Canton, Amoy, Foochow, Ning-po and Shanghai to British trade. The United States and other European powers, quickly benefiting from the British victory, gained these and other privileges, including the principle of extraterritoriality: each nation would now try its own citizens for crimes committed on Chinese soil, even if against Chinese citizens. Christianity and Western women also gained official entry into China in the 1840s.

Missionaries and traders looked forward eagerly to entering

An old engraving shows the "Victorian Vikings" or British soldiers attacking and capturing Chuenpi, one of the forts protecting Canton, on January 7, 1841, during the Opium War.

the city of Canton with its thick gray stone walls hiding an incredible maze of streets. But the British, having aggravated antiforeign feeling with their looting and burning, especially in Canton, were met by continuing riots. Kept out of the city, the missionaries set up their schools, such as the Morrison Education Society, in the new British colony of Hong Kong. Businessmen, too, made use of this haven. Some Westerners began to venture up the coast into the new treaty ports. Here the people were less hostile to foreigners, perhaps because they had not yet had such abrasive contacts with them as the people of Kwangtung.

The British grew increasingly angry over the failure of the Cantonese to live up to the treaty. In 1846 a new British fleet threatened to bombard the city. As a result, Ki-ying, the viceroy at Nanking, was forced to promise that the gates of Canton would be officially thrown open to foreigners two years hence.

Among the missionaries who had reached Canton in 1846 and witnessed the confrontation between Ki-ying and the British warships was William Speer. Within six months of his arrival he had buried his young wife and infant daughter. He had seen placards in the streets of Canton and the nearby villages denouncing foreigners. Nevertheless, his faith had risen triumphant above these obstacles. With a few other daring men, he ventured into the streets to learn Cantonese and meet the people. Ever hopeful, he felt that the work of the few missionaries in the city was beginning to "create a kindly feeling."

Other missionaries and traders were not so lucky. A colleague of Speer's, while returning from Shanghai to Ning-po on a Chinese boat, was thrown overboard by pirates. And seven young English clerks from the factories, out sculling near the village of Hwang-chu-kee, were surrounded by villagers and slashed with pikes and swords. Only one survived. In both cases the Americans and British demanded and got the arrest and execution of the principals involved in these murders. Apparently, they approved pitiless Chinese justice as long as Westerners were the injured parties.

New missionaries and traders kept arriving to replace those

lost in such tragedies. But the ethnocentric pride of the Westerners met the ethnocentric pride of the Chinese, and little real understanding resulted. The small-town background of most missionaries made it difficult for them to comprehend Chinese civilization; often they were repelled by it. They were roused against such practices as the subjection of women and the "backwardness" of Chinese schools, which were concerned only with teaching the literary language, the key to advancement in Chinese official circles.

From the opposing point of view, the Chinese saw the mission school as subversive of the social order. By educating women, it introduced a disturbing element into the Confucian bond between husband and wife. By teaching modern Western knowledge instead of the works of Confucius, it undermined the Chinese social and political order.

In another incident of the Opium War, superior British ships and weapons overwhelmed the obsolete Chinese junks and guns during the naval engagement at Chapu near the mouth of the Yangtze River above Shanghai on May 18, 1841.

Still, the missionary schools began a slow penetration of Chinese philosophic ideas with Western political and Protestant religious ideas. Perhaps the threat to the Chinese system would not have been so serious if these alien ideas had been spread in peaceful, prosperous times. Westerners, however, had reached China at a time when the Ch'ing or Manchu dynasty was entering its final period of decay. According to an important Chinese theory that predates Confucius, when a dynasty becomes corrupt and can no longer rule the people justly, it loses the "mandate of Heaven." Then the dynasty is bound to fall, and the people are justified in helping to drive it out so a new, virtuous dynasty may rule. This is the Chinese version of the right of rebellion.

Signs that a dynasty is losing the mandate of Heaven are floods, famines and peasant revolts, aggravated by official corruption and wickedness. The signs of Ch'ing decay were already appearing. Because of the peace and prosperity of earlier Ch'ing times, the population of China had reached 400 million by the middle of the nineteenth century. Nowhere was the pressure of too many mouths to feed felt more acutely than in the mountainous semitropical land of Kwangtung, which had always been one of the most crowded of Chinese provinces. Then, in 1846 to 1848, flood and famine, the twin scourges in China's long struggle to feed her millions, swept the Middle Kingdom.

Finally, the pressures of overpopulation, corrupt and unresponsive mandarins and weakening imperial authority brought open battle in the turbulent south. The militia raised by the gentry contested ownership of the precious fields with the clans and stranger Hakkas. The secret societies, always the refuge of malcontents, rebels and landless peasants in an authoritarian society, began stirring, wakened by the rumblings of dynastic decay. Branches of the most famous secret society, the Triad Society, known as the Hung-men Hui (Heaven and Earth society), became embroiled in the Red Turban revolt, recalling their earlier history as Ming supporters against the Manchus.

All this civil strife paled, however, in the face of the bloodiest civil war to shake China before the convulsions of our own century. It was the Taiping rebellion, led by Hung Hsiu-ch'üan, a poor but ambitious Hakka, who had failed several times in the imperial examinations. Inspired in part by a Christian pamphlet that had fallen into his hands, he became convinced that he was destined to save mankind. During a brief stay with an American missionary in Canton in 1847, he studied Christianity. He began to develop a new religion, combining imperfectly understood ideas gleaned from the Bible with the traditional Confucianism of his Chinese scholarly background. In Hung's creed, God was the all-powerful father, Christ the son and Hung His younger brother, sent to create a new kingdom on earth. Hung made little use of Christ's teachings about brotherly love but developed a version of the Ten Commandments. In 1851 Hung raised the banner of the *Tai-p'ing T'ien-kuo*, the "Heavenly Kingdom of Great Peace," with a growing army of converts at his command.

During its thirteen-year existence, the Taiping army half a million strong conquered, looted and burned almost every city in the Yangtze valley. They established their capital at Nanking. Unfortunately, Hung and his lieutenants, with one exception, lacked the leadership qualities to sustain their early victories. Their cruel devastation of the countryside, which they abandoned to wall themselves up in the cities, alienated both peasants and gentry. Their use of pseudo-Christian ideas probably increased the gentry's distaste for both Christianity and foreigners. In record time Hung and his court had abandoned their ascetic ideals for the traditional corruption of a decaying dynasty. The vice and cruelty of the Taiping leaders encouraged the Ch'ing officials to suppress them with bloody ferocity. In 1864 Hung committed suicide amid the ruins of his kingdom. Twenty to thirty million people are estimated to have lost their lives in the rebellion.

Yet the legacy of the Taiping long outlasted their kingdom. The ideas Hung had borrowed from his brief brush with Christianity, from ancient pre-Confucian descriptions of a primitive communist utopia and from the almost wordless desire of the common people for some improvement in their hard lot found temporary expression in the social order the Taiping envisioned. Their emphasis on human equality, women's rights, land reform and even simplification of the Chinese language has influenced and inspired every Chinese revolutionary down to Mao Tse-tung.

The immediate effect of the Taiping rebellion and the revolts and disorders in Kwangtung on the people of the south of China was disastrous, however. The poor peasant had suffered a crushing blow in his struggle for existence. Family survival demanded emigration. Fortunately, a new alternative to the plantations and mines of Southeast Asia had become available. In 1848 word reached up into the hills from Hong Kong and Canton that gold had been found across the Pacific in California.

Peasants coming down from the mountains to trade in the markets took home word of *Gum Shan*, the "Mountain of Gold," where the daring might win lifelong ease by one lucky dig. Here was a gamble worth taking. Ships were constantly sailing from Hong Kong to the Golden Gate. Just as the Atlantic shipping companies of the time balanced their budgets by the notoriously overcrowded steerage trade from England and Ireland, so the Pacific companies had found a new means of profit—human cargo. Those Chinese who hadn't the price of a ticket could borrow from kinsmen or brokers in Canton. Relatively few Chinese came to America under the contract labor system that became notorious in Southeast Asia and South America.

The students gathered around the mission schools were naturally affected by the news. When William Speer was declared physically unfit for the China mission because of a recurring lung weakness and started home by way of Capetown, some of his former pupils were planning to set sail for the Golden Gate. The magnet that drew them and their countrymen in increasing numbers to California would shortly draw Speer and other of his missionary colleagues to a new challenge. The drama of American aspirations for the Chinese and Chinese response to them would be reenacted on American soil.

CHAPTER *3*

MINING:
THE FIRST
FRONTIER

*The Chinese bid fair to overrun the country. People are
getting really alarmed at the great number coming.*
FRANKLIN BUCK, *A Yankee Trader in the Gold Rush*

SAN Francisco during the early gold rush was largely a
provisioning stop for miners en route to the goldfields.
And the Cantonese, driven by the adventurous spirit and desire to
save their families that had launched them across seven thousand
miles of perilous seas to the Golden Gate also went on almost
immediately to the mines.

Every spring the San Francisco newspapers sent reporters
down to the steamer landing to record the regular departure of
miners for Sacramento and the northern gold rivers or for Stockton
and the southern mines. Each year the reporters noted, at first with

genuine, if patronizing amusement, but later with growing acerbity, the Chinese contingent in this exodus. In 1850 a reporter hoped they would "get dust enough to build pagodas of gold"; two years later, a dour commentator from the same paper, the *Daily Alta*, was finding them the "least profitable of miners. Their wants are few and supplied in a cheap and peculiar manner, and as they are saving, penurious and apt at trade, society seldom gets the benefit of their earnings. When they have a few hundred dollars they go back to China."

Hostility to the Chinese surfaced suddenly in cosmopolitan San Francisco in the spring of 1852. The early Californians dreamed of building up their state rapidly to rival the wealth of the older, more settled and, of course, more tradition-bound states of the East. They envisioned a new paradise of perfect democracy blooming from the coastal beaches to the top of the Sierras. Of course, building the paradise required the rapid development of California's incomparable natural resources. Massive labor would be needed to achieve this miracle, and free white Americans were not eager to perform it.

Sen. George B. Tingley of the California legislature had a solution to this problem. Why should he not introduce a contract labor bill which would allow Chinese workers to sign contracts for up to ten years of service at fixed wages and then provide that the state government enforce the contracts? In recent years those few Chinese who had sold their services for several years' wages in order to get to California had often disappeared into the mines, like free white Americans, long before the contract had run out.

To the intense surprise of its sponsor, the Tingley bill set off a loud cry of indignation from most Californians. In a politically expedient speech which reflected the popular mood very well, Gov. John Bigler, who was running for reelection, articulated the idea that California was to be a white man's country, not a land for a "servile" class of "coolie laborers." From this speech there arose the specter of the "coolie"—a term not previously applied to the Chinese—who would undercut the white worker's wages and reduce his family to starvation. This monstrous image greatly distorted in size and fearsomeness the reality of the Chinese immigration.

Several reasons have been given for the sudden emergence and growth of this political issue. The first was a connection perceived by some Americans between gangs of Chinese laborers and gangs of black slaves in the South. Such Americans did not know or care that most Chinese came to California of their own free will. Then there were the distinctive physical characteristics and customs of the Chinese, which made them an easy target of other men's frustrations, and the low opinion that many Americans were developing about them from unfavorable books on China. Finally, and underlying all the others, was the American prejudice against the Chinese because of their race, their dislike of any color except white.

While the fight over the Tingley bill was heating up, the Chinese at first continued to mine in relative peace, though any outsider touring the mines might have sensed a more hostile and frenetic atmosphere than usual. One such observer was Hwang Apo, a former pupil of the Reverend William Speer at the missionary school in Canton, who had come to California with his brother, a rice merchant. Though barely out of his teens, Hwang regularly traveled through the goldfields, collecting orders for his brother's firm.

If Hwang headed for the northern mines by way of the Sacramento steamer, he would of course stop at local Chinese stores in the larger centers, such as Marysville. There the back room would be set up for tea and perhaps a fan-tan game. As Hwang traveled along the banks of gold-bearing streams, he might stay with a lone miner, endlessly pouring water over the sand in his rocker or cradle. More often he would stop at the camp of a typical Chinese mining party, a group of thirty or forty Chinese miners who lived and worked together with an English-speaking boss and a cook to serve the customary rice, vegetables, meat and fish. Group living gave the Chinese protection from the vague menace of a frontier community full of men who had fled the restraints of civilization to pursue dreams of quick riches.

Even in these early days the Chinese often took over claims abandoned by white men rather than try to establish their own. If their diggings were too rich, a party of white miners was sure to jump the claim, and the Chinese stood little chance of ever recovering it.

Working together, the Chinese would operate a "long tom," an oversized rocker into which a couple of men could shovel dirt at one time. Or they would construct a wing dam of logs shaped like an

Characteristic of the worldwide interest in the California Gold Rush was this picture in a German publication, showing two Chinese washing gold-bearing earth in a giant rocker or cradle while a lone European prospector used the more primitive pan. (SAN FRANCISCO PUBLIC LIBRARY)

"L" extending from the shore out to the middle of a stream and then turned at right angles and continued downstream leaving one half the river bed bare. Into this dam they would patiently shovel earth, wash the dirt away by diverting the water and catch the gold-bearing particles in a riffle box lined with mercury.

Hwang had had many opportunities to observe the average American or European gold-seeker, whose disappointed hopes could so easily flare up in violence. He hardly fitted the definition of a good Christian that Hwang had learned in Dr. Speer's school.

The neatness of the Chinese, who generally bathed each evening after work, contrasted sharply with the unshaved faces and unwashed bodies of the usual Caucasian miner. And Chinese hospitality was also conspicuous in the dog-eat-dog world of the mining settlements. Hwang often found white miners dropping in for supper at some of the Chinese camps and accepting the proffered share of rice. As one traveler discovered, "The Chinese invariably treated in the same hospitable manner anyone who visited their camps and seemed rather pleased than otherwise at the interest and curiosity excited by their domestic arrangements."[4]

In early May Hwang Apo returned to a Chinese store in Marysville, the northern mining center. By this time the debate over the Tingley bill had spread throughout the mines, bringing increased harassment of the Chinese there. Over a cup of tea Hwang listened to a story even more disquieting than any he had yet heard. A miner who was also drinking his tea had been working alone at Foster's and Atkinson's Bar on the Yuba River. There were several companies of Chinese miners and a large number of Americans and Europeans working in smaller groups. No trouble had arisen between the races there until recently. But the Chinese were well organized and had unusually rich claims. Several unsuccessful miners had remarked that the diggings were too rich for the Chinese.

On May 2 the white men had been ominously absent from the river. When the thunderous tread of many feet reached the ears of the lone miner, some instinct led him to conceal himself on a shelf of rock above the river. Shortly, several hundred miners appeared over the hill, led by a man whose profanity and ill luck in mining were notorious. He announced that by unanimous vote of the citizens of Yuba County, all Chinese were to cease work in the Yuba River and depart at once for other diggings, preferably for the flowery hills of the Celestial Kingdom. This was white man's country and from now on they intended to keep it that way. And if the China boys didn't make tracks, they'd soon find themselves swimming back to San Francisco if their heads weren't bashed in.

Without waiting for a translation, the Chinese began to retreat—some walking, some running, some carrying rolls of bedding or a precious shovel or rocker. Their whiskey-primed assailants speeded them on their way with kicks and punches and by firing rifles in the air. The lone miner huddled among the rocks saw rice spilled all over the ground, tents slashed and rolls of bedding ripped open. Only toward evening did he dare to start back toward Marysville, carrying the remnants of his mining supplies.

As Hwang Apo hurried back to San Francisco to warn his brother of the trouble in the mines, leaders of the Four Great Houses (as the early district companies were called) were meeting with American advisers to deal with the crisis. The riots threatened the hopes of emerging capitalists like As-sing, who wanted to build a fortune in California's tax-free paradise. The simple sojourners who had risked their lives and those of their families to make the long trip to California faced an even bleaker future if they returned home empty-handed.

The Four Great Houses' defense of their community against this sudden explosion of hostility took several forms. Upon the immediate advice of their American advisers, the leaders helped compose a letter which the newspapers published on April 30, signed by Tong K. Achick and Hab Wa. Despite his youth, Tong was proving an invaluable aid in the crisis because of his English education. The letter attempted to defend Tong's countrymen against the unjust charges made by Gov. John Bigler during his reelection campaign. Bigler had led the political attack on the Chinese, claiming that they had come to America under coercion, that they were "coolie laborers" undercutting the wages of white workingmen, and so on.

In June, Tong also led a delegation of a more traditional Chinese stamp to Sacramento to see Bigler. Tong brought gifts, such as shawls with elaborate and unusual designs, rolls of the finest silk and seventy beautifully embroidered hankerchiefs. In the best politician's style Bigler clicked champagne glasses with Tong, then proceeded on his anti-Chinese crusade as soon as his guest was gone.

Meanwhile the disorder in the mines grew alarmingly. In Jacksonville, in the San Joaquin valley, the miners expelled all the Chinese from their diggings. The local authorities, whether from conviction or sympathy with the white miners, claimed they could not intervene on mining premises. And, of course, the atmosphere of mob rule encouraged the casual crime against the Chinese that was already common. For example, some ruffians who attacked a Chinese tent near Chili Gulch wounded the occupant so seriously that he died. In this case a fair-minded sheriff brought the villains to trial, but juries rarely convicted such criminals. More rarely were they punished even for a "hanging" crime.

Tong K. Achick took a leading part in a partial and temporary solution to the problem, which was one of businessmen among businessmen. In the spring of 1853, Tong testified before the Committee on Mines and Mining of the California legislature. He promised increased trade between China and California if only his people and their property might receive protection. To accomplish this he suggested that the tax on foreign miners, first imposed in 1850, might be retained or even increased, and that the revenue be kept in the district where it was collected.

This strategy of the Chinese leaders actually succeeded for twenty years. The collection of the foreign miner's tax, which the companies promised to help collect and which was directed mainly at the Chinese, created tax havens for all the American property owners in the mining country. Because of it the Chinese were tolerated in most such areas. In fact, with the decline in mining and the rise in railroad construction in the 1860s, many mining counties lamented the loss of Chinese miners to the rails.

Nevertheless, the protection afforded to the Chinese in the hills by the collection of the foreign miner's tax was fragile at best. Though the counties that benefited from the tax licenses did not wish to eliminate a source of revenue, they paid little attention to how the tax was collected, provided no one was killed, and sometimes not even then.

Nothing better illustrates the methods of many collectors of the tax than the uninhibited diary of Charles E. de Long, who laid the foundation of his future political success while serving in Yuba County in 1855–56. The tone is that of a young man playing pranks, until we realize the cruelty and callousness to human beings that he unwittingly reveals. By boasting of his exploits, de Long sadly documents the low opinion most Californians held of the Chinese:

> *July 30, 1855—hunted Chinese in the night, done very well, collected about 80 licenses. . . .*
> *August 16, 1855—Had a China fight. Knocked down some and drawed our tools on the rest and they put out . . . .*
> *(Average take $2904 for August, $2736 for September, $3000 for October, and $4066 for November.)*
> *October 23 . . . Had a great time, Chinamen tails cut off.*

The impunity with which a tax collector might injure or even kill a Chinese miner was reinforced by the hostility to the Chinese that developed during the debate over the Tingley bill. In addition, the lawlessness and violence of the frontier certainly contributed to it. One would have thought that time would have cured the first cause of unrest, since the Tingley bill was never passed. Indeed, a general decline in Chinese immigration followed the hostility aroused by that debate. And as law and order were gradually imposed on the countryside, one would have expected the frontier violence to subside. In fact, the violence against the Chinese continued in the mining country all during the 1850s and 1860s. And the tax collector was not the only villain. One of the most important factors undermining the position of the Chinese was a landmark court decision which was handed down by Chief Justice Hugh Murray of California early in 1854. It was one of the most momentous and damaging cases ever to involve the Chinese. It struck at the very roots of the ability of the Chinese to defend themselves against the terror and injustice of which they were all too often the victims.

This case, known as *The People* v. *George W. Hall*, began in a bare country courtroom in Nevada County in the late summer of 1853. One of the main observers and participants was the Reverend William Speer, who had been asked by a Chinese delegation including Tong K. Achick to become "their chief in this country. They need a general superintendent, well acquainted with foreign customs and business, in whom implicit confidence could be placed and who would shield them, if an American, from many annoyances, and acts of injury and plunder, to which they are now daily liable."[5] It was a sure sign of the mutual confidence between Speer and the Chinese that they had chosen him for such a position.

Because of his relation to the Chinese and his knowledge of their customs and language, Speer had been invited to help interpret the evidence in the case by Judge William T. Barbour, an honorable and intelligent man who had left his native Kentucky for the Wild West. The background of the case was described by Speer in a letter:

> *Two brothers named Hall (from Illinois or Indiana) and a person named Wiseman were "prospecting" on Bear River. Near sundown, on the 9th of August, they came upon a Chinese camp. The Halls, with little or no provocation, fell upon and cruelly beat one of the Chinese whom they met alone, and, as he says, searched him for gold, though without obtaining any. The man, as soon as released, fled crying for help "to save his life." The Americans started upon his track, carrying their baggage and rifles. As they passed by some tents*

at a little distance, the cousin of the man, hearing his cries,
ran out, and was immediately shot down by the elder Hall. . . .
The whole testimony in the case was Chinese. . . .

In his bare country courtroom Judge Barbour was attempting
to impose order and civilization upon the natural anarchy of the
mines. He confided to Speer his apprehension that the local mining
community might resort to mob violence if the Halls or Wiseman
were convicted on Chinese evidence alone. One of the most common
anti-Chinese stereotypes of the time was that they constantly
perjured themselves in court. But Judge Barbour was determined
not to let his fears affect his judgment.

Under the suspicious eyes of the white miners, it was a tense
moment when the five Chinese witnesses were sworn in, using the
form of oath already accepted in the courts of San Francisco and
Hong Kong. A pledge to truth before Imperial Heaven was written
upon yellow paper. The paper was then burned before their eyes.
According to Speer, "their testimony was direct, clear and, after
severe cross-examination, to every mind unbiased, convincing."
Judge, jury, even the attorney for the defense, confessed themselves
impressed. George, the elder Hall, was found guilty of murder in
the first degree, the other two were acquitted (Wiseman having
given evidence against George Hall). Sentencing of Hall was
delayed till the next term of the court in December.

Speer returned to San Francisco to celebrate with his Chinese
friends the victory of justice over bigotry. He and they were sure
that the conviction of Hall would discourage many of the injuries,
robberies and killings that were so frequently committed against
the Chinese. Now that the protection of the courts had been
extended to them, they were sure that ruffians would hesitate before
singling them out as victims.

Alas! Within a few months their high hopes were dashed by
the resurgence of racism in the courts. In early 1854, the case of
The People v. *George W. Hall,* was appealed to the California
Supreme Court. Chief Justice Hugh Murray delivered the land-

Chinese miners at work and at rest in a typical California Chinese mining camp of the 1850s were portrayed as exotic but not ridiculous or degraded as in many illustrations later in the century.
(NEW YORK HISTORICAL SOCIETY)

mark decision. In rendering his opinion, Murray quoted Section 14 of the Criminal Act stating that "no Black, or Mulatto person, or Indian shall be allowed to give evidence in favor of, or against a White man." Since the words *Indian, Negro, Black* and *White* were generic terms designating race, Murray said, Chinese and all other peoples not white were included in the prohibition. Murray ruled that the intent of the statute was to protect white men from the influence of any testimony except by others of the same race; therefore, George Hall, who had been convicted purely on Chinese evidence, was free.

Lest anyone fail to understand his position, Murray pictured the horrors that would follow from Chinese testimony in the courts. Soon they would be allowed to vote, sit on juries, even on the bench and in the legislature. All of these were things that men of good will, like the first editor of the *Daily Alta*, had hoped that the Chinese would do as soon as they became accustomed to American ways. On the other hand, they were the sorts of things that racists often blamed the Chinese for not taking an interest in. From then on the Chinese were frequently caught in the double bind that racism imposes on its victims; they were criticized for not taking an interest in American ways or American politics while both law and custom forbade them to participate in such activities in any meaningful way.

In his opinion Murray also confessed himself appalled by the spectacle of "the distinct people, living in our community . . . differing in language, opinions, color and physical conformation; between whom and ourselves nature has placed an impassible difference . . . for them is claimed . . . the right to swear away the life of a citizen. . . ."[6]

By his opinion Murray had summed up all those current views of the Chinese that regarded them as set apart, inferior and not quite human. Whenever a people is officially put in such a position in relation to the majority of the citizens of the country where they live—whether the Indians of the Great Plains, black people in the South, Armenians in Turkey or Jews in Nazi Germany —the results are usually individual cruelty, mob violence condoned or encouraged by the authorities and unpunished crimes against people and property.

Denied equal rights in the courts by the Hall case, the Chinese received another setback late in 1854. A Chinese named Chan Yong applied for citizenship in the federal district court in San Francisco. The newspapers noted that he was more "white" than most Chinese. However, the federal judges unanimously ruled that Chinese were not "white" under the law and therefore could not be citizens. This decision struck at the hopes of precisely those educated Chinese who would have had the greatest interest in and understanding of American ways.

The immediate effect of this court decision and of the denial of citizenship on the Chinese ability to defend themselves against robbery and violence is well illustrated by a story told of Ah Sam, the boss of a Chinese mining company working in 1856 on the

American River not far from the site of John Marshall's original gold discovery near Sutter's Mill. One day as Ah Sam's men were busy sifting through the river sand for gold, a Mexican bandit swooped down on them. Finding them unarmed, he began to tie their queues together so he might rob them. When Ah Sam returned to the river and saw the bandit at work, he seized a gun and held it to the man's head. The other miners tied the bandit to a pole, and like a pig for the market, he was carried to the nearest courthouse in Auburn. When the judge saw their strange cargo, he asked only one question, "Where are your Caucasian witnesses?" Ah Sam told him there were none, so the judge dismissed the case.

The reception of Ah Sam's case against the bandit certainly underlines the reason why more Chinese did not resist their tormentors, and Ah Sam's perplexed response of "What for?" sums up the chances of a Chinese for justice in the mining communities. It also explains why the Chinese generally took care of their own problems, a practice for which they were often criticized.

It would be a mistake to imagine that all Chinese in the mining country were helpless victims who never raised a hand to defend themselves. Though they were generally more murdered than murdering, they had their rascals as well as their models of filial piety and diligence. Though they generally worked in gangs, as much from choice as from necessity, they had their free spirits who roamed the hills much like the Western loner of American myth, half-hero, half-outlaw. The most fascinating tale of such a Chinese desperado is the story of Fou Sin.

On November 7, 1857, in Jackson, California, Fou Sin, plotting with several countrymen, murdered M. V. B. Griswold, an equally restless adventurer, scion of an old New England family settled in upper New York State. Griswold had knocked about the West Coast and Pacific islands, often among warlike Indians. "He had frequently been in positions where dangers of dire character confronted him, but his tact, energy, quick decision and boldness had always carried him successfully through." His nineteenth-century white man's contempt for Indians and Chinese may have irritated his murderers and led to his death; it may also have made him unsuspicious that they were capable of harming him.

Twenty-six-year-old Fou Sin, the son of a poor Cantonese stone-cutter, had lived a life strikingly similar to that of his victim. He had gone to sea at twelve on a British ship, then traveled around the world as a sailor on various ships till he reached San Francisco in early 1857. There he proved equally ready to defend himself in a fight with a knife or his fists. After one fight too many, he was unemployed and hungry when his fellow Cantonese Chou Yee, a cook on the Q ranch, accompanied him to Jackson. The local Chinese stagecoach agent found him a job as cook for a Mr. Horace Kilham, a mine owner and money changer. Griswold, having also drifted penniless into Jackson, had gone to work for Mr. Kilham as business manager and clerk.

Robbery was obviously the prime motive for the murder, since Griswold held the key to Kilham's safe. The whole escapade was carefully planned by Fou Sin, whom all acknowledged to be the leader. He possessed an uncommonly keen, if thwarted, intelligence. After Griswold was killed with a blow on the head from a club, both he and the murder weapon were concealed under Fou's bed and a board nailed over the side reaching to the floor. Three other men played a part—Coon You, Coon See and Ah Hung, a man from Indian Creek.

All the men escaped, and the body was not found till the next day; some weeks later Fou Sin and Chou Yee were betrayed, probably for the reward, by Ah Cow, with whom they had then refuge, and shortly afterward, Coon You and Coon See were caught as well. Coon See claimed he was standing watch outside, but the other three were convicted and hanged on April 16, 1858, surprisingly "the first Chinamen who have ever been convicted, in a civilized country, of the murder of a white man." Coon See, destined to be tried as an "accessory after the fact," hanged himself in his cell.

A contemporary pamphlet describing the murder offers fascinating life stories of the Chinese participants, especially Fou Sin, and the graceful lyrics they wrote as their own epitaphs and sent home to their families. The contrast between his haunting poetry and the brutal crime struck one perceptive editorial writer for the *Daily Alta*. It set him to speculating on the mysteries of the Chinese spirit so little understood by the white men around him.

Fou Sin revealed the struggle between the traditional Chinese view of life and the modern skeptical man when he wondered about the all-important fate of his body:

> *I think my brother and my father will send for my bones after I am dead and take them home to China. . . . I would some rather they would send for my bones, but do not care very much. I have seen so many people buried at sea, their bones cannot be buried. But I would a little rather they would send and take me back to the Flowery Kingdom; I hope and think they will. Then hath the spirit peace forever.*

Even more interesting is Fou Sin's advice to his brother, born of the bitter ending of a wasted life:

> *Your brother still lives. Listen to me. He has words for you; I warn you. My words are those of a true affection. When you become a man, be not wild, nor frivolous, nor fond of wild plays. Let your words be truth. Avoid idle talk. On you is centered the affection, so complete, of a whole house. Whilst this I say, still you are my brother to all time. "One thousand leagues shorten one's existence!" . . . my younger brother . . . must not cease to hold me in remembrance.*

> [*Epitaph*]

> *Green spring, I await you in gladness*
> *Who can obstruct or impede the vast harvest of the grain.*
> *True felicity must come from self, otherwise 'tis nothing.*
> *After joyful spring, comes tedious autumn.*[7]

So across an ocean a condemned murderer sent wise words of Confucian duty and right conduct to his sober, stay-at-home brother, and one of those graceful, melancholy lyrics that evoke the rich farming country of south China. So two young men, far from home, seeking their fortunes, collided and met their deaths in the explosive atmosphere of the California mining country.

As the 1850s waned, a change came over gold mining in California. Nuggets were no longer to be found lying about in stream beds. The individualistic miner of the gold rush, dressed in high boots, slouch hat, old trousers and a red flannel shirt, panning gold by himself or with a partner, could no longer make a living. Increasingly, he pushed north and east. As early as 1852 there were miners in the Rogue River valley in southern Oregon, and Chinese were among them. New mining frontiers continued to lure the most adventurous miners still farther afield in the late 1850s and early 1860s. Many Chinese also joined the trek—to Pike's Peak, Colorado, in 1858; to the Comstock Lode in Nevada for silver in 1859; to Idaho in 1860; to Montana in 1864.

Mining in California, though it remained the state's first-ranked industry until 1867, gradually passed into an era dominated by the large mining company, with individuals working merely as employees. Quartz mining, which required rock-crushing machines to extract the gold dust, and hydraulic mining, which involved a large-scale diversion of the river to wash the gold, replaced the cradle, the long tom and the sluice, which could be built and worked by a relatively small group of men.

With the easy gold gone, the Chinese came more and more into favor as miners because they were generally quiet and hard-working. A few figures will tell the story of the shift. In 1855 there were 120,000 miners in California, of whom about 20,000 were Chinese. In 1861 the over-all number had dropped to 100,000, and the percentage of Chinese was increasing. In 1870 there were only 36,000 miners left in the state, and 9,000, or 25 percent, were

Chinese. Most of these Chinese miners were either working for large companies or belonged to a small Chinese company that had bought up a claim abandoned by white men and were patiently sifting the sand for every last trace of gold.

With the failure of many individual prospectors, with the shift of the remaining white miners from entrepreneur to employee, the Chinese became more than ever a convenient scapegoat. At the same time, wages for the most menial labor in California, which had been abnormally high in the gold rush, were slowly dropping to more normal levels. They were by no means as low as in the East. However, men who had come West to get rich quickly were not eager to work for a laborer's wages. Employers were naturally

Cartoons warning an employer against the use of "Chinese cheap labor" reflected the campaign of boycott and intimidation against Chinese workers and their bosses by white unions that helped reinforce the "coolie" stereotype.

(NEW YORK PUBLIC LIBRARY PICTURE COLLECTION)

happy to hire the Chinese, who found their pay scales quite satisfactory. Such action on the part of the Chinese aroused still greater hostility from white miners. For example, in 1869 the Miner's League of white workers at Sutter's Creek went on strike. In a day when strikes rarely ended well for the strikers, they succeeded in forcing the company head to fire all his Chinese workers.

The enmity aroused by Chinese miners followed them to all the other mining states to which they traveled. It also pursued them into other kinds of mining, such as quicksilver and coal. This smoldering resentment of white workers against the Chinese was destined one day to explode. When it did, it would be a tragic day for Chinese miners.

All the threats to Chinese rights in America, with their consequences in physical danger, created a climate of crisis around Chinese communities. Yet despite this atmosphere and despite the loneliness as men alien and apart, the Chinese endured in California. Some even found success. There were two sets of reasons for this survival. One had to do with the support that the Chinese received from employers who appreciated their abilities as workers, from missionaries who offered them education, medicine and friendship even when they could not convert them and a few enlightened journalists and judges who tried to see that America treated them justly. The other, and perhaps more important, reason had to do with the structure of the Chinese world. That structure protected the sojourner, helped him in his work and gave him the strength to pursue his lonely existence. In the streets and behind the doors of the Chinese quarter, the real life of most sojourners went on; it is there that one must look for the secret of their survival in America.

CHAPTER 4

CHINATOWN:
THE SAFE
HARBOR

The Chinese will not become permanent residents and they are not desired to become such; they will not assimilate, and are not wanted to assimilate; they are an inferior race and they supersede the Caucasians in labor. . . .
REV. ALBERT WILLIAMS, *A Pioneer Pastorate and Times*

FROM the first, China Street, soon to become Chinatown, was a major tourist attraction in San Francisco. Visitors from abroad and from the East in their innumerable travel articles and books about gold-rush California almost invariably commented on the most exotic and alien people in that cosmopolitan city. Many of these reporters went sightseeing along Sacramento and Dupont streets, stopping to look at exquisite porcelains, silks and ivories in Chinese stores, attending Chinese theater productions, observing Chinese gambling houses or eating in Chinese restaurants. Some were charmed by the colorful atmosphere of this Canton-by-the-bay.

For others it was a filthy and overcrowded slum, inhabited by a "degraded" people, worse than the Five Points—then the toughest section of the nation's biggest city, New York.

Whatever their reaction to Chinatown, these writers generally had a very superficial view of Chinese life in America. Like the tourist of today, they saw Chinatown as a series of postcard views, either quaint and charming or poor and miserable. They had, with few exceptions, little sense of the people who inhabited these crowded buildings. For example, many people who commented in the 1850s on the overcrowded dwellings did not realize that most Chinese did not live there permanently. There was a great turnover of Chinese, coming and going to the mines, using the houses of the district companies as hotels. Thus, if we wish to understand the daily life of the Chinese in America, including the significance of the institutions that shaped their lives, we must penetrate this façade.

The average Chinese laborer, usually a former peasant, often illiterate and speaking but a few words of pidgin English, left little written evidence of his adventures. Yet his story can be pieced together from the autobiographies of the few who rose to wealth or fame, from the few facts in old newspapers or from chance quotes in old books and letters. From all these sources we learn of the series of parallel or interlocking associations and organizations that gave meaning and order to the life of the Chinese sojourner.

Because of these organizations, the Chinese sojourner just debarked after his journey across the Pacific was not quite so lonely as he often seemed to the outside observer. He had probably already received the greatest help in reaching San Francisco from the group that had looked after him and given focus to his life in China—his family. In America small family groups of directly related immigrants (*fongs*) and larger family-name associations, consisting of people with the same surname, such as Lee, provided the first line of assistance to the Chinese in America. Regardless of whether he had family members in America, the arriving Chinese was certain to need the services of his district company. These larger organizations, the next step up the ladder of Chinatown associations, provided mutual aid to sojourners from the same part of Kwangtung, with similar dialects and customs. Side by side with the district companies and in some cases serving the same individuals were the secret societies, or *tongs*, whose exact nature and purpose has so fascinated and bewildered the outside world. In later years unions or guilds of Chinese in a particular trade added to the complexity of Chinatown's structure.

At the top of the pyramid was the organization that came to be known in the 1860s as the Chinese Six Companies, a loose federation of leaders of the district companies. The Six Companies attempted to unite the other groups, to arbitrate their disagreements and to speak with a semiofficial voice when threatened by the hostile majority. We have already seen them, in their earliest form, as the Four Great Houses under Tong K. Achick, defending Chinese interests in the California legislature against the agitation caused by the Tingley bill. Naturally, they had little direct contact with the average immigrant.

Completely outside the structure of the Chinese world and yet offering services of a special kind to its residents were the missionaries and their missions. The missions were not a part of the social structure of Chinatown, and yet they were a part of the Chinatown scene. Thus they often were of most help to those Chinese who did not quite fit into the usual organizations, or who desired most strongly to draw away from the Chinese world and closer to the American one.

Even before he embarked on his adventure, the young Chinese sojourner, who was usually between fifteen and twenty-five, received essential aid from his family. With their help or that of the elders of the clan in the village he had raised the money for the ticket which must be repaid from his earnings. Often a field had been mortgaged or a pig sold to provide security for the loan from a ticket broker in Hong Kong. Often, too, the young Chinese left behind a wife and a child or two. Almost always he left behind parents and younger brothers and sisters in need of some support.

If he were lucky, the arriving sojourner would find relatives or members of his family-name association already established here. After the early pioneering days, many Chinese arrived to find such a family enclave among the Chinese immigrants. He might even find a job waiting at a business run by his family; more likely, members of the family could direct him to the boss of the place where they were working. If the older generation eventually retired to Kwangtung, there would always be someone of the same name in America to provide continuity into the next generation.

The immense importance of family names in China is shown by two facts. To begin with, the proper order of a name in China is surname first and personal name second. Thus Tong K. Achick belongs to the Tong family and Sun Yat-sen to the Sun family. In the second place, all people of the same surname in China are assumed to descend from the same ancestor and are forbidden to marry anyone with the same surname, even if no direct relationship can be traced. Eventually, as more Cantonese arrived, the ones whose surnames were most common, such as Wong and Lee, began to form associations of considerable influence. (The Chinese communities of certain cities came to be dominated by certain families such as the Fongs in Sacramento, the Moys in Chicago and the Tongs in Phoenix, Arizona.)

Whether or not he already had relatives waiting for him in California, the new immigrant often got his most immediate and tangible help from his district company. These mutual-aid societies, dominated by the merchant princes, provided essential services that only a formally organized and businesslike body with greater power than his immediate kin could provide. No sooner had he reached the pier than agents of the district companies were trying to reach him and identify the part of Kwangtung from which he had emigrated. According to one observer, the agents and workers identified each other by "some incomprehensible freemasonry of signs"; more likely, it was by accent and local dialect. As soon as he had cleared customs, the new arrival would shoulder his carrying pole, hung with rolls of bedding and bundles of clothing. He would then follow the agent to a wagon destined for the headquarters of the district company. If too many laborers had arrived at once, many had to walk behind the wagon. If they were lucky, they reached the district house without being bloodied by stones tossed by the hoodlums of the city, who considered such target practice great sport.

The house of the district company became a true haven for the sojourner, who was probably as bewildered by the strange look and smell of the *fan qui* ("foreign devils") as he was by their hostility. For all practical purposes single, even if he had a wife in China, he needed a place to sleep among friends. In most cases he also needed a job and a place to bank his money. The district company provided all these essential forms of assistance. At times the company also functioned as a hospital and, when life had faded, as a funeral parlor. Most important of all to a homesick Chinese was the promise of the company to send his bones back to China to repose forever in the soil of his native village, so his soul at least need not wander homeless after death, a promise that was kept right down to the days of the Communist revolution. It remained his strongest tie to the Pearl River delta.

The members of the district companies received other benefits from their membership. The companies served as chambers of commerce for businesses run by members, maintained contact with families back home, protected members against injury and mediated disputes that might be misunderstood or unfairly judged by outsiders. The exercise of this semijudicial function by the companies led Americans to accuse the Chinese of having their own laws, outside the laws of the state. In fact, the Chinese settled disputes among themselves only with the tacit consent of white officials who did not wish to be bothered with the quarrels of an alien people.

The newly arrived sojourner might also have gotten a feeling of protection from the company posters offering rewards for the apprehension of murderers and robbers of members. Unfortunately, this action was about the only one the companies could take after the Murray decision stripped the Chinese of their equality before

In 1862 San Francisco was young and vigorous with a population approaching 60,000. Clipper ships from around Cape Horn and across the Pacific foreshadowed her future importance as a crossroads of Far Eastern trade.

the law. The futility of company efforts in tracking murderers emerges from a report submitted to a committee of the California legislature in 1862. Eighty-eight murders of Chinese had been documented, and many others doubtless went unrecorded for lack of witnesses. Of this number, eleven were known to have been murdered by collectors of the foreign miners' tax, and only two murderers had been convicted and hanged.

The question of whether the district companies were "flooding" California with "coolie laborers," as charged by anti-Chinese politicians, is a complicated one. Undoubtedly, the company leaders did recruit workers and lend money to them, but the initial demand came from American businessmen, some of whom made a business of importing laborers. Ever since the rise of industrial society in the early nineteenth century, the more developed countries of the world have required large quantities of cheap labor. The Chinese merely supplied this need in the West as landless laborers from the British Isles, especially Ireland, did in the East. Since the Chinese, unlike the Europeans, could not become citizens, their various associations provided them with "many of the services the political machine gave to the enfranchised European immigrant."[8]

As their names imply, the district companies soon divided along geographic lines. The first mutual-aid society, the Chew Yick Kung Shaw (Luminous Unity Public Office), dominated by Norman As-sing, began to break up into groups with differing dialects and customs. In 1851 the Sam Yap Wui Kun (Three Districts Company), representing Canton city, seceded from the unified society. In that same year the numerous sojourners from the rustic mountainous district of Sinning joined the peasants from neighboring districts to form the Sze Yap Wui Kun (Four Districts Company). During the next ten years three companies further divided the Punti or native Cantonese, and one was formed by the Hakka families. This brought the number to six by 1862 and led to the formation of the Six Companies.

The rise of the district companies gave many, but not all, of the Chinese sojourners the kind of help they needed in adjusting to their difficult life. Some, especially those from weak clans, those ostracized by their clans or those from the poorest, most remote country districts, naturally had the least influence in the district companies. For the benefit of such a sojourner another organization was growing up in Chinatown. It was the tong, or secret society.

The tongs were a peculiar American development of the secret societies by which Chinese peasants, landless laborers and clan outcasts had for centuries tried to defend themselves against the recurrent tyrannies of emperors and officials. The most recent and active Chinese version was the Hung-men Hui (Heaven and Earth or Wide-Gate Society), one of the many names under which the Triad Society masqueraded. The slogan of the Triad was "Down with the Ch'ing: Restore the Ming." Periodically, the Triad had risen in rebellion, only to be bloodily suppressed, and during the Taiping rebellion, it had been involved in its own Red Turban revolt.

When the Taiping was suppressed, many former soldiers, as well as peasants ruined by the conflict, joined the migration to America. Among them were members of the Triad Society, who established branches in America. Inevitably, though gradually, the tongs became a power to be reckoned with in Chinatown. A Chinese maxim aptly conveys the importance of the tongs to the poorest sojourners: "The Mandarin derives his power from the law, the people from the secret societies."⁹

In America there was no corrupt dynasty to oppose, but there was a hostile society which offered little help to the sojourner. The tongs had several kinds of assistance to give him. These included diversions to soften his loneliness, secret rituals that gave him a feeling of importance, brothers to defend him from his enemies and the warmth of celebrations that he remembered longingly from home.

Some tongs also began to supply recreation and the companionship of women. In this way they expanded their power through the control of those extralegal, but popular activities which have always attracted the forces of organized crime—drugs, gambling and prostitution. For example, the Hip Shing Tong (Hall of Victorious Union) was the gamblers' society, while the On Leong Tong (Chamber of Tranquil Conscientiousness) and Kwong Dak Tong (Chamber of Far-Reaching Virtue) were rivals in the slave-girl traffic. During the criminal phase of tong activity in America, the revolutionary aims of the societies were all but forgotten. Yet one acute American observer prophesied that when the Chinese awakened politically to the benefits of liberty, the societies might well inspire a revolution in China.

The sojourner joining a tong was certainly attracted in part by the elaborate and mysterious rites which have drawn people to secret societies in every age, including our own. The existence of the tongs first came to light in San Francisco on the morning of January 4, 1854. Headlines in the *Daily Alta* exclaimed: "Conspiracy among the Chinese. Three Hundred Arrested." A police raid in "little China" had surprised a large group of men "dressed in gorgeous robes and armed to the very teeth." They were held on a complaint similar to that formerly leveled against Norman As-sing, that they had taken on themselves the power to punish and tax their poorer countrymen. Not surprisingly, witnesses called against the leaders had difficulty in remembering anything. The case was dismissed. However, Tong K. Achick gave the newspapers the first solid information about the nature, purpose and rituals of the secret societies.

A Chinese neophyte desiring entrance into the society approached the guardian of the tong hall on his knees. The guardian questioned him searchingly about his purpose to determine whether he desired to join the tong in good faith and keep its secrets and rules. If his answers satisfied the guardian, he swore an oath and was led—still on his knees—to the altar of the war god Kuan Kung, protector of the society. There he drank a potion of chicken blood, wine, sugar and so on, mixed with his own blood to seal his oath of secrecy before heaven. Bound by a code which emphasized secrecy, mutual aid to brothers and respect for each other's wives or concubines as well as punishment for disloyalty, the new "soldier" of the Hung army celebrated his induction at a banquet.

Both the illegal activities and the secret rituals of the tongs became favorite targets of anti-Chinese propaganda in later years. Yet the tong had a more positive side. It gave the sojourner far from home companionship and helped him celebrate lavishly the festivals that lend joy and meaning to the Chinese year. In China, he would have celebrated them with his family. The most important was New Year's, falling in late January or early February of the Christian calendar. Nightly banquets kept Chinatown awake then for a week, though police set a three-day limit on the setting off of firecrackers.

Two other important festivals, which the sojourner celebrated with his tong, were the Spring Offering, called *Ch'ing-ming* (Pure Brightness Festival) and the Autumn Offering, or Spirits Festival, called *Shao-I* (Burning Paper Clothing). Both are celebrated by visits to the family tombs. A colorful procession led by two men on horseback and bearing gifts of food on wagons wound out to the cemetery. The sojourner marched after them with several hundred of his brothers. In the spring the tombs were cleaned symbolically with willow branches to drive away evil spirits, they were weeded, and a feast was offered to the spirits of the dead ancestors. The fall

The 1871 San Francisco celebration of Chinese New Year found sightseers of every race and nation joining in while firecrackers illumined the night.

festival was similar, except that paper money and clothes were burned so the spirits might return to visit their families.

Complex as was the structure of Chinatown in San Francisco, a new Chinatown usually began very simply. A pioneer sojourner would open up a store in a mining community or other small town to sell food, supplies and clothing to Chinese and Caucasians alike. The store owner might start serving tea to his kinsmen and soon be running a restaurant where the delicacies of home were served side by side with beefsteaks for American miners. If he prospered, the storekeeper would offer other diversions to lighten the drudgery and pockets of the sojourner on vacation. He might set up a gambling table for fan-tan or dominoes in a back room. A singsong girl might eventually furnish solace for the lonely. In the largest mining towns, such as Weaverville, elaborate "joss houses" (corruption of the Portuguese *Dios*, "God") or temples, were erected by local Chinese leaders or groups. They were decorated with gilt statues, carved altars, silk-embroidered banners and bronze gongs. Here the lonely immigrant could burn incense sticks and paper invocations to the gods and offer a prayer for a safe and prosperous return to his distant village.

The heavy imbalance of men to women which prevailed throughout the West in the early days made prostitution inevitable. "Painted women" were found in the wide-open railroad towns like Reno or Dodge City and in the mining camps of Weaverville and Grass Valley. Chinese women were only one small part in the picture of prostitution, but the eyes of racists perceived them as being somehow more degraded than white prostitutes. Most of these Chinese women led hard lives, except for the lucky few who became concubines or second wives to comfortable merchants.

Chinatowns sprang up in all the major towns and cities of the Pacific Coast, notably Los Angeles, Portland, Seattle, San Jose, Denver and Butte, Montana. And with the movement of the Chinese over the Rockies around 1870, a major Chinatown in the East naturally developed in New York. There were also substantial settlements in Chicago, Boston and Philadelphia. Yet, for all these new settlements, Chinatown in San Francisco never lost its position as the capital of the Chinese in America. Though much of it was crowded with dirty tenements in narrow, foul-smelling alleys, there were beautiful temples, restaurants, shops and the buildings housing the district companies. Their frame façades were painted blue, and carved lions guarded wide doors decorated with gilded plaques bearing Chinese characters.

A perceptive traveler of the 1860s and 1870s captured the flavor of this long-gone Chinatown:

Above me were terraces, flowers and people like the ones we see without believing on Chinese jars, screens, pictures and furniture. The balconies jut out over the street. Their doors are closed by latticed frames or cages. They are hung with lamps dangling crimson silk tassels and embellished with flowers especially imported from the Orient.[10]

Despite the apparent distance between them, the Chinese and American worlds in California influenced each other. Beyond the tourist level, Chinatown possessed other attractions for San

Whenever a Chinatown grew large enough one or more joss houses (temples) like this 1871 shrine in San Francisco were built. Here a lonely exile could light a joss stick (incense), burn a paper message to the gods and pray for a safe return to his distant home. (NEW YORK PUBLIC LIBRARY PICTURE COLLECTION) HARPER'S WEEKLY

Franciscans. Chin Tan Sun, a poor boy from Sinning who reached the Golden Gate in 1870, became one of Chinatown's first multimillionaires by adapting the Chinese lottery to American tastes. Another rich resident of Chinatown was Dr. Li Tai Po, who practiced herb medicine, advertising his skills on brilliantly colored balloons that floated above his house. Dr. Li, owner of the Eastern Glorious Temple, was often glimpsed bowing out a richly dressed Caucasian customer while clad in a colorful damask robe embroidered with dragons.

As the presence of the Chinese in America became a political issue, the newspapers grew ever fonder of denouncing the dirt of Chinatown, the misfortune of having such a miserable slum set down on "some of the best real estate in the city" and the disease which such dirt must surely bring. At the same time many of the most respectable businessmen in the city were collecting the rent on the tenements along Dupont and Sacramento streets, profiting from Chinese use of their stagecoach and steamer lines and employing Chinese in their factories, on their ranches and later as servants in their houses.

Apart from these businessmen who merely profited from their labor, the Chinese, though increasingly segregated by the hostility around them, did have a few American friends. The missionaries, like William Speer, despite the limitations of their viewpoint, remained the closest and most sympathetic friends of the Chinese in America. At least their work gave them an opportunity to become acquainted with individual Chinese and see them as something other than oddities or "human machines." Despite their denunciations of heathen ways, the missionaries, especially the Protestants who were most active in the United States, were often drawn beyond the religious demands of their work into becoming genuine defenders of Chinese rights. Moreover, the missions provided help that the Chinese sojourner could find nowhere else. Their work had a special attraction for those Chinese who either could not or would not find a place in the structure of organizations that sheltered most Chinese in America.

The first Protestant missionary in California, the Reverend William Speer, offered most of the services found in later missions. In addition to Sunday schools, prayer meetings and religious services, he established a night school for teaching English, geography, astronomy and mathematics, using modern techniques such as the magic lantern and the telescope. A former medical missionary, he opened a much-needed clinic, aided by charitable local doctors.

Equally important, Speer became one of the most active and eloquent spokesmen for the Chinese in America. He became the

The subversive (to the conservative Chinese) practice of educating women was carried on at mission schools such as this one run by Methodist ladies. Characteristically, there was an American teacher with a Chinese translator or reader.

(NEW YORK PUBLIC LIBRARY PICTURE COLLECTION)

first lecturer ever to speak to Californians on the rich ancient civilization of the Middle Kingdom. In 1855, Speer started a weekly newspaper called *The Oriental*, or *Tung Ngai San Luk*, to help inform Chinese and Americans about each other. While Speer himself addressed Americans in the English pages, Lee Kan, a friend of Tong K. Achick from the Morrison School, edited the Chinese section.

Unfortunately, Speer began to suffer from a recurrence of lung trouble brought on by the fogs and mists of San Francisco Bay. Despite a restorative trip to the Sandwich Islands (Hawaii), his lungs would not heal, and in 1857 he was forced to take leave of his Chinese friends. The tantalizing mixture of success and failure he had experienced was to challenge and frustrate missionaries in both California and China. For during his four years of service at the mission church, Speer's congregation had never numbered more than four members, all previously converted in China except one. That one was his sole California convert—a failed miner named Yeung Fo. Yet William Speer had won the affection of the Chinese community—wherever he went, they greeted him as "teacher"—and Americans had gained some understanding of Chinese culture from his lectures and writings.

In view of the lack of converts and in spite of the support for the mission by San Franciscans, Speer was not replaced until 1859. His successor, the Reverend Augustus Loomis, a shy man, lacking Speer's self-confidence, arrived in San Francisco in September. Loomis was offered Speer's position as official defender of the Chinese community in January 1860. But having little political skill or interest and wishing to devote himself exclusively to his religious duties, Loomis suggested a local lawyer to speak for the Chinese in the state legislature. Though he never became an official spokesman for the Chinese, Loomis soon found that it was not so easy to separate political and social problems from religious teaching. Natural sympathy with the people he was to serve so long drew him into a constant defense of their interests.

The conscientious Loomis tried to make contact with the

Chinese at their arrival, literally meeting them at the boat with his interpreter Ha Chien. Most met his overtures as they had Speer's —with personal friendliness and complete indifference to his message of salvation. However, many came to his school, especially ambitious young men, to learn English and something of the customs of the United States as an aid to business advancement.

Gradually, for a few, especially the more thoughtful, a different bond of fellowship and hope gradually began to grow. It drew them away from their Chinese world and toward the culture of their new country. Those few became a tiny band of converts, centered in the mission. Through the quiet kindliness of Loomis and their own searchings, they began to find meaning in the *fan qui* religion that their countrymen ignored or scorned. By 1866 a dozen members regularly attended Loomis's church.

Dr. Loomis's most impressive conversion at this time was the former Buddhist and vegetarian Au Yeang Shing Chak. After almost six years of attendance at services and Sunday school, Shing Chak invited the Loomises and all his friends to his room for a feast dominated by a symbolic roast of beef. In November 1865 he was converted and began an active career as a Chinese evangelist. He became the first of a sturdy band who wandered through the fields of great ranches and along the dusty main streets of mining towns in California and the mountain states, speaking and distributing tracts.

Slow as was the rate of conversion, there was an increase toward the end of the 1860s coinciding with an increase in immigration. One reason was the signing, in 1868, of the Burlingame Treaty, the first such agreement between China and the United States. For the first time the Chinese officially recognized the right of their subjects to emigrate. To prepare for the influx, new denominations showed an interest in sending missionaries to greet the Chinese in San Francisco. The Reverend Ira Condit arrived to augment the efforts of the Reverend Loomis in the Presbyterian mission. Most influential of the newcomers was the Reverend Otis Gibson, who established the first Methodist mission in 1868.

So the missions became an important, but not a dominant strand in the fabric of Chinatown life. Especially to young men who were attracted to American life and culture, they offered a halfway house between the traditional Chinese culture and the unwelcoming white world. Beyond the confines of Chinatown, Californians refused to accept a Chinese as a full human being and citizen. As all missionaries came to recognize, it was precisely this refusal which, along with the Chinese clinging to old ways and looking to return to China, prevented their taking any deep interest in adjusting to the New World. As Speer observed in 1855, the Chinese will "never in numbers recognize the Lord Jesus Christ" and "look favorably upon American institutions until discriminating legislation is repealed and they are treated like men and the heart of our people opens to them for good instead of for evil."

The center of the private world of the Chinese sojourner did not lie in the mission but in that structure of institutions, both protecting and restricting, that culminated in the Chinese Six Companies. The merchants who gained control of the Six Companies were becoming the highest class of Chinese in America by default, since scholars rarely emigrated unless ruined by war in China. The merchants' inner world of dainty, small-footed wives and equally delicate children was rarely glimpsed by the Caucasian outsider. The stories of their wealth were often exaggerated. Yet the heady get-rich-quick climate of California was good to many, some of whom retired to Paris and champagne.

Mysterious as was their private life, the Chinese merchants had mastered whatever aspects of American political and community life were open to their participation. They hung out flags on Washington's Birthday and the Fourth of July, which they greeted with firecrackers. They continued to participate in parades, until banned, and they were noted for their liberality. In ten minutes they raised the $170 required to meet their expenses for Lincoln's funeral procession.

The search for a common level of discourse between Chinese and American businessmen probably achieved its greatest success in the banquets given by the Chinese merchant princes on such occasions as the opening of a direct route to China by the Pacific Mail Steamship Company in December 1867. The most interesting such banquet, however, was one given for two Republican politicians who had been touring "the new West" in August 1865. The party consisted of Schuyler Colfax, Republican of Indiana and Speaker of the House of Representatives, and William Bross, lieutenant-governor of Illinois, together with two reporters, Albert D. Richardson, of the New York *Tribune*, and Samuel Bowles, editor of the Springfield *Republican*.

On August 17, 1865, the four Easterners, together with thirty-five prominent San Francisco businessmen and thirty Chinese merchants met at the Hang Heong Restaurant at 308 Dupont Street at 6:00 P.M. The presidents of the Six Companies greeted their guests in the second-floor banquet hall.

Both journalists wrote books about their Western travels; their reactions to the dinner differed markedly and amusingly. Richardson described the scene admiringly:

> *The food was all brought on, ready cut, in fine pieces. . . . There were three hundred and twenty-five dishes. Whatever was lacking in quantity was made up in quality, for the choicest cost one dollar per mouthful. Mr. Bowles partook from about a dozen; Mr. Colfax from forty; I suspended somewhere in the seventies; but Gov. Bross religiously tasted every one. Here are a few: bamboo soup, bird's nest soup, stewed sea-weed, stewed mushrooms, fried fungus, reindeer sinews, dried Chinese oysters, pigeons, ducks, chickens, scorpions' eggs, watermelon seeds, fish in scores of varieties, many kinds of cake, and fruits ad infinitum. . . . Neither butter nor milk is used in cooking.*

At the end of three and one half hours they were served strong, well-flavored black tea in tiny cups. Then they retired to an alcove where "cigarettes, digestion and oriental music" were enjoyed.

According to Chinese etiquette, the presidents retired amid mutually translated complimentary speeches. Then important younger merchants joined the party. The three at Richardson's table were highly intelligent and, unlike their elders, spoke excellent English. Richardson blasted another American myth about Chinese look-alikes. He noticed that each merchant "had strong individuality."

At the last course, more farewells were followed by a group of still younger merchants to occupy dessert. At the same time, a man of whom we find little record was responsible for a historic first: "Toy Chew made the first English speech ever attempted by a Chinaman on the Pacific Coast. With point and fluency he complimented Mr. Colfax, touched upon the wonderful growth of the United States and the warm interest in it felt by all his race."

Bowles, a Yankee distrusting unfamiliar victuals, had counted only 60 dishes against Richardson's 325. By this time he was hungry, thus becoming the first American ever to remark that Chinese food was "not very filling." One of his fellow diners, a San Francisco banker, invited him to "a good square meal" at an American restaurant immediately afterward. There the two men tucked away a Dickensian repast of mutton chops, squabs, fried potatoes and champagne.

Very different was Richardson's final reaction: "At midnight ended this novel banquet—the world's oldest civilization striking hands with its youngest. The occasion was curious and memorable. Hereafter, upon every invitation, I shall sup with the Celestials, and say grace with all my heart."[11]

The trail blazed by this political junket was soon to draw one of the greatest migrations in American history. In the same era, the new spirit of commerce triumphant, the fervent desire to get rich quick began to submerge earlier values of religion and ethics which had been the cement of society. For the purpose of the politicians was the building of a railroad. And the railroads which were to link the two coasts would bring homesteaders west in unprecedented numbers. It would prolong California's shortage of labor when there was an exceptional need for it. The Chinese were to play a significant role in filling that need.

CHAPTER 5

CONQUERING
THE WALL
OF ROCK

A large part of our force are Chinese, and they prove nearly equal to white men in the amount of labor they perform and are far more reliable. No danger of strikes among them.

CHARLES CROCKER TO C. P. COLE, COLE PAPERS

O NE of the sights that Colfax and Bross observed with greatest interest on their Western expedition was the progress of the transcontinental railroad. To the homesteaders they had visited along the way, what a difference the completion of that line would make! Albert Richardson, among other travel writers, observed, "The rugged mountains looked like stupendous anthills. They swarmed with Celestials, shoveling, wheeling, carting, drilling and blasting rocks and earth. . . ."

Richardson did not realize that as recently as the beginning of 1865 not a single Chinese had been at work on the transcontinental railroad. The Central Pacific section was being backed by the "Big Four" of San Francisco commerce—Charles Crocker, Leland Stanford, Mark Hopkins and Collis P. Huntington. Starting in Sacramento, their roadbed had to climb precipitously from sea level to seven thousand feet in the first hundred miles. In over two years less than fifty miles had been finished. Meanwhile the Union Pacific was starting west across the plains from Missouri to meet them.

J. H. Strobridge, the hard-bitten construction superintendent, told his boss, Charles Crocker, that he had only eight hundred of the five thousand men needed to complete the project. Every time gold or silver was discovered in the nearby mountains, his white workers shouldered their picks and melted away. Crocker was "the engine that drove everything ahead." His answer to Strobridge was "hire the Chinese." (Ironically, his partner Stanford had campaigned for governor on an anti-Chinese platform.) Strobridge merely snorted in disgust at first. He did not believe that those little men, barely five feet tall, could perform such strenuous work.

Desperation over his lack of manpower finally drove Strobridge to try Crocker's suggestion. He collected an experimental party of fifty Chinese from nearby worked-out mines and started them on the simplest tasks, filling and then driving away the one-horse dump carts. Next he gave them picks to break up the earthen sections of the roadbed. They performed every task with ease and skill. After that Strobridge discovered that there was no type of work, no matter how skilled, that the Chinese could not either pick up immediately or quickly learn—even masonry, tracklaying, blacksmithing and the use of explosives.

Convinced at last of the value of Chinese workers, Strobridge sent agents to comb first the mining camps and then the streets of San Francisco. Finally, he called on agents of the Six Companies to recruit laborers "right off the boat."

Meanwhile, the increasingly outnumbered white workers began to grow restive. Mostly Irish, they had performed in the East and Midwest most of the hard physical labor on canals, railroads, bridges, and so on. One day they confronted Crocker with a demand that he hire no more Chinese workers. Crocker delivered an ultimatum: "We can't get enough white labor to build this railroad, and build it we must, so we're forced to hire them. If you can't get along with them, we have only one alternative. We'll let you go and hire nobody but them."[12] Out of the white workers' resentment developed the nickname for Chinese railroad workers— "Crocker's pets."

With Chinese labor becoming essential to completion of the western portion of the railroad within the time required by acts of Congress, Crocker approached the big labor contracting firms in San Francisco. Cornelius Koopmanschap, of Dutch birth but long a resident in California, was asked to start recruiting young men directly from the Pearl River delta. Judge E. B. Crocker, brother of Charles, joined another firm, Sisson, Wallace and Company, in a similar effort. Placards were set up in the public squares of market towns in the Sinning and Sinhwui districts, source of most of the workers, seeking help for a long-term project in the Golden Hills. Any young men wishing to take advantage of this opportunity who could not raise the money among his clansmen went to credit ticket brokers in Hong Kong. They advanced his fare—$25 for the two-to-three month voyage on a sailing ship or $40 for a month on a modern steamer. Then his family signed the agreement to repay the money.*

---

* There is little evidence that the notorious "pig" or contract labor business operated to the United States during this period, as it certainly did to South America and Southeast Asia. Under the contract labor system laborers were "recruited" by crimps, who received $7 to $10 a head, and delivered to barracoons or coolie stations. The laborers —prisoners captured in clan wars, kidnapped men or men who had lost at gambling and were tricked into using themselves as payment— were sent to brokers in Cuba, Peru, Malaya and so on, where their contract for a fixed period of years was bought by an employer. The conditions under which they were transported and housed have been compared to the Atlantic slave trade.

In late July 1865 the first gangs of laborers that Koopmanschap had hired in the hills of Sinhwui and Sinning reached camp. Already organized into messes of twelve to twenty men, with a cook, they had a Chinese section head for leader and interpreter. His smattering of English would be their only link to their bewildering new world.

It was a hot dry summer—the building site was aswirl with the red dust of the earth and the gray dust of the perpetual blasting. The Chinese were quite content to settle down for the summer in tents, while learning the work. Strobridge made a deep and daunting impression on the Chinese, as he did on most of his workers. "He was well over six feet tall, thin, agile and tirelessly energetic. His profanity and temper were spectacular." Strobridge looked yet more fearsome because he had lost an eye in a blasting accident. The Chinese, exasperated by his constant pushing, used to express the wish that he would "shoot 'em two eyes."[13]

Not long after the first Chinese arrived from Canton, Strobridge and Crocker came up against a literal stone wall, a nearly perpendicular cliff, called Cape Horn, that rose fourteen hundred feet above the American River at an angle of seventy-five degrees.

A Chinese interpreter approached Strobridge and said that in the Yangtze valley it was often necessary to build along the faces of cliffs as steep as these. Let him bring reeds up from San Francisco to weave baskets. Soon the Chinese were sitting up late around the campfires weaving round, waist-high baskets big enough to hold a man. It was an immemorial pattern used for high work in China. At each of the positions of the four winds, an eyelet was woven into the basket. Symbols were printed on it to repel the evil spirits.

When the whistle blew at 6:00 A.M., the Chinese marched off with the baskets suspended between two of them, a rope secured to each eyelet. At the top of the precipice the four ropes were further lashed to a central cable. Then, with two men to haul each basket, one man got in and was lowered along the cliff face. Swaying in the wind, he chipped and drilled into the face of the rock and inserted his powder charge. Quickly, he scrambled up the cable while the charge spluttered and flashed, erupting at last in a spray of pulverized stone.

At the end of the long day the Caucasians and Chinese marched away to their separate quarters and their well-earned dinners. But first each Chinese filled his tub with hot water from a giant boiler that his mess cook had ready. Behind the tent, he sponged himself and changed clothes, to the astonishment of his white neighbors.

In the summer of 1866 Chinese workers on the Central Pacific at Owl Gap Cut near Blue Canyon were hauling away rock from the blasting site in horse-drawn carts, but shortly after they had mastered the most complex skills needed in construction.
(SOUTHERN PACIFIC RR)

The evening rice was made savory with an array of imported delicacies—oysters, abalone and cuttlefish, mushrooms and bamboo shoots, exotic fruits and vegetables, seaweed—all dried and imported from China, then mysteriously revived with warm water. Absolutely essential was the tea which was served to them on the grade several times a day by a coolie who carried it in powder kegs, filled from thirty or forty gallon whiskey jugs. Probably the better health and endurance of the Chinese resulted partly from their better-balanced diet. The Caucasian workers ate beef, beans, bread, butter and potatoes eternally. The water they drank was sometimes unintentionally a cause of illness.

All summer and fall and into the winter, the dangling Chinese worked at their perilous task. It took three hundred men ten days to "clear and grub a mile of right of way." Not every cable held, not every Chinese shinnied up the rope in time. An occasional basket or wide coolie hat could be seen bobbing on the surface of the American River far below. But no count was kept of Chinese casualties. By winter, the monument to the labor of the living and the dead was a roadway wide enough for several men to pass abreast, and it rounded the corner of the promontory.

With Cape Horn rounded, the highest peaks of the Sierra separated the railroad workers from the sunny slopes of Nevada. The plan called for drilling eighteen tunnels, each at least a thousand feet long, through the seven-thousand-foot-high Donner Pass, then slicing through the second, or lower, range of the mountains to Truckee Meadows near Reno, Nevada. Another obstacle—the heavy winter snows—was scheduled to be controlled by plows. Naturally, many critics were skeptical of the feasibility of this plan.

Deaf to the critics, Crocker prepared an immediate assault on the string of tunnels, numbers 3 through 13, which lay between Cisco and Lake Ridge, a distance of twenty miles. At the approach to each tunnel, a party of workers, mostly Chinese, started simultaneously to drill, blast and chip at the rock. The remaining men shoveled and carted the chips away. They worked day and night in eight-hour shifts. And in each cycle of twenty-four hours, they progressed exactly one foot.

The longest tunnel was the Summit, 1,659 feet long. Here Sam Montague, Strobridge's assistant, sank a shaft 73 feet deep into the center of the tunnel so that Crocker could work four parties at once—two starting back to back in the center of the tunnel and one at each end. Desperate for greater speed, Crocker sent to

Every Chinese construction crew included a tea carrier like this one who brought the steaming drink in old whiskey barrels to the workers on Tunnel 8 of the Central Pacific Railroad, 105 miles east of Sacramento. (SOUTHERN PACIFIC RR)

Virginia City for experienced Cornish miners. Then, to their dismay, he started them in the middle of the Summit Tunnel, back to back with the Chinese. Each day he measured their progress, and inevitably the Chinese cut more rock than the Cornishmen. "And there it was hard work, steady pounding on the rock, bone-labor."[14] In disgust, the Cornish miners quit, and "the Chinamen had possession of the whole work."

By the time the Sierra snows began piling up at the entrances, the men had progressed far enough inside twelve of the tunnels to work beyond the reach of the weather. But each day they had to burrow like gophers through a passage to the work sites. Inside the tunnels, the Chinese gangs lived a strange subterranean life amid the earsplitting din and billowing smoke of blasting and chipping. In one of the worst Sierra winters on record, death came out of the silent snow in the sudden roar of an avalanche which dropped on a whole shack or simply engulfed a lone, unlucky worker. Or it came to the careless or unlucky in the tunnel blasts. Sometimes no supplies would reach the workers for weeks as the teamsters vainly goaded their floundering oxen through the powdery, bottomless drifts. Only the spring thaws disclosed the number and location of the dead.

The perils of blasting were increased early in 1867 when Crocker and his partners decided to use the new and dangerous compound nitroglycerin, just patented in Europe by Alfred Nobel. At this early stage, no safe means of transporting it had been found. However, the formula for the treacherous oily liquid was known to many chemists. So Crocker had a Scottish chemist named James Hawden brought up with separate batches of the basic ingredients of the explosive—nitric and sulphuric acids and glycerin. Each day Hawden mixed just enough nitroglycerin to take care of the day's blasting. The Chinese would then drill holes, fifteen to eighteen inches deep, stopper them with hay, sprinkle them with powder and imbed a fuse in sand. After an initial caution, the Chinese grew casual with the deadly oil, and the casualty list mounted. Most of the nitro was used on the Summit Tunnel.

As the spring of 1867 edged toward summer with the tunnels near the Donner Pass still incomplete, Crocker pushed the shifts in the tunnels to ten, even twelve hours. In June, sensing perhaps some unusual restlessness among the normally peaceful Chinese workers, he offered them a raise from $30 to $35 a month. Then a shocking thing happened. The Chinese raised a banner amidst murmurings of discontent. A spokesman stepped forward and

Late in 1866 a junket of politicians and reporters stared in awe at the road bed along the nearly perpendicular 1400-foot Cape Horn cut, where not long before Chinese workers swaying in baskets had set charges of dynamite and chipped away the rock.
(NEW YORK HISTORICAL SOCIETY)

A scene from the life of a Chinese work gang in a summer tent camp of the Southern Pacific Railroad drawn by an artist for Frank Leslie's Magazine: *a cook fried fish in giant woks while in the background three laborers ate morning rice.*
(SAN FRANCISCO PUBLIC LIBRARY)

announced they would need $40 a month with an eight-hour shift in the tunnels—or they would strike! Beginning on Tuesday, June 25, the Chinese lay on their bedding smoking opium pipes; they gambled and joked and drank tea all day long. On Friday Crocker delivered his ultimatum. They must go back to work on Monday, or he was sending for freedmen from the South: $35 a month was his last offer, and no supplies were coming in. With no recourse and no solidarity with white workers, the Chinese had to go back to work again on Monday. Crocker assured inquiring reporters that they were working with "greater energy than ever." "Designing persons," he told *Alta,* had circulated pamphlets in Chinese to stir them up "for the purpose of destroying their efficiency as laborers.

All summer the Chinese workers blasted and raced to complete the tunnels before the next winter's snow. By November the road stretched almost 107 miles from Sacramento to the eastern end of the Summit Tunnel, then after a gap of 7 miles, twenty-four miles more proceeded down the eastern slope into Nevada.

On December 7 the unvarying days of the workers were interrupted by a ludicrous scene. A group of dignified-looking white men were romping about in the early snow just beyond the Tunnel. A reporter noticed that a rousing snowball fight was in progress "much to the demoralization of high-crowned hats and immaculate snowy collars." Through the windows of a railway coach, a group of ladies watched the exhilarating game. The Central Pacific had organized a public relations junket for legislators, state officials and journalists, with their wives, over the newly finished tracks. Much liquor and food had smoothed the minor mishaps such as stalls, uncouplings and a suffocating cloud of smoke from the woodburning locomotive in a tunnel.

Warned by the snow, Crocker was determined not to be stalled in the Sierra tunnels another winter. The Union Pacific, building westward to meet him, had completed 500 miles of track to his 131. Vowing that no eastern-financed railroad would come near the border of California, he began moving his whole operation across the seven-mile gap between the Summit Tunnel and the Truckee slopes. First oxen pulled the rails, the hardware, even the railroad cars across the gap on sleds of logs. Then five thousand workers marched to Truckee and built a shack city. Here they could work all winter on a sunny slope where snows in the lower elevations at Truckee Meadows were rarely deeper than six inches. Only two drilling teams of Chinese would remain behind in tunnels number 12 and 13 for the winter. Crocker was sure the two portions of his line would meet by New Year's, but he was wrong. The winter of 1867–68 was as severe as the previous one. The lines remained unconnected.

Nevertheless, on New Year's Day, 1868, Crocker made another

vow—a mile of track would be laid every day of the coming year. On the Nevada side his highly trained teams worked swiftly and efficiently, whereas the Union Pacific was bogged down in the Rockies in one of the worst winters of the century. In April Crocker was able to send his Chinese crews back up to the Summit Tunnel to complete the link. At the same time, sawmills were turning logs into timber for a series of sheds to protect the most vulnerable stretches of track from the snows of a Sierra winter.

Superintendent Strobridge of the Central Pacific lived and worked in this headquarters train which sat next to a tent camp for Chinese workers during the push east across the Nevada desert during the summer of 1868. (SOUTHERN PACIFIC RR)

At last, on June 18, the two rails touched, and 154 miles of continuous track connected Sacramento with the city of Reno, newly sprung from the Nevada desert. Working days were long that summer. It was 8:30 P.M. when H. H. Minkler, one of Strobridge's assistants, drove the ceremonial spike at Strong's Canyon to unite the rails.

The usual sightseeing notables traveled on the first train to Reno as the Chinese were preparing to move east. Watching them,

A construction crew on the Central Pacific laid rails to the right rear while in the foreground other Chinese workers rested in their tent camp on the Nevada desert during the summer of 1868. (SOUTHERN PACIFIC RR)

an *Alta* reporter had an unusual insight into the Chinese understanding of the significance of their work.

> *As the first through passenger train sweeps down the*
> *eastern slope of the Sierra, John,* comprehending fully the*
> *importance of the event, loses his natural appearance of*
> *stolidity and indifference and welcomes with the swinging of*
> *his broad-brimmed hat and loud . . . shouts, the iron horse*
> *and those he brings with him. . . . John, with his patient toil,*
> *directed by American energy and backed by American capital,*
> *has broken it [the great natural barrier] down at last and*
> *opened over it the grandest highway yet created for the march*
> *of commerce & civilization across the globe."*

Once the Humboldt desert was reached, the pace of the work
quickened. The work trains would set off before sunrise. Even after
dark, brush fires would cast eerie shadows over the barren stretches
of sagebrush and rugged canyons while the work continued.

When the year ended, Crocker had fulfilled his proud boast—
350 miles of track had been completed in 1868. Just as important,
the border of California lay far behind. As the engines of the
Central Pacific chugged each day across the newly laid track, they
came ever closer to the westward-moving Union Pacific crews.
Now everyone in camp became aware of the mounting tensions.
The drive to meet the Union Pacific began more and more to
resemble a contest. When the Chinese blasting crews came within
sight of those of the Union Pacific, Crocker determined to beat the
opposition once and for all with a tracklaying record that couldn't
be topped. In 1868 Gen. "Jack" Casement's men on the Union
Pacific had laid four and one half miles in one day; Crocker's had
come back with over six; then Casement had raised the total to
eight. When the final reunion, set for Promontory Point near
Ogden, Utah, had been agreed upon, Crocker asked Strobridge if
he could beat the eight-mile record. The reply was, "We can beat

---

* John—short for John Chinaman, colloquial epithet for the Chinese.

them, but it will cost something." "Go ahead and do it," said Crocker.

Strobridge planned his winning strategy with care. Only fourteen miles of track remained to be laid when the competition was scheduled for April 28, 1869. Five trains of sixteen flatcars each were brought to the front, each train holding enough supplies to lay two miles of track.

At seven o'clock, workers and spectators were lined up for action. There was a blast from the locomotive whistle. At once a large group of Chinese workers jumped on the cars and threw down every rail, spike, bolt and fishplate they held. Sixteen cars were cleared in eight minutes. The first group of workers, called "pioneers," aligned the ties. Next the tracklayers, all Irish, divided in two—the forward gang manipulated the front of each rail and the rear gang the end until it was guided into position. In thirty seconds a rail thirty feet long and weighing about 560 pounds was in place.

Now the Chinese followed. The first group put the fishplates and eight spikes next to each rail. Another group finished bolting the fish joints and driving the spikes. They were followed by track levelers who lifted each rail and shoveled enough dirt under it to keep it level. Finally the biggest gang, the tampers, assured the solidity of the rails.

By seven o'clock in the evening, with time out for lunch, Strobridge's teams had completed 10 miles 56 feet of track, a record never exceeded. They had lifted 125 tons of steel and used 25,800 ties, 3,520 rails, 28,160 spikes and 14,080 bolts. A locomotive rolled over the newly completed line to prove its soundness; then two hundred weary men returned to camp. Casement admitted himself beaten.

On May 10 all was in readiness for the ceremony of the golden spike. Leland Stanford, accompanied by a party of nine, was the only partner representing the Central Pacific. In the Union Pacific delegation were their chief engineer Gen. Grenville M. Dodge, Vice-President Thomas C. Durant of the line and the Casement brothers. First several gold and silver spikes were placed in the holes next to the joining rails. Then various officials and Mrs. Strobridge tapped lightly and symbolically on them with a hammer. Finally a pair of Chinese workers took out the ritual tie and spikes, replacing them with the real thing. The highest amusement of the day was produced by the failure of Stanford and Durant to hit the iron spike even once. The Chinese finished the job, then walked off to an honorary lunch in the car which was Strobridge's house on wheels. It was the only official gathering at which they were present.

At the grand celebration in San Francisco the next day, Judge Nathaniel Bennett gave the keynote speech. Typically,* it ignored the role of the Chinese completely:

> But our countrymen were composed of the right materials, derived from the proper origins to fit them to surmount obstacles, laugh at difficulties, and to look upon reverses with contemptuous scorn. In the veins of our people flows the commingled blood of the four greatest nationalities of modern days. The impetuous daring and dash of the French, the philosophical and sturdy spirit of the German, the unflinching solidity of the English, and the light-hearted impetuosity of the Irish have all contributed, each its appropriate share to the formation of a national character that is capable of undertaking and executing the greatest deeds under the most adverse and appalling contingencies, and in the shortest possible space of time.[15]

But Crocker remembered them. At a banquet given by the legislature in Sacramento, on May 8, in anticipation of the joining of the lines, he said:

---

* In an incredible modern re-creation of this speech, Secretary of Transportation John Volpe at the hundredth anniversary of the golden-spike ceremony, 1969, said: "Who else but Americans could drill ten tunnels in mountains thirty feet deep in snow, who else but Americans. . . ." The leaders of the San Francisco Chinese-American community, who had come expecting some recognition of their grandfathers' contribution, waited in vain.

The staggering achievement of Chinese workers in building the
Central Pacific Railroad can best be appreciated by pictures such
as this which shows a locomotive rolling through some of the
steepest terrain in the west at Ten Mile Canyon, Nevada, shortly
after the completion of the line in 1869.
(NEW YORK HISTORICAL SOCIETY)

> *In the midst of our rejoicing, I wish to call to mind that
> the early completion of this railroad we have built has been in
> great measure due to that poor destitute class of laborers called
> the Chinese, to the fidelity and industry they have shown—
> and the great amount of laborers of this land that have been
> employed upon the work.*[16]

An equally good tribute to the Chinese was indirect. J. H.
Beadle, a writer who rode the railroad soon after it was opened,
gave this description of the Cape Horn cut:

> *The finest view is at Cape Horn but the sight is not good
> for nervous people. An awful chasm, at first apparently right*

before us, and then but a little to the left, opens directly across the range; and standing on the steps of the car, it seems as if the train were rushing headlong into it. The first view allows the sight to pierce a thousand feet almost straight downward to the green bottom where the trees shrink to mere shrubs, and the Chinamen working at the lumber seem like pigmies; a little further down the gorge, the wagon bridge, hundreds of feet above the bottom, appears like a faint white band, and still further the sight is lost in a blue mist.[17]

If one of the original young men from Kwangtung, hardened, bronzed by the sun, had survived those four years of nitro blasts, avalanches, swaying in a basket over canyons and rockslides, he had three choices. He might with luck, and resistance to gambling, have saved $20 a month. With this small fortune, he could return to the Pearl River delta, marry and settle down to a life of comfort. If his earnings had slipped through his fingers or if the rough life of the road had gotten in his blood, he could build one of the other railroads that were linking the West Coast to itself and to the East— the Northern Pacific or Southern Pacific, for example. Or if he preferred the homier air of Chinatown, he could return to San Francisco to look for a job in a factory or construction site. Many made the latter, fateful choice.

CHAPTER 6

NEW FIELDS
TO CONQUER

*"Finally the blue-jacketed stream of coolies, 1200 in number,
surged down the gang plank. . . . Behind them four hundred
millions of the most patient, ready, apt and industrious toilers
on earth. . . .*

"FROM THE ORIENT DIRECT,"
Atlantic Monthly, NOVEMBER 1869

*A*s the 1860s ended, the pace of Chinese immigration into
San Francisco quickened. The Chinese were, in fact,
reaching the city from two directions—from China and from the
completed transcontinental railroad. In 1868, 1869 and 1870, more
Chinese passed through the Customs House than had reached the
port in any year since 1854. The building of the railroads, which
created the demand for Chinese, and the Burlingame treaty, which
permitted them to emigrate, accounted for the upsurge. Events in
China around this time had created a climate favorable to such a
drastic change in Chinese official policy toward the outside world.

This change took place during the period of relative peace and prosperity which followed the defeat of the Taiping rebels in 1864. The hero of that conflict, the scholar warrior Tseng Kuo-fan, had personally led his Hunan braves to victory against the Taiping "Heavenly Kingdom of Great Peace." For twenty years thereafter, he and his protégé, Li Hung-chang, dominated the government, becoming the first two mandarins to attempt to incorporate Western knowledge into Confucian society in a conservative and orderly way.

Improving on the old Chinese principle of "using barbarians to fight barbarians," Tseng and, after Tseng's death in 1872, Li brought about significant changes in Chinese policy. For the first time relations were officially established with other countries, and barbarian science was used to strengthen China's military and economic position. The hope of these neo-Confucians was to preserve the basic fabric of Chinese society while enabling her to defend herself against the Western nations who were competing around her borders for ever more trade.

Among the immediate fruits of these policies were the Burlingame treaty and the official exchange of ambassadors and consuls between China and the nations of the West. Within China itself the first foreign office, or Tsungli Yamen, was set up to handle this new branch of the government. Factories were organized to manufacture modern guns and shipyards to produce warships. The first coal mine was opened. The army and navy were modernized, and telegraph lines were planned. Then Yung Wing, a former student of the Morrison School and the first Chinese graduate of Yale (in 1854), was given permission to carry out a lifelong dream. In 1872, with the blessings of Tseng and Li, he led to the United States the Chinese Educational Mission, composed of 120 Chinese students who were to study at eastern colleges and universities.

These changes were important, but they did not go deep. They could not progress far against the opposition of the reactionary majority among officials, who sensed a threat to their power. The strength of this conservatism was personified for most Chinese and foreigners by the square, unbudging figure of the real ruler of China during the next thirty-odd years—the Dowager Empress

Tzu-hsi, who came to be known as the Old Buddha. Yet actually, Tzu-hsi was more equivocal than this description implies. Her real game was to win the most power and, to gain it, she gladly played reformers of every stripe against conservatives and vice versa. A consummate politician, she usually won whatever game she played, using the spoils as she pleased. For example, she spent money intended for the navy on rebuilding her summer palace. Her pursuit of personal power plus the die-hard opposition of the conservatives explains why China did not attempt the all-out modernization that transformed Japan into a strong world power during the same period.

Nevertheless, the Burlingame treaty at least temporarily encouraged immigration to San Francisco. Shortly afterward, the railroad workers began returning from the Utah desert. In the decade from 1860 to 1870, the population of Chinatown jumped from two to twelve thousand. To some concerned observers it seemed as if a tidal wave of Chinese was flooding the port of San Francisco. Though the number of Chinese was not so large as the image suggests, far more were reaching the port than was indicated by the ten thousand increase in Chinatown's population. For example, 11,085 (in 1868), 14,994 (in 1869) and 10,869 (in 1870) Chinese arrivals were recorded at the San Francisco Customs House.

Most of the laborers found plenty of jobs awaiting them. With the decline in mining and railroad building, "a hundred different branches of industry" depended on the Chinese. The most important were local manufacturers, various kinds of construction, and agriculture, which was replacing mining as California's major industry.

Since the young girls who performed light factory work back East were in short supply on the Pacific Coast, the owners of woolen mills, boot and shoe factories, work clothes and other clothing makers, were eager for help from the Chinese. Powder mills, jute mills and tanneries employed them. They were especially adept at making cigars. In 1867, *Alta* listed thirty-eight cigar manufacturers in San Francisco who were Chinese themselves, including the third and fourth largest. The white-owned companies employed mainly Chinese as well. It was the workers in these factories who crowded the Chinatown tenements in San Francisco.

The city Chinese were also found in large numbers in the business which has become so strongly associated with them in this

In a nineteenth-century American Chinatown such as the one in San Francisco, all the traditional Chinese service occupations flourished: the cobbler sewing slipper soles from cardboard, the barber shaving the head around the queue, and the apothecary pounding medicinal herbs in a mortar.

country—the laundry. The Chinese had early gone into the kind of "woman's work" which was badly needed in the male society of the frontier—especially cooking and washing. Not alone in San Francisco, but in the Chinatowns of every city and town in which they migrated, the Chinese started laundries. Besides being non-competitive with white men, laundry work required little knowledge of English, could be started on almost no capital and was in demand everywhere.

When large institutional laundries began to develop in California, the Chinese generally supplied the manpower; in the Palace Hotel laundry they operated a steam-driven washer and a mangle for ironing sheets. (SAN FRANCISCO PUBLIC LIBRARY)

Early travelers described with a good deal of interest the Chinese method of ironing with flat-bottomed copper kettles while sprinkling the clothes with a fine spray of water from the mouth. This way of dampening the clothes, which the Chinese had raised to a high pitch of proficiency, was abandoned later in the century with the rise of better irons. However, it caused trouble for the Chinese when Americans first began to become aware of the connection between germs and disease.

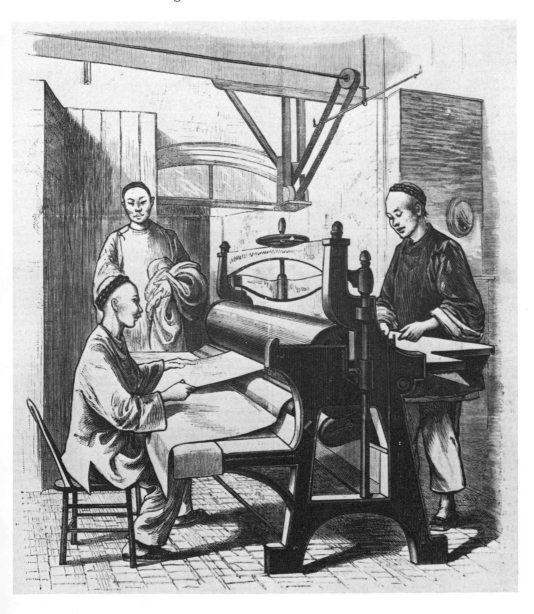

The role of the Chinese was even more important in the rise of California's immense agricultural industry, for farming, rather than laundry, factory, mining or construction work, was the original occupation of most Chinese sojourners. In 1860, on one of his earliest trips around the Bay, Dr. Loomis had observed a small colony of Chinese agricultural workers at Oakland. They were tending the strawberry and raspberry vines that served the city markets, picking the fruit and showing their expertise as "hoeing hands."

By the "feudal seventies," the large ranches that still control California's agriculture were developing out of the haciendas of the Mexican era. According to Charles C. Dobie, one of the most famous American historians of Chinatown in San Francisco: "The marshes were reclaimed by Chinese working in muck up to their waists and irrigation ditches were dug through the arid country by lean coolie laborers sweating but not groaning under a temperature of 110 degrees in the shade in the San Joaquin country."

Most of the California grain was plowed and planted, harvested and bound in sheaves by the Chinese. Two-thirds of all vegetables were cultivated by them. In the wine country of Napa and Sonoma especially beautiful and tangible memorials of the Chinese role in the early development of California wine-making survive, for the countryside is dotted with picturesque wine cellars, bridges and walls made of rocks cemented together by Chinese laborers.

California's fruit growers, who still supply most of the produce for America's tables, were almost totally dependent on Chinese workers from 1870 to 1890, when the Japanese began to replace

The importance of Chinese from Kwangtung in California food production of the 1870s and 1880s is evident from these sketches of the Sacramento Valley. At top, a Chinese fishing village; in the center, a worker carrying grapes while two others load produce; at bottom, fishing boats on the river.
(SAN FRANCISCO PUBLIC LIBRARY)

them. The perpetual shortage of labor, the seasonal nature of the work made the Chinese ideal, because of their lack of families. Beyond these reasons, the innate skill of the Chinese in cultivating fruit led even their enemies to acknowledge their value.

Often the Chinese helped their employers, inexperienced in fruit culture, to improve old and develop better new strains of fruit. At least two documented cases of this Chinese gift for improving the species exist. Many more probably went unrecorded. In Oregon, a Chinese laborer known as Ah Bing worked with his employer to develop the all-time favorite among American cherries—the juicy, deep-red Bing cherry, named in his honor. In Florida, which ranks second in the citrus-fruit market, a Cantonese immigrant named Lue Gim Gong did research for many years on improving varieties of oranges. Working on the farm of Miss Fannie Burlingame, a cousin of Anson Burlingame, who negotiated the first treaty with China, Lue Gim Gong evolved an orange which was cheaper and hardier than current Florida varieties. He thus enabled it to compete with the California orange in the markets of the East. It became known in his honor as the Lue Gim Gong Mediterranean Valencia Orange.

Though, because of the investment required, not many Chinese were in a position to start their own farms, the more enterprising groups of laborers sometimes rented or even leased outright a part of a field. Building their own cabin upon it, they worked it completely from plowing to harvest and then paid the owner with a part of the crop. They sold the rest and divided the profit in equal shares.

Finally, there was another important Chinese occupation which the seagoing Cantonese had pursued on the shores of the South China Sea and transplanted to the California side of the Pacific. That trade was fishing. Those Chinese who left the mines in the early 1850s because of "impolitic taxation" had set up a pioneer fishing village at Rincon Point, which was one of Dr. Loomis's frequent ports of call.

Fishing was an occupation which survived for a long time

among the Cantonese, spreading up and down the coast. Shrimp fishing, which centered in San Francisco Bay, was dominated by the Chinese during its years of importance in California. At Monterey the Chinese began catching abalone, now regarded as a delicacy by white Californians, but then looked on with contempt. A reporter was amazed by the cool way in which the Chinese waded out into the shark-infested waters to pick up the large and beautiful abalone shells with their pearly interiors, much prized for ornaments. In a moment of good humor, the reporter conceded that the abalone steaks drying on the roofs and walls of their huts were "not altogether unpalatable when made to yield their flavor by long and severe cooking" in soups. (Abalone fanciers today know that heavy

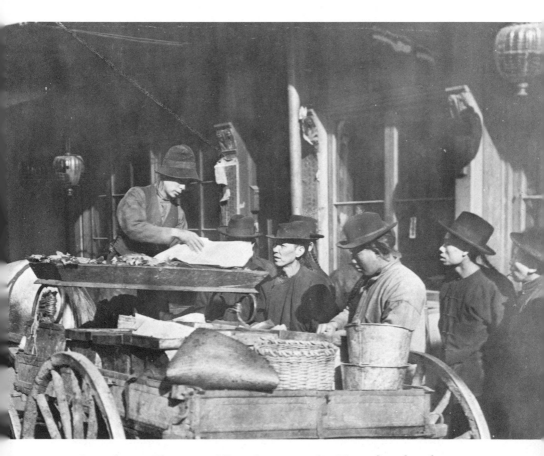

Around 1900 Chinese peddlers always met the fishing fleet, bought the catch and carried it by horse and wagon to the doors of San Francisco houses all over the city.
(CALIFORNIA HISTORICAL SOCIETY)

pounding followed by quick cooking best enhances the flavor and tenderness of abalone.)

With reforms under way at home and with their services so much in demand in America, one would have thought that the Chinese were about to enter a period of unprecedented hope and progress. Dr. Loomis certainly caught something of this feeling in his 1875 report on his mission:

> *The Chinese young men who come to this country are enterprising and energetic. Reforms have commenced in China & they will extend to every portion of the country & affect every class of society, & the many thousands of the people who have lived in this country will form a very important element in shaping these social and political revolutions.*

Unfortunately, Loomis's rosy prophecy was premature. Mighty forces latent in California since the days of the Tingley bill were operating to increase the jealousy and suspicion of the Chinese.

In the 1870s the industrial revolution was beginning to transform the Eastern and Midwestern cities, drawing thousands from the farms into the factories. In California where the railroads had brought so many Americans in search of a better life, the laborers were especially aggressive and articulate. They had come first to mine, then to earn the unusually high wages that had once been paid in the state even for simple ditchdigging. But an increasing supply of labor had naturally caused wages to drop toward but not entirely down to levels more usual in the East. The California workers were quick to notice that a good deal of competition for factory and construction jobs was coming from the Chinese.

Hostility to the Chinese had been blunted by the labor shortage of the Civil War years and then by the involvement of so many Chinese in building the Central Pacific Railroad, but it had never totally died out. Ironically, the civil rights granted in theory to black people after the Civil War, particularly the right to testify in court, were not extended immediately to the Chinese. But as the direct competition between Chinese and Caucasians for jobs increased, anti-Chinese sentiment began to rise again. There were two immediate results of this hostile feeling—one was a series of anti-Chinese ordinances and laws passed in California and the other was an increase in mob violence directed against the Chinese.

Even in the 1850s and 1860s various laws were passed levying special taxes on the Chinese or trying to discourage shipmasters from bringing in persons "ineligible for citizenship." For example, Dr. Loomis visited the fishing camp at Rincon Point in 1860 when the fishermen had just been subjected to a head tax of $4 per man per month. The tax collector had attached their boat in lieu of the money. While appealing the law to the Supreme Court, the fishermen had to pay the tax collector $300 to go on fishing for a month. Though both state and federal courts often upheld the rights of the Chinese against discriminatory laws, they might be driven out of a particular occupation while waiting for the case to be settled.

In the 1870s San Francisco passed several nuisance ordinances to harass the Chinese—among them the Cubic Air Ordinance, the Laundry Ordinance and the Queue Ordinance. The Cubic Air Ordinance forbade anyone to rent rooms where there was less than five hundred cubic feet of air per person—a direct blow at the Chinatown tenement. It was declared unconstitutional three years after its passage. The Laundry Ordinance levied a heavier license fee upon laundrymen who did not own horse-drawn carts than upon those who did. Since the Chinese rarely had delivery carts, it discriminated directly against them. The Queue Ordinance required that all prisoners in the city jail must have their hair clipped short, a great humiliation for a Chinese. The mayor vetoed both ordinances, but the Laundry Ordinance was passed over his veto. It was then declared unconstitutional; two years later the Laundry Ordinance was passed and declared unconstitutional again. Even though many of these ordinances did not remain permanently on the books, they accomplished their purpose of making life difficult for the Chinese; they also clearly indicated the general attitude of the people of California toward the Chinese in their midst.

Even more dramatic and disturbing were the violent attacks

upon the Chinese, which increased in the 1870s. The symptoms of a coming crisis were not missed by Loomis. In February 1870 he wrote, "The persecutions of Chinamen on the streets are becoming more frequent and people who interfere to defend them are likewise set upon by the rabble & the police contrive *to keep out of sight*. Oh Lord, how long."

If the police were generally ineffective in San Francisco, they were nonexistent in the rural areas, where mob action and murder for gold took many Chinese lives. Then, in 1871, in the sleepy southern agricultural center of Los Angeles, a more terrible outrage attracted the attention of the country and the world. Two bands of feuding Chinese were set upon by a mob, who lynched nineteen by hanging and shooting. Trials of the rioters proved a mockery, ending in acquittal or brief prison terms. The Six Companies and, for the first time, the Chinese government, protested to Washington. Indemnities were paid by the United States government to the families of the victims.

Unfortunately, this outbreak of mob violence did not shock public opinion into a revulsion against the violently anti-Chinese propaganda that had led to such cruelty. It was merely an introduction to the darkest pages of Chinese-American history.

The anti–Chinese riot of November 20, 1880, in Denver, Colorado, followed the tragic pattern of so many other racial flare-ups. A mob of white men, on some minor pretext, rampaged through Chinatown, breaking down walls, burning homes and businesses and beating their occupants. (NEW YORK HISTORICAL SOCIETY)

CHAPTER 7

VIOLENT
CONFRONTATION

*The Chinese labor question is destined within the next ten
years—five years, perhaps, to become what the slavery
question was a few years since, to break down, revolutionize
and reorganize parties, completely change the industrial
system of many of our States and territories and modify the
destination of our country for generations to come. . . .*

"FROM THE ORIENT DIRECT,"
Atlantic Monthly, NOVEMBER 1869

THE anti-Chinese movement in California, which eventually grew into a national phenomenon, did not spring
up overnight, but in the 1870s it assumed a new and more menacing
form. The main reason for this change had nothing to do with the
Chinese directly. That reason was the vast social and economic
dislocations produced by the progress of the industrial revolution
across the once predominately rural American landscape. The
Chinese in America were incidental losers in the accomplishment
of this revolution, whose effects on our lives we are still trying to
assess and control. With the new industrial age came new tensions
and new beliefs to intensify anti-Chinese sentiment.

In the first place, theories of social Darwinism, which were currently popular in the United States, did indeed convince many that the Chinese were "an inferior race" ready to overwhelm native stock. In this racist interpretation of Darwin, Anglo-Saxons were seen as the pinnacle of evolution and therefore intended by nature to dominate the "lesser breeds without the law"—that is, Asians, Africans.

Second, the Chinese were becoming "medical scapegoats" because of increasing sensitivity to the connection between dirt and disease without accurate knowledge of how disease is spread. Disease was thought to be caused not by germs but by "foul vapors" arising from the filth of Chinatown.

Third, the arrival of Chinese strikebreakers in the East in the 1870s served to crystallize the vaguely unfavorable view of the Chinese already implanted in the Eastern mind. They were used at a shoe factory in North Adams, Massachusetts, a steam laundry in Belleville, New Jersey, and a cutlery factory in Beaver Falls, Pennsylvania. Reaction from the press and the unions was generally hostile. Chinese also appeared as workers on a few Southern plantations and railroads. Despite the hostility, or perhaps because it was less overt than in the West, most Chinese headed for the nearest city at the end of their contracts, or even before. They started groceries in the South and laundries in the North.

The growing anti-Chinese sentiment throughout the country coincided with a period when the California legislature was frustrated again and again by the courts in its attempts to pass anti-Chinese laws. Californians began to realize that they had to seek anti-Chinese laws at the national level.

At the suggestion of California congressmen, a Joint Congressional Committee to Investigate Chinese Immigration met in San Francisco in November 1876. Businessmen, clergymen and lawyers, city and state officials were questioned. Leaders of the Six Companies, Americanized Chinese like Lee Kan, Dr. Speer's former editor and an interpreter for the Bank of California, and Chinese Christians were subjected to a veritable inquisition. The congressmen who conducted the questioning seemed determined to prove that, regardless of the evidence, the Chinese were a degraded race, their labor unfree, their community filthy and overcrowded, with every second house a brothel or gambling den, and that no Chinese could be a sincere Christian. Just to make sure the message got across, the California legislature conducted a similar investigation in 1877. The report of their committee was sent to Congress with a petition for an end to Chinese immigration.

With every hand turning against them, the Chinese had need of a strong defender, but few were forthcoming. Among sympathetic clergymen, neither Dr. Loomis nor his newer colleague, the Reverend Ira Condit, had the temperament to be a political activist. Their place was taken by the fiery Otis Gibson of the Methodist mission, who became the most militant and audacious defender of the Chinese presence in California. In his speeches and in his book, *The Chinese in America*, Gibson flew in the face of current hostility to the Chinese. So unpopular did his outspoken words make him that he narrowly missed being thrown out of the legislature when he came to testify against the anti-Chinese reports and legislation.

In all but their religion, Gibson found the Chinese high in intelligence and capable of learning anything:

> *If the Chinese are the inferior race which they are constantly represented to be—if they lack the capabilities of brain power, moral restraints, physical endurance or enterprising industry, the superior race in all these qualities certainly has no cause to fear their competition. . . . But if the Chinese are simply our equals in intellectual and moral capabilities, in push and enterprise, then the competition is fair and healthy on both sides. If they are superior, which I do not believe, then the Anglo-Saxons have a chance to improve by contact and assimilation.*[18]

Unfortunately, Gibson was part of a small minority, growing ever smaller. White church members and even their pastors were finding it "no longer expedient . . . to be too demonstrative in favor

The Rev. Otis Gibson (standing with beard), fieriest defender of Chinese rights in the 1870s, addressing a group of worshipers at his Methodist mission, 620 Jackson Street, San Francisco.

of the Chinese," as Loomis discovered. One reason for their timidity was a sudden, dramatic increase in the potential for danger from the anti-Chinese movement.

In the late spring of 1877, a strike paralyzed the Eastern railroads. On the night of July 23 a meeting called by workingmen in San Francisco to express solidarity with these striking brethren was interrupted by a noisy gang of young men from the Anti-Coolie Club. Gathering strength, they rushed pell-mell in the direction of Chinatown, "hooting and yelling in a fearful manner."

Primed with liquor from a grocery store they had broken into, they came upon their first Chinese house. It was a two-story frame building with a laundry in the basement, and a fruit store and apartment on the first and second floors.

The vicious gang rushed into the washhouse, beat the Chinese inmates who had not effected a retreat, scattered the clothing upon the floor, smashed the windows, battered down the doors, and broke oil lamps against the walls. A portion of the crowd made a raid on the fruit stand, and threw the contents into the street. The burning oil set the building on fire, and in a few minutes the house was in a blaze.

The mob swept on toward Chinatown, attacking laundry after laundry, breaking everything in sight, beating up any Chinese workers they encountered. They tossed stones against the windows of Otis Gibson's Methodist mission, howling that they would have his blood to drink along with any Chinese he might try to protect.

"Lawlessness Rampant" howled the headlines of the newspapers next morning. As the riots continued for several days, and as word kept coming of violence in the Eastern strikes, the business and political leaders of San Francisco became alarmed. The Chinese Six Companies were warning their countrymen to stay off the streets and even buy guns to "fight to the death" if necessary. A new Committee of Public Safety was organized. Because of the relative political strength of workingmen in California, as compared with the East, the committee issued soothing statements about removing that "disturbing element," the Chinese, "from our midst." At the same time, quick action by federal troops broke up the mobs.

The riots died down, but the issue remained. The workingmen had found an extremely effective agitator named Denis Kearney, a disappointed miner turned teamster. As fall approached, Kearney continued to address nightly meetings, by the light of bonfires, with his two favorite themes. In the very shadow of Crocker's and Stanford's mansions on Nob Hill, he harangued the crowd: "The Central Pacific men are thieves, and will soon feel the power of the workingmen. When I have thoroughly organized my party we will march through the city and compel the thieves to give up their plunder. . . ."

Even more satisfying to the mob were his violent threats

against the Chinese: "The Chinamen must go. If they don't, by the eternal we will take them by the throat, squeeze their breath out and throw them into the sea."

Attempts to prosecute Kearney for his violent language failed and only increased his popularity with his followers. His political power grew, and he continued to end every speech with a chant like a drumbeat of menace: "The Chinese must go!"

Gradually, over the next years, businessmen came over to the side of politicians, laborers and newspapers. By 1880 Chinese immigration had become so poisoned a topic in California that the most liberal politician or crustiest capitalist would not publicly say a word in its favor. The workingmen helped elect a mayor in San Francisco in 1879, and a new state constitution adopted in that year reflected the strong influence of the Kearney faction upon politics. It contained many anti-Chinese provisions, such as a ban on the use of Chinese labor in public works. Though declared unconstitutional, it had its effect—no Chinese was used on any public works in California until 1914.

Across the Pacific the Chinese government was losing interest in the move toward modernization that had been sponsored by the forward-looking mandarins, Tseng Kuo-fan and Li Hung-chang. Though Li had retained his position as viceroy of Chihli, the most influential of court posts, since Chihli included Peking, he was under increasing pressure from the conservative faction. The conservative Dowager Empress Tzu-hsi was emerging as the real power in the government. The officials around Tzu-hsi attacked Western methods and Western machines. They were especially opposed to Western education.

Not surprisingly, the Chinese Educational Mission to the United States under Yung Wing came under heavy fire from the conservatives. The anti-Chinese agitation in the United States played into the hands of Yung's critics. A politician above all, Viceroy Li Hung-chang was not likely to support the mission much longer.

Congress had made its first attempt to pass a bill limiting

Denis Kearney, the leader of the sand-lot riots in San Francisco in 1877–1878, was jailed for the violence of his language against Chinese laborers and the railroad kings, but on his release, shown here, became more popular than ever with workingmen.
(NEW YORK PUBLIC LIBRARY PICTURE COLLECTION)

The anti–Chinese movement became a rallying point for discontented white workers during meetings in the sand-lots in San Francisco during the 1870s.
(NEW YORK PUBLIC LIBRARY PICTURE COLLECTION)

Chinese immigration in 1879. Vetoed by President Rutherford B. Hayes, the Fifteen Passenger Law would have limited the number of Chinese on each incoming ship to fifteen. As a result, Hayes, a Republican, was denounced as "anti-labor." But he had no greater love for Chinese immigration than had any other politician. The obstacle, he explained, was the Burlingame treaty, which permitted unlimited Chinese immigration. There was to be an election in 1880, so the Burlingame treaty must go. Hayes therefore appointed a negotiating team of three able diplomats to give it decent burial.

Within two years the Burlingame treaty had been revised. A new treaty gave the United States government the right to make "reasonable" adjustments in the flow of immigration. Predictably, this chilling of the American welcome to Chinese immigrants helped precipitate Viceroy Li Hung-chang's decision to recall the Chinese Educational Mission in 1881. By so doing, he was seeking favor with the conservative faction that now dominated the court of Tzu-hsi.

All during the years when the debate over Chinese immigration was generating such intense emotions, the agitation against the Chinese in California continued at an especially high pitch. Even the Reverend Otis Gibson began to wonder whether so many Chinese should come. And the faithful Loomis began to feel that his age was rendering him unfit for his work. In despair he wrote to the secretary of the Board of Foreign Missions in New York:

> The mob have it all their own way—they threaten to drive the Chinese entirely away from their present quarters—blood and arson if they don't go—Kallock, the Mayor, is with the mob—he out-kearneys Kearney—the sand lot has an organized, armed & equipped military company or regiment. The governor signs the anti-Chinese bills as fast as they are passed . . . good people seem paralized [sic] . . . .

Yet at other times Loomis could not believe that Congress would do anything so wrongheaded from the point of view of our relations with China and so contrary to American tradition as to limit Chinese immigration. Other men of goodwill agreed with him.

Alas for the bright hopes of the Reverend Augustus Loomis and the Chinese community he served! The people who elected the congressmen of the 1880s had experienced three decades of attempts to pass anti-Chinese legislation in California, two decades of anti-Chinese propaganda in the press and seven years of debate at the national level. In 1882 Congress passed and President Hayes signed into law a ten-year ban on the entrance of Chinese laborers into the United States.

The movement to suspend the immigration of Chinese laborers was a landmark in American history, the first time this country had repudiated its policy of welcoming immigrants, regardless of race, religion or national origin. It was the beginning of a trend toward exclusion of immigrants on just such grounds, and it was to grow from the late nineteenth into the early twentieth century.

Nationally, the Chinese issue was partly related to the closeness of presidential elections in this era. California's electoral votes were important and eagerly courted by both parties. Sacrificing the unpopular Chinese to get those votes was easy for most politicians. Not surprisingly, congressional legislation against the Chinese continued to occur in election years.

To the Chinese in America and their few friends, the true nature, import and extent of the new laws were not immediately clear. Ch'en Lan-pin, who had served as first Chinese ambassador to Washington since 1878, believed that the new law meant just

Ch'en Lan-pin, China's first official ambassador in Washington, together with his staff, was received by President Hayes and his cabinet on September 28, 1878.

(NEW YORK PUBLIC LIBRARY PICTURE COLLECTION)

what it said, that his government and the United States government understood it in the same way. The law stated that there was to be a ten-year suspension, but not a total prohibition, of the immigration of Chinese laborers into the United States. The law also stated that other classes, such as merchants, teachers, students and so on, were to be admitted. At the same time, the naturalization of Chinese was definitely prohibited. Ch'en Lan-pin believed that this suspension would remove the cause of agitation by American workers and help protect the Chinese already in America. He believed that the Exclusion Act of 1882 would be the last such act to be directed at his people. Unfortunately, Chen was to be proved wrong.

CHAPTER 8

ORDEAL
BY FIRE

Well, the sworn exterminators of every thing Chinese are working on in the same line—while the contracting of our funds is starving our work they are growing more bold & fiendish in their plots to drive the Chinese out of the country. . . .

REV. A. W. LOOMIS TO REV. F. F. ELLINWOOD, JULY 25, 1887

*F*AR from appeasing the anti-Chinese faction, the Exclusion Act of 1882 was merely the beginning of a long nightmare for the Chinese immigrant. Newspapers lost no opportunity to tell horror tales of Chinese cruelty or degrading tales of Chinese vice or contemptuous tales of the peculiar customs of the "heathen Chinee," whether in America or China. America seemed to be determined to prove to herself that she had been right in preventing the immigration of such a people by blackening the character of the Chinese past the point of absurdity.

For the individual Chinese, there were still some means of

escape, none totally satisfactory. The most obvious response to the outpouring of "simple hatred" was for the Chinese to go home for good, and many of them did. One of Dr. Loomis's best assistants, tired of being spat upon and shoved into the gutter, left in 1885 to become a missionary in China. After twenty-five years with the Bank of California, Lee Kan, the Morrison School friend of Tong K. Achick, decided to go to the Sandwich Islands (Hawaii) in 1881, on the eve of passage of the Exclusion Law. Other Chinese set out to try their luck in the Midwest and the East.

During the sand-lot agitation of the late 1870s and the national debate over Chinese exclusion, anti–Chinese cartoons marked by a virulent racism flourished. This one by Johannes Keppler from an 1878 Puck was typical: "A Picture for Our Employers—Why they can live on 40¢ a day while they can't." The portrayal of the Chinese overcome by opium and eating rats reinforced the worst features of the Chinese stereotype which, consciously or unconsciously, poisoned the American view of the Chinese for decades. One of the few sympathetic cartoonists was Thomas Nast of Harper's Weekly who showed "un-American" mob law chasing black people from the South and Chinese from the West, ironically titled "The Poor Barbarian Can't Understand Our Republican Form of Government." (GENERAL RESEARCH AND HUMANITIES DIVISION, THE NEW YORK PUBLIC LIBRARY, ASTOR, LENOX AND TILDEN FOUNDATIONS)

But there was no general exodus. If the Chinese were chased from the mines, they went into the fields; if they were chased from the fields, they went back to the city. With unions boycotting Chinese factory workers, the majority opened laundries or went into domestic service.

Dr. Loomis observed the changed spirit of his students with mixed feelings: "Since the revision of the treaty the Chinese seem to apply themselves to money-making more than before—servants and farm laborers are more in demand & people are fully awake to their opportunities & are disposed to make all the hay they can while the sun shines."

"Chinese cheap labor" was cheap no more as wages, particularly for house servants, rose in response to an unfilled demand. In contrast to the anti-Chinese propaganda which filled the newspaper columns, well-born Californians lamented the difficulty of getting those most desirable and satisfactory of servants—the Chinese. The "leprous" Chinese with their "filthy" living habits, as reporters insisted on calling them, were most sought after by rich Californians to cook their meals, clean their houses and care for their children.

Their acceptance into the homes of the rich and well-born did not, of course, improve their standing with the mass of Californians. If anything, it fed the hatred of citizens on the West Coast by proving the Chinese to be clearly on the side of the bosses. By the middle eighties, economic warfare and vigilante violence against the Chinese were reaching a hysterical pitch. Anti-coolie leagues spread from the newly emerging labor unions in the cities to the rural districts. Bombings, burnings and assaults terrorized the fruit and vegetable belt in California's fertile valleys. Nevertheless, the Chinese remained dominant in agriculture for another decade till the coming of the Japanese.

Reports of the terror in the countryside are reflected in missionary letters of the time. The Reverend Ira Condit went south in 1885 to serve a Chinese community of three thousand that worked in and around Los Angeles, especially in the citrus groves. He termed the violence against Chinese farm workers almost a "race war to drive them from our shores." Miss Wilson wrote Dr. Loomis from Santa Rosa in the Bay area that the "daily papers . . . fanning the anti-Chinese flame" had helped set the stage for a horrible murder, which went unpunished and which the "better people" ignored.

The year 1885 represented the peak of anti-Chinese hysteria and violence, and the most horrifying atrocities occurred in the mountain states and the Northwest.

The state of Washington witnessed murders of Chinese hop-pickers and miners. In November 1885 anti-Chinese agitators in Seattle rioted and threatened to drive out the whole Chinese population and to shed blood if they did not go. Many Chinese left, selling their property far below its worth. The mayor brought together the anti-Chinese labor leaders and the Chinese leaders to negotiate. The Chinese stalled for time, and the arrival of government troops helped quiet the agitation. Eventually, the anti-Chinese leaders were tried and acquitted, and the violence was never repeated on such a scale.

In Tacoma, on the other hand, the whole Chinese population was packed into boxcars one stormy winter day and sent to Portland. That city had its own riots in 1886. The missionary there, the Reverend W. S. Holt, wrote sadly to Loomis that many Chinese would like to go home but were unemployed and lacked the money.

But all other horror stories pale beside the Rock Springs Massacre, which sent reverberations across the country and across the ocean to China. At this time, Wyoming Territory had only about fifty thousand people. Rock Springs, in the southwest, was the site of a large coal mine, owned by the Union Pacific Railroad. To the force of mostly immigrant labor that worked this mine, the company had recently added four hundred Chinese who had just finished a railroad construction job.

On September 2, 1885, a Welsh miner entered a chamber in the mine where a group of Chinese were at work and ordered them to leave, claiming they were not supposed to be working there. The Chinese stood their ground, and in the argument that followed, a Welsh miner struck a Chinese miner with a shovel. He fell dead from the force of the blow. Attracted by the shouts, other miners closed in on the Chinese. The sight of the dead Chinese seemed to stir all the hidden animosity of the workers, turning it from the company toward a nearer target—the Chinese. Once again the Chinese were caught in the crossfire between capital and labor.

In a burst of fury the mob drove the Chinese out of the mine and back into the Rock Springs Chinatown. A barrage of gunfire punctuated their flight. By this time almost the whole neighborhood, men and women alike, had joined the hunt. Chinatown was set afire, trapping many Chinese, and the wounded were thrown to perish in the burning houses with those trapped inside.

Turned away from almost every door where they sought sanctuary, the fleeing Chinese were driven out into the surrounding wasteland, one of the most desolate in the West. Some lucky Chinese stumbled up to the door of the Pacific Hotel in nearby Green Springs. There the lady who ran the hotel took them in and hid them. This "only true Christian" in the countryside faced the mob as they rattled the door and shook their weapons. Mincing no words, she told them to get off her company's property and leave the poor Chinese in peace. Perhaps their tempers had cooled; perhaps some of the mob were beginning to feel ashamed of their day's work. They retired and left the hotel untouched. But riots continued throughout the state for a month until Governor Warren called in federal troops. Estimates of the number of Chinese killed range from twenty-eight to fifty.

In the wake of the Rock Springs Massacre, humanitarians held protest meetings in the East. They urged Americans to reject violence in their reception of the Chinese and called on the government to protect Chinese residents on our shores. Diplomatic protests were lodged with the State Department by the Chinese ambassador. Fair-minded Americans who had no great love for the Chinese were shocked at the atrocities committed against an inoffensive people.

The Rock Springs Massacre had two important results. The United States government paid about $150,000 to the families of the victims. However, the grand jury called to investigate the massacre refused to indict the miners. Their reason spelled out the attitude of most Wyoming residents to the problem: "While we find no excuse for the crimes committed, there appears to be no doubt abuses existed there that should have been promptly adjusted by the railroad company and its officers."[19]

The worst violence against the Chinese during the bloody 1880s was the Rock Springs Massacre in a Wyoming coal mining community which ended only after Chinatown had been burned and at least 28 Chinese workers had been killed.

(NEW YORK HISTORICAL SOCIETY)

Life for the Chinese in San Francisco, though they were subject to humiliation and harassment, was far more secure than in the countryside. The city was entering its most colorful era. On the boundary of Chinatown was the flamboyant and notorious Barbary Coast, playground for sailors from the Seven Seas. One visitor, though deploring the poverty, dirt, gambling and opium smoking of Chinatown, found its neighbor "a far more objectionable region . . . inhabited by the vilest class of poor whites."

Certainly the San Franciscans had a beam in their own eye when it came to wide-open indulgence in the deadly sins. Yet they did not have the decency to show restraint in attacking the mote in the eye of their Chinese brothers. Despite their own vice mills, they always reserved their most virulent charges for the sins of the Chinese. Periodically, state and local authorities, with much help from journalists and reformers, raised a hue and cry about the need to clean up Chinatown, "the rankest outgrowth of human degradation that can be found upon this continent."[20]

In defense of their people during the dark 1880s, the Chinese Six Companies evolved into a more formal group that survives to this day—the Chinese Consolidated Benevolent Association. There now being seven companies, the president of each district—except Yan Wo, which represented the Hakkas—held the presidency of the association for two months of the year. With legitimate business declining in Chinatown, the companies were under more pressure than earlier from the tongs, who began to compete with them for community leadership. Meanwhile the tongs reaped good profits from gambling, drugs and prostitution.

Most pathetic of the victims of the criminal phase of tong activity were the girls, who were often kidnapped or tricked into believing that they were going to be married. The most dramatic work of the missions was performed in the rescue of young children from domestic slavery and young women from prostitution. Both Methodists and Presbyterians established women's homes for rescued or escaped girls. The most famous was the Presbyterian home under Margaret Culbertson and, from the turn of the century, the most famous of all such crusaders, Donaldina Cameron, known as Lo Mo, or "Little Mother."

Of course, not all prostitutes wished to exchange their life for the "plain living and high thinking" of a mission. But a goodly number of those who wished to escape eventually did. A grapevine grew up between the girls and their rescuers. Using hairsbreadth escapes through cellars and over rooftops and acquiring a helping hand from friendly lawyers and judges, the Misses Culbertson and Cameron collided head on with politicians who winked at this nefarious trade.

Unfortunately, tong involvement in gambling, drugs and prostitution was as much grist to the journalistic mills then as Mafia stories are today. All during the 1880s and 1890s they were grinding out stories to prove the unsuitability of the Chinese to enter the United States, let alone participate actively in American life. The most serious result for the Chinese was the passage of new anti-immigration laws.

The first was the Scott Act of 1888 which went much beyond the first exclusion law. It positively forbade the entry of Chinese laborers into the United States. The prohibition applied even if the Chinese were merely returning from China after residence in the United States and possessed a valid reentry permit. By this cruel act, twenty thousand laborers who had gone back to China to visit their families were permanently barred from returning to their homes and jobs in America. The same law also defined more narrowly the five classes which might enter—officials, teachers, students, merchants and travelers.

The prohibitions in the Scott Act contravened the provisions of the treaty of 1880. Worse, the act undercut a treaty that had just been negotiated by the Chinese minister to the United States, Chang Yin-huan. Under this new treaty the United States would be allowed to prohibit the immigration of laborers for twenty years but required to permit laborers who had returned to China to reenter the United States if they met certain qualifications, and it would pay $276,619.75 to Chinese victims of mob attacks other than Rock Springs. While Peking was considering this treaty, Chang Yin-huan went to Peru to check conditions among Chinese laborers there.

It was during his absence that Congress passed the Scott Act, with provisions even more severe than allowed by the proposed treaty. In indignation Chang protested officially to the State Department, but he never received the courtesy of a reply. When, six months later, Chang went to see Secretary of State Thomas F. Bayard, Bayard disclaimed any responsibility for the act.

Though Chang's superiors such as Li Hung-chang sympathized with his difficult position, his fellow Cantonese blamed him for the harsh provisions of the new act. Discouraged by both the law and his discourteous treatment in Washington, Chang returned to Peking in 1890. He was not replaced until President Harrison's term of office ended. During those years, the consul in San Francisco was the ranking Chinese diplomat in America.

Up to this time the Chinese had always found that they were treated with greater fairness by the courts than by any other branch of the American government. The courts had found unconstitutional the unfair laws directed against them: the nuisance taxes, the Queue Ordinance, the Laundry Ordinance, the Cubic Air Ordinance and so on. Relying on this record of court protection, Chae Chan Ping, one of the twenty thousand stranded laborers, brought suit against the United States. The Scott Act prohibited his return to his home and job in California, but he claimed that the government, having given him a reentry permit under earlier legislation, and in the light of treaties between this country and China, had made a contract with him which it was now proposing to break.

The brief filed for the government denied there was any such contract. Congress, it argued, had the power to regulate immigration, and it might bar or deport any alien it wished, regardless of the rights granted to Americans under the Constitution or any treaties made with foreign governments.

The court upheld the government, saying that it had the power to reverse itself and bar any alien to whom it had earlier given permission to return. One statement in the government's brief is especially significant:

> *Under the law of nature and nations the right of a man or body of men, to leave one country and pass into another, for any purpose—that other being free and sovereign—must in the end, come to be a right represented by force alone, and end in a question of the strongest arm and best guns.*[21]

In the end it came back to the weakness of the central Chinese government. As long as China yielded to the demands of colonial powers at home, her people abroad could be abused with impunity.

In 1892 Congress passed another anti-Chinese law to squeeze the Chinese community in America. The success of the attempt may be judged by the census figures for Chinese residents. Between 1880 and 1890, despite the Exclusion Law of 1882, the Scott Act of 1888 and all the violence, the Chinese population of the United States rose slightly, from 105,465 to 107,488. But in the next decades the Chinese population began a long decline. It sank to 89,963 in 1900 and continued to slide until 1930, when it began to rise slightly.

The 1892 law was known as the Geary Act. It provided a sad response to those diplomats who had thought that the exclusion law would bring an improvement in American attitudes toward the Chinese in their midst. The Geary Act, however, went beyond merely extending the previous laws. It struck at the status of the Chinese already resident in America. It forbade the use by Chinese of writs of habeas corpus in cases where they had been arrested. All Chinese in the United States were required to register with the government and obtain a certificate attesting to their eligibility to remain here. If a Chinese should be picked up without his certificate, the burden of proving that he possessed one fell upon him.

The Chinese consul in San Francisco, the ranking Chinese

diplomat in America, could not believe that the courts would uphold an act that so clearly violated the constitutional guarantees of the Bill of Rights. He and the leaders of the Chinese Consolidated Benevolent Association advised resident Chinese not to register under the provisions of the Geary Act.

Anxiously the Chinese awaited the verdict of the courts on this challenge to the constitutionality of the Geary Act. Among the Chinese who lacked certificates of residence were two laborers, Fong Yue Teng and Wong Quan. They sued in court to stay deportation proceedings against them instituted on the day the Geary Act went into effect, a year and a day after its passage. Despite two ringing dissents, the majority of the Supreme Court ruled for deportation. Moreover, lack of a registration certificate had been made a crime punishable by a year of hard labor. This provision was later struck down, as were later attempts to deport someone without a hearing. Yet an important precedent had been set—the government had power to deny due process to aliens, and the power later would be used at times against citizens as well.

The reaction in the nation's Chinatowns was immediate. From San Francisco to Chicago, to New York and Boston, the leaders who had advised their countrymen not to register reeled under the blow. The shock waves fanning out from this failure shook the complex and delicate structure of Chinatown to its very foundations. Many Chinese now stood in danger of immediate deportation unless they conformed to the provisions of this unjust law.

The failure of the leaders of the Benevolent Association to repel the government attack on the Chinese communities naturally brought a challenge to their discredited leadership. There had, of course, always been grumblings about the Six Companies' running things. Now they burst out into the open. Generally, the more sophisticated city folk from Canton (the Sam Yap) had wielded the greatest influence among the companies. But the country folk from Sinning (Sze Yap) had long been most numerous among Chinese immigrants. The branches of the Triad Society, such as the Chee

Kung Tong, were especially strong in these mountainous districts where there had been so much unrest recently in China itself. The secret societies as a source of power had always been looked down upon by educated Chinese, but they played an important role in breeding rebellion in times of dynastic stress and change.

All through the 1890s Chinatown in San Francisco and, to a lesser extent, the Chinatowns of other large cities were terrorized by the worst outbreak of tong violence that America was ever to see. These so-called tong wars were outward signs of an inner struggle for control of Chinatown among the fighting tongs and between the tongs and the companies. The techniques of the tongs followed in the familiar vein of American organized crime. They used hired gunmen, called "hatchet men" (after their traditional Chinese weapon) or "high-binders," extortion and blackmail to obtain the acquiescence of legitimate businesses, and strong-arm tactics to silence anyone who knew too much.

The suppression of tong violence would have required co-operation between American courts and police and Chinese leaders, and that was impossible in the early 1890s. American hostility, the indifference or corruption of police and courts, threw the Chinese back upon their own resources and left them at the mercy of the power struggle. Neither the leaders of the Six Companies nor the Protestant missionaries could strike at the true cause of the "tong wars"—the bachelor society. Instead of being a temporary phase of pioneering days, the bachelor society had become for most Chinese in America a permanent way of life. Deprived forever of a normal family life, they depended on the illegal substitutes supplied by the "fighting tongs." Even so unfriendly a witness as Jacob Riis, who could find nothing good to say about the Chinese in his report on the slums of New York, put his finger on the core of the Chinese problem and proposed the solution: "Rather than banish the Chinaman, I would have the door opened wider—for his wife; make it a condition of his coming or staying that he bring his wife with him. Then, at least, he might not be what he now is and remains, a homeless stranger among us."[22]

Arnold Genthe caught one side of the "bachelor society" in pre-earthquake San Francisco's Chinatown in this famous photograph "The Street of Gamblers." During the tong wars of the 1890s the walls carried proclamations announcing the objects of tong vengeance. (NEW YORK PUBLIC LIBRARY PICTURE COLLECTION)

The advice of Jacob Riis was not heeded; only merchants were allowed to bring over their wives in the 1890s. Meanwhile, the activities of the fighting tongs merely confirmed what Americans had suspected all along—that the Chinese were "natural criminals" who "wallowed in vice." The Fu Manchu image of the Chinese— cruel, though of course brilliant in a twisted way—and the opium-den, slave-girl view of Chinatown reached their peak in the bloody nineties. Unfortunately, the image long outlasted the reality.

Meanwhile, in the countryside and on the labor front, where most Chinese led their drab lives away from the glamour of a city Chinatown, blood of a different sort was shed. Rural vigilantes and labor unions continued their drive to oust the Chinese from the farms and factories. And no one accused the Americans who initiated the violence of being by nature "cruel" and "criminal."

About this time, there was an increase in the immigration of Japanese laborers, so ranchers could begin to substitute one form of Asian labor for another. At almost the same moment the anti-Japanese movement began; eventually it would merge with the anti-Chinese movement in the growth of Asiatic Exclusion Leagues.

The average Chinese worker, barely literate in his own language and often totally ignorant of English, knew the world around him to be hostile; he rather expected it to be. If one had to live among barbarians, one must not be surprised when they behaved like barbarians. The Chinese sojourner clung to the hope of returning home and consoled himself with Chinese festivals, Chinese food, Chinese dress and an occasional pipe of opium or game of fan-tan.

It was the Christian Chinese, small in number, but closest to the white world, who understood the racist insults most clearly and suffered most sharply. As the turn of the century neared, their country was on the defensive both at home and abroad against a triumphant West. Young men who had absorbed Western ideas of democracy and national independence could find little reason to rejoice in the plight of their country. Around her borders, aggressive European nations squabbled among themselves about treaty rights and seemed on the verge of carving up their country "like a ripe melon." Within China's borders, the decadent and reactionary government of Tzu-hsi seemed to hold the land in a death grip.

At first glance, the outlook for ambitious young Chinese in republican America would seem little more cheerful. In view of the violence of the 1880s and 1890s, it would seem impossible that any Chinese could prosper, or even survive. Yet some few men, tenacious, talented and lucky, managed to gain recognition on the shaky bridge between the Chinese and American worlds. They gained strength from the difficulties of their life and determined to try to change the conditions that led to oppression in China and persecution in America. Among the Chinese who worked longest, hardest and most effectively to improve the situation of the Chinese in America, and who exerted an influence on events in China as well, was Ng Poon Chew.

An Arnold Genthe photograph of pre-earthquake San Francisco called "Waiting for a Car" showed one of the Chinese families which were then a minority in Chinatown because of the cruel laws prohibiting the entry of wives of Chinese laborers.
(CALIFORNIA HISTORICAL SOCIETY)

CHEW'S
JOURNEY

CHAPTER 9

PEASANT BOY
FROM KWANGTUNG

*Naturally these able-bodied young peasants aspire for some-
thing greater, something by which they can better their own
economic conditions and secure the ease and comfort of life.
At home such excellent opportunities are lacking. They have.
to seek them abroad.*

PYAU LING, "CAUSES OF EMIGRATION,"
FROM *Annals of San Francisco*

*I*N the 1870s *Gum Shan* (the "Mountain of Gold," or
California) was no longer a fairy tale to a boy growing
up in one of the districts of southern Kwangtung. For often one or
more of his male relatives had made the trip across the Pacific.
"Those who returned imparted fabulous tales of wealth," as one of
them remembers, and these tales whetted the appetites of young
boys for the journey.

One youth affected by these tales was Ng Poon Chew. Born
on March 14, 1866, the son of Ng Yip and Wong Shu Hok, he
lost his father, and perhaps also his mother, at an early age, for he

was later described as an orphan. He was also, apparently, an only child.

The death of the father may explain the importance of the grandmother in the early life of Ng (his real family name). She was a devoted follower of one of the three major Chinese religions —Taoism, which emphasizes a mystical contemplation of the natural world, in all its contradictory aspects. Taoism urges avoidance of useless striving for wealth and power and a "natural" acceptance of life as a defense against the evils of the world. Popular superstitions and local gods were absorbed into Taoism; magic and the search for the elixir of life led later Taoists into a kind of early science and medicine.

Young Ng was destined by his grandmother to be a Taoist priest, and he served as an assistant in the shrine near the village. He also had to attend the village school to learn the Confucian classics which were the foundation of a Chinese education. It is likely that the money sent home by *Gum Shan Hok* ("guests of the Golden Mountain"; that is, the Chinese in California) helped support the village school.

Among the memories that stayed most vividly with Ng throughout his life were the hardships of school life. He recalled rising in summer at 3:30 A.M. and rushing out of the house without a mouthful of food, pulling on his clothes as he ran. In his mind the Confucian classics came to be associated with the early morning chill:

> *In the old method when I was a boy . . . we were compelled to study, but we were not required to know what we were studying about. We were simply set to memorize the Confucian classics, endeavoring hard to transform our heads into first-class phonographic records.*[1]

At nine the children were allowed to go home to breakfast but had to return once more to study till it grew dark, with a break for supper at 4:00 P.M. Naturally this left little time for play except on holidays; the Chinese week contained no regular day of rest. In their brief hours of freedom the students played the usual games of village boys—swimming in the pond with the water buffaloes, throwing stones across the pond, fishing, catching and training crickets, playing blindman's buff or shooting marbles.

Whether Ng began at this early age to question old habits and attitudes, old teachings and beliefs cannot be determined. Most of his own memories of such change and rejection of the past belong to a later period after he had radically changed the direction of his life. We have only two clues to anything unusual about his childhood—his dedication to the priesthood (in deference to his venerable grandmother) and his constant reiteration that Confucian knowledge was "cold."

The turning point in Ng's life came suddenly. Among the villagers who had made the overseas journey to California was an uncle of Ng's, a brother of his late father. Probably after his father's death, Ng, his grandmother and his mother, if still living, came under this uncle's protection. One fall evening Ng saw this uncle coming up the road from the Tam River, dusty and travel-worn, but grinning at his fast-growing nephew and the wife he had left so long ago. In the outside world, the year was 1879, and Ng was thirteen.

Once in the house, surrounded by his family, the uncle reached into the folds of his traveling blouse and brought out eight sacks and laid them on the rustic wooden table. In each sack were a hundred Mexican silver dollars. Before Ng's unbelieving eyes the uncle took out a dollar and held it close to the flickering brazier. Here was a fortune not found by the alchemy of the Taoists but by simple hard work.

Ng's feelings about his future were changed forever. He could think of nothing but finding a way to reach the Golden Mountain. However, his uncle, having made his fortune, wished only to settle down and enjoy a comfortable family life. With $800 he could buy land, hire a poor peasant to work it, put on the robes of leisure and join the village elders in study. But as a man of influence, he could perhaps find another cousin to take Ng to California. Not all sojourners had brought back fortunes.

Of course, those who had built up prosperous businesses in the United States could not afford to leave them for long; some took sons or nephews back to work with them; a few progressive merchants even brought wives and young children. There were other villagers for whom the call of *Gum Shan* had become a siren song. Year after year they worked but were never able to keep their small savings away from the lottery and the fan-tan tables. Even on the return ship and in Canton itself, there were professional gamblers looking for peasant boys returning from *Gum Shan* weighed down with bags of gold. For those who arrived home with a fraction of their original earnings, the only solution was to book passage and return again to California. And some who kept commuting across the Pacific were restless young men, spoiled by city life for the simplicities of the village.

More than a year passed over the Sinning hills before the uncle yielded to Ng's plea and found him a suitable relative to accompany to the United States. Ng was jubilant. He hardly believed it when his uncle told him that only the simplest labor, probably in domestic service, would be open to one of his age and experience. His uncle also warned that the *fan qui* workers had become jealous of the sons of Han (as the Chinese call themselves) and their ability to work hard and live on little. Sometimes they beat up and robbed his countrymen. Some had even died by violence. Ng must have been puzzled by these reports if he even heard them in his youthful excitement. If America were so big, beautiful and rich as all men reported, was there not enough work there for all?

In the spring of 1881 Ng was scheduled to set off with his cousin. This man was returning to San Jose where he worked for a Chinese contractor, who leased a plum orchard from a rich *fan qui* rancher. Early one morning the two cousins set off toward the river. Wrapped in Ng's bedroll was his grandmother's parting gift—an herbal medicine to guard his health. Written on his heart were her parting words, the only thing she could bequeath him, realizing she would probably never see him again. It was an old Chinese proverb, "If you will, you can," that was to guide him through difficult moments for the rest of his life.

Ng's chief memory of his trip to America was of the heavy, slow-moving cargo junk that carried them down the Tam River, into the mouth of the Pearl River and across the bay to Hong Kong. He recalled asking a boatman about the eyes painted on the bow—and being told that they enabled the boat to see where it was going. This trip of perhaps one hundred miles consumed six days.

By 1881 most transpacific travel was by fast steamer. Liners of the Pacific Mail Steamship Company regularly made the voyage from Hong Kong to San Francisco in a month or less. Since 1873 all arriving ships from the Orient had been required to anchor in the bay. Then the quarantine officer would examine each passenger, especially the Chinese, for Americans had begun to fear more than ever that they were carriers of dreaded Asiatic diseases such as cholera, typhus and yellow fever.

Ng and his cousin landed in San Francisco at a time when the debate over the exclusion law was generating intense emotions. We do not know if they suffered from attacks by hoodlums.

It would be interesting to know whether Ng and his cousin heard Dr. Loomis when he came to address arriving sojourners in the district houses. There is no evidence that they did. Within a short time after arriving in San Francisco the two kinsmen proceeded to San Jose where the cousin's former boss leased his orchard. Many men from their district supplied the labor for tending and harvesting the plum, apricot and cherry trees that gave San Jose the name of the "garden city."

The cousin's boss was glad to welcome back his former laborer, but he had another suggestion for Ng. Since he was young, intelligent and something of a scholar, the boss would find him a job as houseboy for one of the wives of neighboring ranchers. Boys like Ng were always in great demand for domestic work.

Just as the Chinese boss had predicted, Ng found favor with

Mrs. Travis, to whom he was sent for a job that involved working in and around the house. Such work was paid at the rate of $1.50 to $2.00 a week plus room and board. It was Mrs. Travis who insisted on calling him Chew. Ng was apparently too difficult a name for *fan qui.*

From the beginning Chew found himself working harder on the Travis ranch than he had ever worked before. He was busy from dawn till long after supper: tending the kitchen garden, cleaning the house, watching the children, serving as kitchen help and waiter. But his capacity for work and his determination led him to succeed at everything he attempted. Strangely, his greatest trial in this new life was not the exhausting work, but those breaks in the routine which are usually welcome to a lively young boy. The errands Chew had to run in San Jose for Mrs. Travis soon turned into an agony of terror. He never knew when the bullies of the town, who could not seem to bear the sight of even one small, innocuous Chinese teen-ager, would strike.

One summer day several months after his arrival, Chew decided to evade his tormentors by ducking through an alley where he had never seen them before. His maneuver was in vain, for a gang blocked his exit, and when he turned to run back out of the alley, they were hard on his heels. The bullies were in their late teens, mostly a head taller than he was and close to twice his weight. No one was in sight on the quiet residential street except a small, middle-aged lady with light, graying curls. Chew ran toward her.

To his surprise she called to his assailants in a firm voice, "Sammy, Clifford, Robert, what wicked tricks are you playing? Has this small China boy done you any harm? You are worse than heathens if you harm him."

Chew understood only a word or two of this speech, but he could recognize the voice of a woman scolding naughty children and gauge the miraculous effect on his tormentors. Muttering, "Sorry, Mrs. Carey, we were just having a little fun," they looked down and shuffled slowly away.

In his rudimentary English, Chew tried to convey his thanks

to his rescuer. They smiled at each other in friendship and frustration. Then Chew had an idea. He mentioned the name Travis.

Mrs. Carey nodded and looked pleased. "Mrs. Travis is a good Presbyterian. I'm sure she'll want to send you to Sunday school and I would love to teach you." She repeated the word *school* in Cantonese, and Chew's face lit up.

Mrs. Travis agreed that it was her duty to send Chew to Sunday school in his spare time. If he should learn English, it would make him more useful. However, soon after, an event took place that almost ended his scholastic career before it started.

One hot August night, Chew was wakened from sleep by a shout. Mr. and Mrs. Travis were dressed and sitting on their wagon, ready to start for town. They motioned to Chew to ride in back, saying something about Mrs. Carey, his new friend. As they approached the Chinese Presbyterian mission, Chew was horrified to see the two-story school afire, with flames darting out the windows and up toward the roof, charring holes in the shingles.

Mrs. Carey stood watching, and moaning, "My school, my school!" She wrung her hands, then covered her eyes as if the blaze were literally painful to watch. Nearby stood a young Chinese student, who was guarding a jumbled pile of furniture, books, Chinese scrolls, an organ and a melodion, which he had helped rescue from the building. He told Chew that he and several friends had been sleeping on the second floor when some lucky crash had wakened him. He had run to the fire station to give the alarm. " 'They' set it," he murmured darkly. " 'They' wish to destroy our school." Chew was not quite sure who "they" were but remembered the bullies who had chased him and the "anti-coolie league" of the Workingmen's party of which his cousin had spoken.

Just then the wind fanned the flames to a louder roar, and part of the roof collapsed. Mrs. Carey let out a small scream and collapsed on the ground, moaning, "My eyes! My eyes!"

Next morning Dr. Loomis, who had been summoned by telegraph, arrived on the train. The firemen had saved part of the structure, but the landlady refused to repair the roof, saying she wanted to sell the whole building. With his funds tied up in a new San Francisco mission, Dr. Loomis could not afford to buy it.

In September Mrs. Carey, her eyes still inflamed, was back at work, under the ruined roof. Chew came to school and made his first concerted attempt to learn the English language that floated in tantalizing snatches around him all day. When Otis Gibson's active organization came down to buy the San Jose mission, many Chinese were attracted to the newer school. But Chew would not think of leaving the benefactor who was becoming almost a mother to him. Also, Dr. Loomis rented new rooms for Mrs. Carey and offered her the aid of his most active and promising assistant, Soo Hoo Nam Art.

Soo Hoo, who had come to California in 1875 at the age of twenty, had been attracted to the mission and its message during the troubled years of persecution. Soon Dr. Loomis was reporting that Soo Hoo was "very popular with his people and with ours." His "work in San Jose was blessed." In Napa, in San Rafael, he "revived interest" in the schools.

This charismatic young man played a central role in influencing Ng Poon Chew toward the dominant religion of his new land. For the first time Chew beheld the model of a young, dynamic, intelligent Chinese Christian. Soo Hoo was particularly important to Chew because between visits the San Jose Presbyterian mission began to languish. Mrs. Carey never really recovered from the fire. However, Chew always honored her for her part in his early education. Even after he became famous, for as long as she lived, he made a pilgrimage each year to see the "quaint little old lady with the curls on each side of her face."

In January 1883, Dr. Loomis and his new assistant, the Reverend Alex J. Kerr, fresh from Princeton, performed the ceremony of conversion for four young men from San Jose, two from San Francisco and one from Santa Clara. Though we lack direct evidence that Chew was one of them, all references to his conversion place it early in 1883.

Between 1881 and 1884 Chew lived, worked and studied in

San Jose. Whether he remained the whole time with the Travis family or worked for others as well, we know only that the work was domestic, tiring and poorly paid. At school, when he could get there, he progressed rapidly, mastering English with exceptional skill. Mrs. Carey wrote of him in 1884 the Sunday school teacher's supreme compliment—"There are not many American boys of his age that can tell more about the characters of the Bible than he."

In late October 1884, Chew announced to Mrs. Carey that he was quitting his job. He had been working too hard with too little time to study. He intended to go to San Francisco on vacation; he would likely stay if only he could study and find work there. Though sad at the thought of losing him, Mrs. Carey promised to write Dr. Loomis.

So Ng Poon Chew set his face toward San Francisco and the hope of a new life.

CHAPTER 10

OLD PROBLEMS
AND
NEW CHALLENGES

*We are not dealing with a dull, stupid besotted people, but
a keen, energetic, intellectual race. . . .*
IRA CONDIT, *The Chinaman as We See Him*

IN October 1884 the former houseboy named Ng Poon
Chew arrived at Dr. Loomis's door and expressed a
desire to study for the ministry. He bore a letter from Mrs. Carey,
emphasizing his willingness to work hard and explaining, "He
knows very little of his own language, but if he learns that as
readily as he has ours, I think you will not regret you have taken
him."

Chew's arrival answered the prayers of the San Francisco
missionaries. Chinese candidates for the ministry in America were
few. In 1879 Dr. Eels of the First Presbyterian Church in Oakland

had gone east to head Lane Seminary in Cincinnati, taking with him two students from the Oakland mission—Huie Kin and Chin Gim. When they finished their studies, Chin Gim was sent to serve the Chinese community in Chicago. Huie Kin, who was a peasant from Kwangtung like Chew, was named to head the mission in New York. Other denominations, especially the Methodist, had also trained a handful of Chinese ministers.

The passage of the exclusion law was starting to dry up the supply of China-trained evangelists entering the United States. Given little supervision in their interpretation of the law, immigration officers could classify incoming Chinese in any way they wished. Sometimes they had been known to call doctors or preachers manual laborers, thus placing them in the class prohibited from entering the country.

With a threatened shortage of Chinese evangelists, Dr. Loomis and his assistant, Alex J. Kerr, were delighted with the promise of a new pupil. Kerr set to work to find a means of support for Chew. By December an anonymous patron in Chicago had pledged $10 a month for six months to cover Chew's "food, clothes, washing, books, etc." Kerr described Chew and his new life with enthusiasm: "He is earnest and intelligent, full of life and decided in his Christian character. . . . We have . . . placed him in our day school for boys. . . . He studies English in the forenoon and Chinese in the afternoon. In the early evening my teacher gives him a Chinese lesson, and later I give him instruction in my advanced classes."

The only hint we have of Chew's own explanation for his life's divergence from the traditions of his countrymen has come down to us through a brief paragraph in his family's sketch of his life: "In many particulars Chew was radically different from most of the Chinese boys. His mind was less tenacious to old ideas. . . ."

Even before coming to San Francisco, Chew had taken a small but radical step away from accepted Chinese custom. One day, reflecting on the sad fact that the queue and non-Western dress of his countrymen were frequent causes of hostility in America, he reached back, grasped his queue and with the recklessness of youth, cut it off. Now, if he went back to China, he would be called disloyal to the emperor and might even lose his head.

Donning Western clothes, Chew went from barber to barber all over San Jose, being constantly rebuffed with the statement that they "don't cut hair for Chinks." Finally, a poor man with a small dingy shop on the edge of town was more impressed by the money in his hand than the color of his skin. Chew became one of a handful of Chinese young men then in California who wore modern dress.

Even Huie Kin had not taken such a step till after he had lived some time in the East. In his old age, Huie wondered if "our people were too slow in adjusting ourselves to the life of the people among whom we lived, moved and had our material well-being." But Huie's explanation hardly covers the complexities of the reasons for anti-Chinese feeling. Different customs are usually more an excuse than a deep-lying cause for persecuting a minority. Certainly, a difference in customs was insufficient to explain the frenzy of persecution of the Chinese that was taking place in the very year that Huie started work in New York—1885. The Rock Springs Massacre and the riots in Seattle and Tacoma were only the most noticeable of the outrages.

In the comparative haven of the East Huie turned his attention from the horrors he could not help to the immediate condition of his people in Chinatown, New York. In his report on the first year of his mission, he analyzed their problems with an insight that few, if any, white missionaries could match. Out of his experience, he offered useful advice to anyone who wished to approach the Chinese sympathetically and win their confidence:

> *Our people are naturally shy when asked to go among strangers. . . . Once* gain their confidence *so that they will trust you as they would one of their own people and it will be an easy matter to get them to church. . . . They are too often made to feel that they belong to a lower class. . . . Now there*

are no social distinctions in that part of China from which
most of them come, and it is a mistake to look down on them
and consider them lower people because they do manual work.
Most of them follow the laundry business because they come
here poor, and this enterprise requires no capital and scarcely
any knowledge of your language. . . . They say, and with
good reason, that they do not *receive the treatment which the*
Christian religion enjoins and this one fact deters numbers
from accepting it.

With the courage and energy of youth, Huie also conducted
a quixotic war against the Mott Street gamblers. He actually
succeeded in closing down the games for a year, but he almost lost
his life in the process. Eventually the police and the politicians lost
interest in Huie's crusade, and the gamblers drifted back to their
old haunts.

Meanwhile Huie fell in love with Miss Louise van Arnam
of Buffalo, who had come to teach in his Sunday school. She
reciprocated his affection. In 1889 they married, overcoming the
objections of family and friends by their determination to let no
racial barriers divide them. So Huie set up a home on University
Place that was to become the haven for many visiting students,
teachers and diplomats, as well as the simple laundrymen he was
to serve so well.

Spurred on by such stories as he heard of Huie Kin or Soo
Hoo Nam Art, his first Chinese mentor, Ng Poon Chew gained in
knowledge and confidence through his years at the school run by
the Women's Occidental Board of the Presbyterian Church under
Miss Baskin and Kerr and Loomis. In his mind China grew
dimmer, and the attractions and promise of America overcame her
defects in his eyes. He regarded the anti-Chinese laws as did his
teachers—a passing aberration of the American spirit from which
it would recover when reason began to replace hysteria.

So highly did Chew's teachers think of him that in the summer
of 1888, with one year still to go at the school, they sent him out

on his first missionary assignment. He traveled among the fishermen in the Bay area, speaking to them, reading to them from the Bible, listening to their problems and offering them the consolidations of Christianity. His sympathy with his people broadened. His wit sharpened. His voice grew in power and expression. At the end of the summer, he was commended as a "young man of promise" who did "excellent work." He was then twenty-two.

Across the Pacific, in China itself, young men were beginning to dream of using the modern knowledge they had gained from missionaries or by study abroad. Despite the distrust of conservative officials surrounding the Dowager Empress Tzu-hsi, then reaching the height of her power, they sought to strengthen their country and resist the domination of the Western powers. Those who had studied in the United States with the Chinese Educational Mission went quietly into useful careers. Among the fields to which they contributed most were mining, railroad building, diplomacy and the navy.

The reactionary trend that followed after the more enlightened Confucianism of the forward-looking ministers Tseng Kuo-fan and Li Hung-chang had a crucial influence on a Chinese medical student who had studied under missionaries in Canton and Hong Kong—Sun Yat-sen.

The life of Sun—like Chew a native of Kwangtung—was also crucially influenced by *Gum Shan*. But in his case events proved that the great risks taken by the early Chinese gold-seekers did not always lead to fortune. In his household lived two aunts who were doomed to lives of celibacy by the Chinese custom that regards the remarriage of widows as immoral. In 1851 their young husbands had been lured by the posters and fine speeches of steamer agents to try their luck in the goldfields. The wives remained in the home of the eldest brother, the father of Sun Yat-sen. Patiently they waited for their absent husbands to return, only to learn, years later, that one had died aboard ship and the other in the mines.

Most important, Sun had a brother, fifteen years older, who had prospered in the sugar-cane fields around Pearl Harbor in the

Sandwich Islands. In 1879 Sun Mei (called Ah Mi) sent for his brother to help him in his business. But first Ah Mi wished his younger brother to gain the kind of education which he had been too busy to obtain. He placed Sun at the famous Bishop's College School, or Iolani School, in Honolulu. The school had been founded and was still run by Bishop Willis for Hawaiian boys. For three years Sun devoted himself to learning English and the usual Western school subjects, along with that most subversive of studies —Christianity.

Like most of the boys in the school, Sun Yat-sen absorbed the idea central to Bishop Willis's teaching—that progress and Christianity were bound together. So persuasive was the bishop's proselytizing that Sun began to speak to his brother about converting. Mostly to counter these dangerous influences Ah Mi sent his brother home to Choyhung. But it was too late. Sun had already inhaled the virus of modern ideas that was shortly to infect many other foreign-educated young Chinese. He was never to be of much use to Ah Mi in his business.

Sun received the first shock to his patriotic sensibilities in 1885, not long after he returned to Kwangtung, when China was defeated by the French in Tonkin and, as a result, lost control of its tributary states in Indochina.

Bitter at the ineptitude of the Manchus, Sun took up medical studies in 1886–87 with the American medical missionary, Dr. John G. Kerr, at his Canton Hospital and School, one of the most famous of such institutions in China. During his studies with Dr. Kerr, Sun found for the first time like-minded friends who shared his dream of driving out the Manchus in a great revolution.

The next year Sun moved to Hong Kong to study at the new Alice Memorial Hospital run by the London Missionary Society under Dr. James Cantlie. Dr. Cantlie was to play an important role in Sun's life. And though Sun left his revolutionary friends behind in Canton, he took his revolutionary dreams with him.

The defeat of the Chinese by the French in Indochina and the passage of the Scott Act prohibiting all immigration of Chinese

laborers marked the dismal years when Ng Poon Chew was growing into manhood and consciousness of the world. He must have
already possessed a good share of the spiritual toughness and
determination which guided his later career. In September 1889
he entered the San Francisco Theological Seminary, located at that
time at 121 Haight Street. Loomis and Kerr felt that it would be
a great contradiction to all the anti-Chinese propaganda to train
a Chinese minister in America.

Chew took the whole course, which included church history,
theology, Greek and Hebrew. Sacred music was added in 1890.
Robert Mackenzie, professor of apologetics and missions and a
famous preacher, helped his students develop a vigorous and
dramatic pulpit style. At the same time, Chew continued the
difficult study of his native language.

While Chew was happily absorbed in these new challenges,
his first spiritual father in San Francisco, Dr. Loomis, was growing
old. In 1890 he announced that he was going to find a resort in
southern California, and Dr. Condit was called back from Los
Angeles to Oakland to oversee the San Francisco mission. In their
report for 1890 Condit and Kerr composed the definitive tribute to
the work of Loomis:

> Much labour and care connected with the general
> interests of the Chinese in California have been laid upon
> him as in former years, owing to the hostile feeling against
> the Chinese, the need of protecting them in the courts and
> giving counsel, not only to those in the city of San Francisco,
> but to those also who are scattered up and down the coast. For
> many, many years Dr. Loomis has been a faithful friend of
> all Chinese in California more or less sustained and supported
> by the sentiments of Christian men and women—but to a
> large extent left without sympathy with the masses of our
> American people. He has stood up firmly for the political and
> social rights of these people until he is known throughout all
> the villages and mining camps of the Pacific Ocean where
> Chinese are gathered as their staunch friend and father.

But like so many men whose lives have been given to an all-absorbing cause, Dr. Loomis was destined not to enjoy the rest he longed for. In July 1891, after thirty-two years of service in San Francisco and ten more in Ning-po, China, he died. The Chinese church was filled to overflowing with his students and converts. All bore witness with tears of gratitude to the fitting epitaph that he was "loved not only in his directly spiritual teaching, but in his kindly and courageous intervention for the defense of the Chinese."

As 1891 drew to a close, Chew had only a few months left before graduation. His professors spoke highly of his intelligence and ability to learn. The seminary itself was about to move to a beautiful new building on a hilltop in San Anselmo, north of the city. Chew, however, was destined to finish his education at the old seminary on Haight Street, near the people he hoped to serve in the heart of the city.

In May 1892, a momentous year for Chew and the Chinese in America, he was to graduate from the seminary and be ordained as the first Chinese Presbyterian minister on the Pacific Coast. As the great day approached, he was already assured of his first post as assistant to Dr. Condit at the mission in San Francisco.

This assurance of work in America was especially important to Ng Poon Chew in 1892. New ties, dating from the last year, bound him to the city of his adoption. At the same time, the worsening plight of the Chinese in America strongly demanded just such help as an educated man from their own background might give them.

Before plunging into this grim business, Ng Poon Chew enjoyed a lovely lyric spring. The harsh outlines, the rigid limitations of the Chinese world in America, were softened for a time. Tucked away on a quiet street near the edge of Chinatown were some neatly scrubbed houses, quite unlike the crowded dirty tenements where most Chinatown residents were forced to live. On this tidy street, the "Chinese Nob Hill," lived the handful of Christian families.

Some of the women had been converted with their husbands.

Some had been brought by Christian husbands to the mission for instruction or had been visited at home by the indefatigable Mrs. Condit, who made as many as a thousand such visits a year. Some were former slave girls, trained at the mission. By 1890 thirty-five such homes had been established, with two hundred children, of

In 1894 when Ng Poon Chew was a young pastor, Market Street was the commercial heart of San Francisco, lined with splendid stores and offices and linked to the rest of the city by cable cars.
(NEW YORK PUBLIC LIBRARY PICTURE COLLECTION)

whom twenty-eight were native born. At the same time, the Methodist mission had added a similar number of Christian homes. Though the daughters of these families stayed at home more than American girls, they were generally less restricted than their unconverted sisters.

One of the quiet apartments on this quiet street held a charming and pretty young girl named Chun Fah (Spring Flower) —just nineteen, and the personification of her name. Often in the spring evenings, after the long days of study and extra hours of helping Kerr or Condit at the mission, Ng Poon Chew would find his way to the house of Chun Fah. Chun Fah was by nature shy and retiring, but she caught a spark of excitement from young Chew as he told her of his hopes for helping his people. He intended to teach the Chinese to be at home in America and, at the same time, he intended to teach Americans to appreciate the fine qualities of the precious and ancient civilization that had nurtured him and Chun Fah.

For Chew, Chun Fah was willing to undertake the life of a missionary's wife—a career unheard of in China. In May 1892, the year of his graduation and ordination, Ng Poon Chew married Chun Fah before their Chinese and American friends in the mission chapel. Condit and Kerr said the blessing over their protégé and his bride.

The refuge of a home of his own must have seemed particularly precious to Chew as he began working in that summer, for it was the year of the Geary Act.

As Ng Poon Chew started his career, he had to deal with this American contempt for the Chinese. With the confidence of youth, Chew resolved that he would untangle the knotted threads of American-Chinese misunderstanding. He would prove that each nation—and its people—was wrong about the other. When most young Chinese dressed like Americans, spoke good English and converted to their neighbor's religion, prejudice (he was sure) would disappear. He, Chew, would help to expand this group of forward-looking Chinese. So, for over a year, he worked as an assistant minister at the San Francisco mission.

CHAPTER 11

CONVERTS
AND
CONSPIRATORS

[In 1896] I found the Chinese in America even more con-
servative than the Chinese in Honolulu. . . .

SUN YAT-SEN, *Autobiography*

S AN Franciscans in the 1890s had grown accustomed to the
Chinese who served as cooks and houseboys for affluent
families. Hardly a reminiscence by a famous Californian who lived
in this era fails to recount anecdotes of the ways and whimsies of
the Chinese servant. All are told with the kind of patronizing
affection that characterizes stories of black mammies and faithful
black stewards in the South.

Despite the condescension, this attitude of the Californian
represented an advance over the earlier one for those who were

thus able to know the Chinese on more personal terms. A man who causes playful laughter is at least a man and not a monster to frighten children like the "hatchet man" or an abstraction to whip up economic fears like the "coolie laborer."

In those days Chinese peddlers came regularly to the doors of all the comfortable and substantial houses in San Francisco. Usually, there was a Chinese cook or servant-of-all-work who dickered with them in rapid Cantonese and kept accounts in Chinese characters on the back of the kitchen door. The peddler brought his wares in two huge baskets, "overflowing with fresh greens and glowing fruits," as one old San Franciscan remembered it. On Friday the fishman arrived with his scales and his slippery, glassy-eyed cargo.

Most fascinating to old and young alike were the more refined peddlers of "silk and brocades, carved ivory and jade in cases wrapped in great squares of yellow cotton." The trader would step softly into the living room, bow and kneel on the carpet, unwrap each precious object and soon spread a "confusion" of Chinese goods before the wondering eyes of his audience.

In this colorful world Ng Poon Chew served his apprenticeship. Most Chinese preachers of the time, like Kwan Loi and Soo Hoo Nam Art, wore the queue and Chinese dress, perhaps because they still commuted between China and America. Only a few Chinese like "foreign devil" Chew, as the conservative Chinese called him, and Huie Kin, with his American wife, stood before the world as self-proclaimed "modern young men."

Poorly paid and endlessly busy, Chew found that his new position as preacher at the Chinese Presbyterian Church called upon all his resources. Unexpectedly, the shy, retiring Chun Fah proved of priceless aid as a missionary's wife. When Mrs. Condit organized the Circle of the King's Daughters, made up of Christian Chinese women, in 1893, she received substantial help from Chun Fah. Mrs. Condit could not praise highly enough the "work of Mrs. Chew, quiet, unostentatious among the heathen women. . . . She is a host for good. . . . No American pastor's wife could care more efficiently nor more lovingly for her flock than does

Mrs. Chew. . . . She is a really rare woman, very handsome and very intelligent."[2]

Within a year of their marriage, Chew and Chun Fah added

In the 1890s the cook in a rich California home was usually Chinese like the one caught in his doorway here by Arnold Genthe, greatest photographer of old Chinatown, San Francisco. (NEW YORK PUBLIC LIBRARY PICTURE COLLECTION)

a new responsibility to their small household—their first child, Mansie Condit Chew, named after the wife of the Reverend Ira Condit. Both Chew's proven ability and the increased financial burden of fatherhood suggested to Condit that Chew was ready for a more challenging assignment. Why not send his protégé to take care of the Chinese mission in California's fastest-growing city?

Los Angeles, the small market center of the 1850s and 1860s, had always been close to Condit's affections. He had first sought out the sunshine of the south in 1876 to restore his health and that of his wife. Providentially, his arrival had coincided with the completion of the Southern Pacific Railroad link between Los Angeles and San Francisco. With this line and the southern connection to Chicago in 1888, the population of Los Angeles increased almost tenfold between 1870 and 1890, when it reached 50,390. From 1885 to 1890 Condit again served the Chinese church there.

After Condit returned north upon the death of Loomis, no missionary had charge of the Chinese church for over three years. Only Mrs. Noble and her assistant, Miss Ida Boone, carried on in the Sunday school.

Early in 1894, Chew set out for his new charge, accompanied by Chun Fah and baby Mansie. How different for Chew was this trip by train as an ordained minister of the Presbyterian Church from that other journey, just ten years before, between San Jose and San Francisco. The loneliness of the orphan had been dispelled by a home and a family. In this new southern city to which he was speeding, Chew's first independent congregation awaited him. Little Mansie, born in America, was a citizen despite the worst that the anti-Chinese forces could do. And wouldn't the other child on the way be the same?

Chew was not disappointed in the devotion of his Chinese church members. As far back as 1883, Ira Condit had remarked on the contrast between their "earnest spirit" and their poverty. Successful merchants, the nucleus, were "as permanent as any of our citizens" and as "much interested in the elevation of their race as any of our churches of American citizens." Scattered over the wide-open spaces of Los Angeles County, the church members clung more strongly to the heart of their little community.

Chew and Chun Fah found the mission a pleasant home where, in quick succession, Effie Bailey, Rose Bullard and, in 1896, Edward Chapin joined little Mansie. Their birth gave added urgency to Chew's mission to bring his countrymen closer to the American world in which they lived and on which they depended for their work and security.

As Chew became better established, he helped other members of the Ng family to emigrate and join his circle in Los Angeles.

For four years Chew worked with single-minded energy and devotion at his chosen field. The mission report for 1895 "commended . . . Chew's wisdom & success." But success is relative. Like so many missionaries before him, Chew found that many young men were willing to come to his school to learn English but that they passed out of the mission in Los Angeles and its smaller branches in Santa Barbara and San Diego as soon as their prime objective was attained. A somewhat smaller number was willing to listen to Bible stories, learn hymns or even sit politely through a prayer meeting. Out of this latter band of interested listeners came the handful who welcomed conversion, perhaps a half dozen a year to keep the church of thirty-eight members from dying. There was a small Sunday school of eighteen young people. Chew's greatest accomplishment, in fact, was the creation of a day school where Chinese youth could learn to read their own language as well as English.

Yet the real life of most Chinese immigrants lay remote and alien from the attractions of America and Christianity. The great, immovable block of Chinese conservatism stood in Chew's path, and he stumbled over it as had so many reformers in the past. Trying to understand this reluctance to change, Chew came to realize that most of the sojourners saw no use in fighting the hostility around them. They looked forward to "returning to their tribal villages." By "retaining their customs," they expected to "fit in easily" back home, he concluded.

The fact that young Chinese in America were more conservative than young Chinese in China and Hawaii came as an even greater shock to Sun Yat-sen. As a medical student in Hong Kong, he and his small circle of friends had a greater ambition: they dreamed of rescuing China from the corruption of the Ch'ing dynasty and the domination of foreign powers. Later, as a young doctor in Canton, he had tried to interest high officials in his ideas of reform. Disappointed, Sun had organized, probably in Hawaii, a secret society called Hsing Chung Hui (Revive China Society). The Hsing Chung Hui used the blood oaths of the Triad Society to hide its revolutionary aims. Among Sun's early supporters were his brother Ah Mi and a successful Shanghai merchant named Charles Jones Soong, educated in the United States.

In 1894–95 another defeat from an unexpected direction struck a new blow to the shaky foundation of the Manchu dynasty. Japan, which had been extending her influence to such Chinese border protectorates as Korea and Formosa, went to war with China over them—and won. Japan had learned Western techniques and used them to manufacture weapons and build an army to a degree that China had not.

In Canton in September 1895 Sun and a group of conspirators were stockpiling weapons for a takeover of the government buildings in the city. The plot was uncovered and their headquarters raided. Seventy of the young rebels were arrested, and three executed, but Sun escaped. Hidden by friends in Hong Kong, he was warned by his former teacher, Dr. James Cantlie, that even in the British protectorate, the long arm of the Tsungli Yamen might reach him. Sun took the first boat to Japan. At the same time, he cut off his queue, put on modern dress and began to grow a moustache. From this time he was often taken to be Japanese.

In less than a year this modern young Chinese, whom even good friends could hardly recognize, was sailing from Hawaii to San Francisco. Little is known of this visit to the United States, including how he escaped the scrutiny of the immigration officers enforcing the Geary Act. Probably, it was his appearance, since Japanese could still enter the United States freely. In fact, Sun was so pleased with his "new look" that he had a photograph taken while in San Francisco—and thereby alerted the Chinese embassy in Washington to the whereabouts of the dangerous rebel Sun Wen, wanted for high treason in Peking. Sun was shadowed during the rest of his three-month stay in America.

Though the Chinese community in America was hardly receptive to Sun's message, he did gain a hearing through his secret-society connections and missionary friends:

> *Everywhere I preached to the Chinese about the crisis in the mother-country, the corruption of the Manchu government, and the necessity of a fundamental national reconstruction in order to bring about national salvation. I also pointed out that it was everyone's duty to participate in the reconstruction. Though I worked hard there were very few who paid any attention to me.*[3]

If Chew heard Sun through the mission, he undoubtedly sympathized with his desire to strengthen China's people through modern knowledge. But, he was no more ready than the other Chinese in America to hear Sun's call to revolution.

After crossing the country to New York, Sun sailed for London in September 1896. Unaware of a trap set for him, he went freely about the city, calling on his old teacher, Dr. Cantlie. Then one day Sun was lured into the Chinese embassy and locked in a third-floor room. From that moment Sun was in mortal danger. The embassy wired Peking for permission to charter a special ship and send him secretly back to China.

Alone, cut off from all help, faced with the sure prospect of an excruciating death, Sun experienced the most agonizing and important crisis of his life: "My despair was complete, and only by prayer to God could I gain any comfort. Still the dreary days and still more dreary nights wore on, and but for the comfort afforded me by prayer I believe I should have gone mad. . . ."[4]

From this "dark night of the soul" Sun emerged with a new

sense of mission, an intense conviction that he was the man chosen by destiny to free his people from the degrading yoke of the Manchu. His Christianity, which had strengthened him in this ordeal, also helped save his life. For by enlisting the sympathy of an English servant for a persecuted Christian, Sun was able to smuggle to Dr. Cantlie a message explaining his plight.

On Thursday, October 22, the London *Globe* revealed in its evening edition that a Chinese subject, kidnapped on British soil, was being held prisoner in the Chinese legation. By the next morning the Foreign Office had taken note of the situation and politely requested the release of the prisoner. And that afternoon Sun walked out of his prison a free man.

An interview with the press made Sun an overnight celebrity. It also transformed him, in the minds of the Manchus, from a minor rebel into a dangerous revolutionary with a high price on his head. But to the world, Sun Yat-sen became one Chinese everyone could remember.

Still, in America, Chinese leaders had much more sympathy with a group of reformers who had followed the famous fiery scholar from Kwangtung called K'ang Yu-wei. K'ang had reinterpreted Confucius to admit the possibility of genuine reform within the framework of the Chinese government. His chief disciple was the Cantonese journalist Liang Ch'i-ch'ao.

For one hundred glorious days during the summer of 1898 K'ang, Liang and their followers had gained the ear of the young Emperor Kuang-hsü, nephew of the dowager empress. Kuang-hsü had issued edict after edict, aimed at streamlining and modernizing the government. Then the conservative officials, fearing for their rice bowls and supported by Tzu-hsi, fearing for her power, imprisoned the emperor on the grounds of "illness." Six reformers were executed, many were exiled, and K'ang and Liang fled to Japan, then the lodestar of young Asian reformers.

Sun, having made his way from Europe to Japan, was glad to welcome K'ang and Liang, whom he felt to be fellow patriots, even if their political ideas were not as advanced as his. Unfortunately, the upper-class Confucian scholar K'ang had no sympathy for a man whose learning was Western rather than Confucian and whose strength came from the secret societies, the lower-class refuge of discontented farmers and laborers.

Touched by these exciting events, Chew began to wonder if the profession he had chosen could be of any solid help to his people. At the same time, he was beginning to feel the pinch of economic need. Chew had four children by 1898, the year of K'ang Yu-wei's ill-fated reform attempt. But his loyalty to the mission was strong.

Then, one evening, Chew awakened to the dread cry of "Fire!" For the second time during his life in California, a mission was burning. This time Chew lost all his personal belongings. The destruction of the mission could not have come at a worse time. After years of debate, the Board of Foreign Missions had decided to support no domestic Chinese missions except the one in San Francisco. All others must become self-supporting.

Suddenly unemployed, Chew found Americans willing to give thousands of dollars to missions in China, but only pennies to a mission for the Chinese in America. This paradox was partly explained by the tong and slave-girl activity, then at its height in Chinatowns along the Coast, and juicily reported by the new breed of "yellow journalists" in newspapers such as Hearst's San Francisco *Examiner*. Such stories helped convince Americans that the Chinese were so degraded that they would, in the words of a senator, "corrupt the sweetness of our national waters."

The young men in Chew's school raised enough money to rent a room for a school, and Chew's family received a generous gift to keep them from going in rags and to provide a place to live. In their temporary quarters Chew and Chun Fah considered the uncertain future. The few posts open to a Chinese minister were filled—by Soo Hoo Nam Art in San Francisco and Huie Kin in New York. (No one even considered the possibility that a Chinese minister might officiate at a white church.)

Spurred on by the need to earn a living and excited, like most young Chinese of his generation, by the possibilities for change in China, Ng Poon Chew's ambition to help his people took a new direction. He had witnessed the immense power of modern mass newspapers, like Hearst's San Francisco *Examiner*, to move their readers. Compared to the influence they exerted, Chew's efforts at education and conversion through the mission seemed a painfully slow way to modernize his people.

The more he thought about it the more it seemed clear to Chew that a Chinese-language daily newspaper would be the best way of informing the Chinese in America about such vital events as the fall of the reformers of 1898 and the imprisonment of the Emperor Kuang-hsü. A newspaper could rally support for the aims of the reformers like K'ang Yu-wei and Liang Ch'i-ch'ao and expose the machinations of the power-hungry "Old Buddha," as Tzu-hsi was often called. It could also alert the overseas Chinese to the dangers of American immigration laws and the fight for civil rights and citizenship. When friends from San Francisco came to visit Chew with offers of help in his predicament, he mentioned the possibility of starting a daily newspaper. Though he had no experience in journalism, he had done a good deal of writing and speaking to both Chinese and American audiences.

His friends laughed. "There's never been a Chinese daily newspaper," they exclaimed. "Besides, even if there were, no one would read it." There was a small weekly in San Francisco called *Mon Hing Yat Bo*, but a daily seemed out of the question.

Chew answered with the turn of humor that was always to be his defense against discouragement. "Our people have some bad habits like opium-smoking and gambling and maybe they will contract another—the newspaper habit."

Undeterred by their skepticism, Chew started to lay the groundwork for his newspaper at once. He had to solve three major sets of problems, dealing with financial, technical and staff needs. A persuasive and dynamic speaker, Chew was able to raise enough money among the Christian Chinese merchants of his congregation to order a press and type. The men who provided this essential capital were Huang T'ing-yup, Ng Yup, Tom Wo Shun and Liu Hay-juk.

A press and type were of no use, however, unless someone had the skill to operate them. Since there were no Chinese papers in Los Angeles, Chew went to work for a local Japanese journal for two months in order to learn the mechanics of typesetting and running the printing press.[5] Finally to fill the need for staff, he chose two members of his clan. Ng Yee Yin, who had taught Chinese at Chew's day school, could serve as Chinese editor since, unlike Chew, he had completed his education before coming to America. Another cousin, Ng See Yee, had the mechanical ability required to oversee the printing. Ng Poon Chew called himself Manager (Managing Editor) and Translator since he was the only one fluent in English. With the self-confidence of youth he expected to take care of all the other jobs, including "compositor and printer's devil," as well as the selling of advertisements. Lacking capital for a daily, he decided to start with a weekly paper.

Chew found an office in a dingy building between Sonora Town (the old Mexican heart of the city) and Chinatown at 117 Marchessault Street (long since obliterated by freeways). He hung up a signboard bearing the last words he had heard from grandmother, "If you will, you can." On May 12, 1899, the first issue of the *Hua Mei Sun Po* (*Hua-mei Hsin-pao* in Mandarin), or *Chinese American Morning Paper*, appeared. Hoping the quality of the paper would win support for his bigger dream, Chew quickly sent copies to his friends in San Francisco.

Meanwhile, he tried to work out the technical problems he would face on a daily. He would need a bigger press and three fonts of 11,000 characters, containing the 250,000 separate pieces needed to provide for repetition of common words. Professional compositors and reporters would also be needed.

As if to mock his hopes, events in China to which he turned his attention as never before were discouraging. For both reformers and revolutionaries, 1899 was a dark year. Foreign powers nibbled first here, then there, at tempting pieces of Chinese territory. The weak Chinese government could only acquiesce dumbly, but the people, especially in the north, channeled their anger and frustration into a new antiforeign secret society called the Boxers or Righteous Fists. The Boxers received covert encouragement from Tzu-hsi and the conservatives in control of the court. The "Old Buddha" remained deaf to the advice of wiser heads such as the aged statesman Li Hung-chang, who called it madness to attack the foreigners with their superior weapons.

The bad news of a repressive regime and foreign encroachments in China was balanced for Chew by stirrings of hope from another source. He knew that the exiled reformers of 1898, Liang Ch'i-ch'ao and K'ang Yu-wei were now settled in Japan and Singapore respectively. Scorning direct collaboration with Sun, K'ang had imitated Sun's journey through the Pacific islands to the coast of North America, then on across Canada to England where he sought help, in vain, from Parliament. But everywhere he was greeted with the respect due a scholar and official, from both Chinese communities and government authorities. Returning in June to Victoria, British Columbia, K'ang had organized among the overseas Chinese of that city the first branches of his own reform society—the Pao-huang Hui or "Protect Emperor Association." Some of his strongest supporters were sent to organize branches in the United States, among them Liang Ch'i-t'ien, a cousin of Liang Ch'i-ch'ao. And some who had been awakened earlier by Sun to the peril that threatened their homeland deserted his banner for the Pao-huang Hui.

The organizers for the Pao-huang Hui reached Los Angeles in the fall of 1899 just as Chew was weighing the merits of moving the paper to San Francisco and making it a daily. Response to the paper by supporters of the San Francisco mission had been highly favorable. Chew, however, like most young Chinese of the time, had begun to feel a greater devotion to the rising national feeling in China than to the direct goals of the mission.

Though the leaders of the Pao-huang Hui were of the gentry class, these organizers were now eager to gain support from all possible groups, even the secret societies like the Chee Kung Tong (Chinese Freemasons) and the Chinese Christians, who were considered suspect, if not subversive, by most Chinese. Certainly one of the most influential Chinese Christians on the West Coast was the Reverend Ng Poon Chew who had just raised $6,000 in additional capital to move his newspaper to San Francisco and turn it into a daily. The exact relation between K'ang and Chew at the time of the founding of Chew's paper had always been shrouded in secrecy. However, in the *Special Magazine/Book to Commemorate the Fortieth Anniversary of the Chung Sai Yat Po*, which appeared some time after Chew's death, there was an interesting report. Probably, it came from the memories of Ng Yee Yin or Ng See Yee, who survived Chew by a number of years.

As the story went, K'ang wrote Chew asking that he and the other editors of the soon-to-be *Chung Sai Yat Po* join the Pao-huang Hui and support it openly in their paper. However, among the articles of the society's charter as described by K'ang was one calling for reverence for Confucius (*pao-chiao*). Chew answered that he and his fellow editors were very much in favor of the Reform party and wished to see the rightful emperor, Kuang-hsü, restored to his throne, but as Christians they could not in conscience support a party which included *pao-chiao* ("Confucius reverence") as an article of faith. When K'ang wrote back agreeing to drop direct references to Confucius, Chew and his colleagues agreed to support the Reform cause in their paper.[6]

The last few months of 1899 were breathless ones for Chew. He had the money to start his modern Chinese daily in San Francisco. Six-sevenths of the stock was to be owned by friends of the San Francisco mission, but he would be able to buy shares from his salary. It was understood, of course, that as a Christian-owned daily, it would have no Sunday edition.

As he prepared for the return to San Francisco, Chew at last had a challenge big enough to match his ambitions. It didn't matter to him that some of his friends thought he had "more ambition than common sense." He was thirty-three years old; now, if ever, was the time for him to strike out on a new venture. Through support of the Reform party, Chew looked forward to being closer to the mainstream of political action. But at heart he was not a partisan politician; his only party was China and his creed whatever would benefit her. Through greater knowledge, he hoped his people would contribute some day to the new age promised by the new century. Inevitably China must change, and his paper might play some small, constructive part in that change.

CHAPTER 12

EDUCATION
OF AN EDITOR

The newspaper is the people's tongue.
CHUNG SAI YAT PO, MARCH 14, 1931

*R*IDING the train north in 1899, Ng Poon Chew was hurrying back to the "Bayside Bohemia," celebrated by so many artists and writers during the eighties and nineties. And it was to one special place in that city of dreams that Chew was hurrying. Chinatown, San Francisco, the quintessential American Chinatown, the fountainhead, was to claim him once again.

It was the first thing which the guides offered to show. Whenever, in any channel of the Seven Seas, two world-wanderers met and talked of the City of Many Adventures, Chinatown ran like a thread through their reminiscences. . . .

Its inhabitants, overflowing into the American quarter, made bright and quaint the city streets. Its exemplars of art in common things, always before the unillumined American, worked to make San Francisco the city of artists that she was. For him who came but to look and to enjoy, this was the real heart of San Francisco, this bit of the mystic suggestive East, so modified by the West that it was neither Oriental nor yet Occidental—but just Chinatown.[7]

Will Irwin, the writer of these words, was a supreme rhapsodist of turn-of-the-century San Francisco, as was Arnold Genthe, the photographer. As they knew, Chinatown could be tough—it was the honky-tonk center for Chinese workers from the

By the turn of the century the tantalizing sights, lilting cries and pungent smells of San Francisco's Chinatown were often recorded by perceptive artists, writers and photographers, like this picture capturing the unconscious artistry of a grocery store.
(NEW YORK PUBLIC LIBRARY PICTURE COLLECTION)

whole Pacific Coast. But it had another side, more important and more lasting, "a real life of homes and quiet industry" which went on in the factories, stores and secluded upstairs apartments. Though the women stayed close to home except on great social occasions, the "children—high and low, rich and poor . . . had the run of the streets. And they were the pride and joy, beauty and chief delight of the quarter."

Before Chew could move his family from Los Angeles to this enclave, he had to lay the groundwork for publishing his paper. In this work he had the help of representatives from the Pao-huang Hui or Reform party which had its strongest American branch in San Francisco. Teng I-yün and several other Reform leaders joined Chew and his kinsmen on the editorial staff in preparing for the first issue of the paper in early 1900. While they debated the proper editorial approach to problems of the day, Chew also had to solve a number of practical problems.

First Chew had to send to Tokyo, Japan, for a press and the three fonts of type. He found an office at 804 Sacramento Street. It was big enough to accommodate his press, his composing room and his editorial office, where he hung his motto, "If you will, you can." Finally he chose a name for the paper, *Chung Sai Yat Po*, or *Chinese-American Daily Paper*.

When Chew found time to look for a place to live, he ran up against the realities of Chinese life in America. His growing family, now increased by a young baby—Caroline, the last born—required an adequate home. After the bucolic atmosphere of Los Angeles, Chinatown in San Francisco appeared to a family man as simply a slum, inhabited by single men and dubious women. Rich merchants' wives, the only respectable class of women that existed in any numbers, still lived in a seclusion little suited to the ideas of a modern Christian Chinese. Chun Fah intended to continue her church work as she had when her husband was still a minister. In vain, Chew searched for an apartment or a house on the wider, cleaner, newer streets of the city, but no one would rent or sell to a Chinese family desiring to live outside of Chinatown, where Americans were glad to charge high rents for a small apartment in poor condition. After a year of vain searching, Chew went back to the quiet street on the edge of Chinatown where the Christian families lived, not far from the mission. He renewed his ties with many old friends such as the Reverend Soo Hoo Nam Art, ordained in China and pastor since 1894 of the Chinese Presbyterian Church.

Even before Chew settled on a place to live, the *Chung Sai Yat Po* made its debut, to the considerable surprise of Chinatown. On February 16, 1900, the first issue appeared, completely printed in the lucky color of Chinese tradition—red. Used for birth and marriage announcements, red contrasts with white, the color of Chinese mourning. Though Teng I-yün signed the early editorials and Chew was listed as translator, Chew was from the beginning and remained the driving force behind the paper's success.

From the first issue Chew strove to maintain the highest standards in its appearance and content. He engaged an adviser to to help the literary quality of the Chinese language used in the paper—Prof. John Fryer of the University of California at Berkeley. The two great causes for which Chew fought all his life were already evident in the earliest issues—a modern strong Chinese nation and equal rights for Chinese both in immigrating to America and in settling there. For Chew in 1900 the Reform party platform seemed to offer the Chinese both at home and overseas the best chance for attaining these goals. And always, whatever his political interests, he strove to report all sides of the news.

Even more than its coverage of foreign and domestic politics, the *Chung Sai Yat Po* probably owed its early success to its feeling for the everyday trials, the petty humiliations and grave injustices that were the lot of the average Chinese in America in 1900. Whether it was a Chinese fisherman harassed by petty regulations about the size of his nets or some army cooks whose queues were cut off by an American sergeant in a fight, the *Chung Sai Yat Po* always made room for their stories. A poignant example is this account of a brave wife who dared the seas to join her husband, as the reporter explains:

Chinese women are mostly illiterate and timid. Most husbands believe they should be left at home. This has often meant hardship and loneliness for the wives back home. Yesterday we received news from Washington of the wife of a Chinese, Lin, who had come here to meet her husband. The immigration officers intended to send her back on the grounds that this is against the regulations. Lin retained a lawyer who appealed to the Justice Department in Washington and Mrs. Lin was released.[8]

Of equal interest was the case of Chu Nan, who sued the city of San Francisco for $5,000 for medical treatment resulting from his alleged beating by an Officer McGill of the police department. As Chu told it, McGill had demanded $25 from him in exchange for not arresting him for loitering. Chu did not have the money, and McGill hit him so hard he broke two of his ribs. The reporter, recounting this incident, denounced the "intimidation of private citizens by officers," which he was saddened to find in free America as well as in authoritarian China. The reporter deduced that McGill, like most policemen in Chinatown, was looking for graft. Otherwise, he asked, why should so many illegal

The masthead of Ng Poon Chew's newspaper, the Chung Sai Yat Po, *in one of the early issues from May 29, 1900.*

gambling parlors flourish undisturbed along Officer McGill's beat?

This aspect of Chinatown was a cause of constant concern to the editors in the early years of the *Chung Sai Yat Po*. Tong violence, condoned or winked at by the police, survived into the 1900s, and with the extreme imbalance of men and women, it lent to Chinatown an air of the primitive frontier that the wild West itself was losing—the wide-open-quick-draw-loose-women-and-whiskey aspect. It survived in Chinatown and, excluding the Barbary Coast, in no other part of San Francisco. In language that blended the Biblical prophet denouncing sin with the Confucian official scolding his unruly villagers, the editor appealed to local Chinese to mend their differences and recover their earlier unity:

EDITORIAL: THE CLAN FEUDS AND THE GORY BLOODBATHS. . . . *Why should we of the same race hate, savagely attack and kill each other as though we desired to eat each other's flesh? . . . The cause of all this tragedy lies in the clan feuds and the hostilities thus aroused. . . . We came here to find a living, not to die, and you know finding a living is not easy over here. The loved ones that we left behind are constantly worrying about us, anxious to find out how we are. They pray to God and appease the Devil that we might be safe. Remember the time when we first got here; we were not used to our surroundings and we didn't know where to begin! Didn't we cling to each other and wish each other well? . . . But now our only companions are wine-meat* friends. At first we thought we were just going around with them for the fun of it. But very often casual acquaintance would lead to total involvement. We might kill someone and end up in prison. Even if we escaped arrest, pangs of conscience would leave us no peace. My friends, it is not too late to repent.*

---

* Literally translated. It denotes decadence, degeneration, indulgence and, by extension, simply bad. The equivalent might be, in English slang, "good-time Charlies."

In a community so fraught with conflict as Chinatown in 1900, the outspoken young editors were sure to arouse opposition. Officials like the Chinese consul, Oxford-educated Ho Yow, and conservative Chinatown officials regarded their support of the deposed Emperor Kuang-hsü, instead of the Dowager Empress Tzu-hsi, as treason, and called for a boycott of the new journal. They even threatened reprisals against the families of Reform leaders still in China. The fighting tongs which had been so strongly attacked made more direct threats. Posters on Chinatown walls began to name Chew and his fellow editors as objects of tong vengeance. One morning Chew even arrived at his office to find that an informant close to some tong leaders had brought word of a bomb planted in the building. But no bomb was found.

What saved Ng Poon Chew from the knife or a bullet? Were the threats less serious than they sounded? There are several reasons why Chew survived and eventually gained the respect of those who had once fought him. First was undoubtedly the stubborn spirit of the man: he refused to be intimidated by his opponents. But just as important was the gradual success during 1900 of the drive against tongs. In this the Chinese consul Ho Yow took the lead. Almost daily he was quoted in the *Chung Sai Yat Po* and American dailies as calling for an end to the feuds. He continually pointed out that the tong leaders were hurting their own people, not in one way but in two: they were making it difficult for legitimate merchants to do business in peace, and they were proving the truth of American charges of Chinese criminality.

Urged on by Ho Yow, the tong leaders in San Francisco declared a truce on March 13. Though this did not put an end to rivalry among the tongs, it marked the beginning of a long decline in violence.

Yet the most important reason for Chew's survival in these early difficult years was the pressure of events outside Chinatown, across the ocean, in China itself. Chew became the staunch defender of Chinatown against all comers, even when the direction of the attack was veiled.

On March 7, 1900, an ominous report appeared on the front page of the *Chung Sai Yat Po*:

> *Chinatown surrounded:*
> *. . . Last night at about* 11:00 P.M. *police surrounded Chinatown from Stockton Street to Kearney Street, from California Street to Pacific Street, blocking all traffic and stopping all passengers from passing. We first thought the police might be tracking down gangsters but by morning we found the cable cars had stopped running, and no mail was delivered. Upon inquiry, we learned that plague is suspected. A Chinese died last night and the American health official suspected that the disease was contagious, and therefore ordered a blockade. The cause of the spreading of the plague is due to the weather and the seasons. It has nothing to do with man . . .*

Chew, as we know now, was wrong, but for this there is some excuse. The knowledge of how bubonic plague spreads was by no means complete in 1900. Though the bacillus that causes it had been discovered in 1894, the method of transmission had yet to be proved. Plague had been largely absent from the Western world in the nineteenth century, and even in Asia, its ancient home, it broke out only sporadically. Then, in 1894, it migrated to Hong Kong from Canton, where 100,000 persons were reported to have died. Ships thereafter spread the disease to seaports all over the world. The consequence was that Chinese were feared as the source of the plague. In Hawaii, Chinatown had even been burned in an attempt to stamp it out, yet it did not stop.

The outbreak of plague in San Francisco in 1900 resulted in a strange, unacknowledged four-year compact in which the Chinese leaders and the state officials of California both sought to conceal that plague was claiming many victims in San Francisco. The Chinese did so because they naturally suspected the motives of the health officers to be purely racist. The officials of the city and state, on the other hand, wished to suppress the news because it would be bad for business. At last, in 1904, when increasing knowledge focused attention on rats as carriers of the disease, a rat eradication campaign was begun and the disease died out. Meanwhile, 121 cases had resulted in 118 deaths.

In the midst of the battle against plague, the echoes of the more dramatic conflict which was arousing both China and Chinatown reached American shores. For the first time since Sun's visit in 1896 a major Chinese political figure landed in San Francisco. Liang Ch'i-ch'ao, one of the two heroes of the Pao-huang Hui, had just spent six months in Hawaii, organizing branches of the society, schools and a newspaper. Now he expected to continue the same work in America. Despite the opposition of officials of the Ch'ing government, both American leaders and Chinese merchants offered him a warm welcome. Liang Ch'i-ch'ao, after thanking the merchants of the Chinese Chamber of Commerce for their hearty welcome, called for a constitutional monarchy, defended his role in the "Hundred Days" reform and asked overseas Chinese to support the deposed emperor. Chew was among the Pao-huang Hui leaders who consulted with Liang before he set off for other cities.

In the summer of 1900 the worst fears for China of both reformers and revolutionaries were realized as a series of events focused the world's eyes as never before on the Manchu Empire. The antiforeign Boxers, growing in strength, began to rampage over the countryside, spurring the peasants to attack railroads, missionaries and converts, as hated symbols of foreign aggression. Unruly mobs of Boxers descended on Peking.

The foreign legations, alarmed, sent for troops from the port of Tientsin. While waiting for help, the foreign community in Peking was cut off from the outside world for six weeks, from the end of June to the middle of August. Every day was a drawn-out agony of suspense, with only a few hundred soldiers to guard them from the mobs besieging their quarters. Meanwhile, with no news of the community's fate the newspapers entertained their readers with fantastic rumors of massacre and destruction.

"The Real Trouble will Come with the 'Wake.'" This cartoon in the comic weekly Puck *portrayed China at the time of the Boxer troubles as a sleeping dragon fought over by the western powers, notably Great Britain, the lion, and Russia, the bear.*
(NEW YORK HISTORICAL SOCIETY)

Actually, the only foreigners killed were a Japanese attaché and the German ambassador, and no Chinese official or general ever ordered an attack on the legations. The schism at court between conservatives and progressives saved the foreigners. Whenever food became short, a truckload of supplies would mysteriously appear. Thus, when the Allied Expeditionary Force reached Peking in August, they found the diplomats largely unharmed. Tzu-hsi fled in disguise to the northwest, taking her royal prisoner, the emperor, with her.

During that suspenseful summer, however, the Chinese in America waited in fear for the latest news in the *Chung Sai Yat Po.*

A July editorial had clarified the ambivalent attitude of many Chinese toward the Boxers, a sentiment little understood by Americans:

> *The massacre of the foreigners is a manifestation of Chinese hatred. We must, on the one hand, blame the stupidity of the peasants, but on the other, the Boxers' slogan "To Help the Ch'ing and Eliminate the Foreigners" is not an aberration but a culmination of ingrained Chinese hatred arising from the continued occupation of our land, disregard for our sovereignty, and trespasses on our rights by the foreigners. Our present unenviable plight is a consequence of their action. We lost our independence. Our people internalized their hatred. Now they find an outlet to channel their grievances. Their action, however, is going to lead to destruction.*

A British detachment including Indian cavalry was among the foreign troops closing in on Peking in August 1900, to rescue the legations besieged by the anti-foreign Boxers.

Regular Chinese troops like these of the early 1900s suffered from lack of modern training and weapons. This led to their defeat by Japan in 1895, and later failure to check foreign encroachments. (NEW YORK PUBLIC LIBRARY PICTURE COLLECTION)

Here the young activists spoke with a strong voice that was to echo through Chew's whole career—that of the fiery patriot and nationalist calling for the strengthening of China. At the same time there was a realistic note advocating restraint when China was too weak to drive out the foreigners.

In mid-July the reformers' contemplation of events in Peking was suddenly diverted toward home. Stirred by reports of cruelty to foreigners in China, a mob gathered around the Chinatown restaurant of Ah Shang, shouting and shaking their fists. When he unwisely came out to investigate, two of the biggest bullies seized him and shouted, "If you Chinese keep killing foreigners in China, we are going to get revenge by massacring you Chinese in America." Fortunately, one of Ah Shang's waiters had slipped out to call the police, and they dispersed the mob. But as to future protection, the

Chung Sai Yat Po sadly warned, "Police are no sure guarantee to a Chinese."

Despite some harassment during the Boxer Rebellion, the Chinese in America actually benefited at this time from a sudden turn in American foreign policy. Secretary of State John Hay was about to reiterate the Open Door policy that was to govern American policy toward China for the next fifty years. After the Spanish-American War and the Philippine adventure, Americans had become more interested in foreign affairs, especially in the Far East. Americans did not wish to see China divided up among the European powers, for then they would lose their equal rights in trading. Since the British agreed with the Americans in this, the two nations jointly influenced the peace negotiations toward that end. The resulting treaty, signed in Peking on September 7, 1901, called for China to pay heavy indemnities and punish guilty officials, but it made no further territorial demands.

When the safety of foreign diplomats was verified late in the summer of 1900, Chinatown erupted in joy. Firecrackers and noisy crowds milling in the streets resembled a Chinese New Year's celebration. But the joy of the Chinese was short-lived. On reflection, they felt humiliated by the whole affair. Daily bulletins from China reported rape, looting and murder by foreign troops occupying Peking, the Germans especially. These events "reverberated" through Chinatown, as Chew's old friends in the mission noted. Dr. Condit sensed an "undercurrent of disaffection felt not against Christian people so much as against the conditions which led up to the war."

Now, for the first time, the bright young men of Chinatown began to follow new paths to modern knowledge and power. These paths did not lead to Christianity but to reform and revolution. For the present, however, the reformers, taking guidance from Liang Ch'i-ch'ao, were in the ascendancy. During the summer of 1900 advertisements and articles in the *Chung Sai Yat Po* called on all Chinese to support the Pao-huang Hui. A new liveliness and excitement gripped Chinatown. Parties of cadets, the young sons of workers and merchants, began to drill in the parks every day. An editorial of July 19 condemned the "stupidity" of the empress dowager and the "reactionary traitors" who had brought China close to destruction. The only solution was "that our emperor be restored. He would be able to stop the Boxers, reconciliate the Powers, calm the people and uproot the causes of disorder. . . ."

While most Chinese, feeling insecure in their temporary homes, turned their eyes more determinedly back toward China, a minority continued to seek rights in America. In September 1901 an ad in the *Chung Sai Yat Po* suggested raising a fund for a "To Become [American] Citizen Society." The Chinese must "debunk the myth that we are unassimilable, so as to change [the Americans'] opinions about us. Although we came from a country with a great tradition, we must cope with the situation realistically. In China we are Chinese citizens; in America, we are Americans."

Despite his interest in a strong, awakened China, Chew shared the hopes of the young men of the "Citizens Society." He understood the connection between the denial of rights to Chinese in America and America's conflicting images of the Chinese—that of the bloodthirsty Boxers and that of the friendly docile nation patronized by the Open Door. Late in 1901 Chew had his first opportunity to "debunk the myth." The Chinese Christians in the Reform party had decided to organize a cross-country speaking tour to help explain to interested Americans the need for change in China. The time was ripe, for the Boxer Rebellion had piqued American curiosity about China as never before. Chew, whose eloquence in English had already proved effective with American audiences in California churches, was the featured speaker and he was accompanied by a trio of male singers including two brothers named Lowe. The most important stop was New York, where Chew was to speak under the auspices of the Chinese mission. Huie Kin, who had been serving as Chinese preacher there since 1885, made the younger man very welcome and initiated a lifelong friendship.

Two of Chew's speeches were reported in *The New York*

Times. The second, and more important, speech was given at the Fifth Avenue Presbyterian Church in early January 1902. In "The Chinese Crisis as Viewed by a Chinaman" Chew explained that Chinese resisted such modern inventions as the railroad and the telegraph because they "bring wants and not happiness; they stir us up and make us miserable." Yet in the face of foreign aggression, China had to turn her face from the past to the future. Already she was starting to adapt modern knowledge to ancient ways. On the brink of great changes, she looked to America as her best friend among the Western powers.

In the next few years, as the *Chung Sai Yat Po* flourished, Chew and his cousins Ng Yee Yin and Ng See Yee, along with Presbyterian elders and merchants, became more than ever the dominant force on the paper. By 1903 Chew was managing editor and had declared the *CSYP* to be independent of any political party. Though his editorials continued to favor the ideals of the Reformers, he covered the activities of all parties. Since his goal of a strong free China remained the dream of his life, he was now more able to support any group that seemed to further that aim.

Though Chew's reputation spread, his adopted country would not adopt him. In 1902 the exclusion law was extended for another ten years. In 1904 the treaty of 1894 expired, and a new one had to be negotiated.

While this new treaty and new laws hung in the balance, a timely visitor was approaching the Pacific Coast on the steamer *Korea*, sailing from Honolulu to the Golden Gate. Sun Yat-sen had found a loophole in the exclusion laws and stretched it to fit himself. When Hawaii was annexed to the United States in 1898, all

On its first anniversary, February 16, 1901, the Chung Sai Yat Po *featured some interesting pictures, including "Manager" Ng Poon Chew wearing a western suit, haircut and moustache in striking contrast to his traditionally robed and queued fellow editors. Note also the composing room (upper left) with its trays holding thousands of characters.*

(BANCROFT LIBRARY, U. OF CALIFORNIA, BERKELEY)

圖粒字放按

角街板百乃號四零八百埠唐人大街在局報本

機用轉印圖報每外餘千印力此印報者印有鑄一百餘做有機電動乃點五紙出機印點三紙出機印點五外散餘機一百餘印墨器本報電動有力

像件各局報本

照盤緯伍報本

Chinese born on Hawaiian soil became American citizens. Through his educational and family connections in Hawaii, Sun had secured an affidavit of Hawaiian birth, and he had gone before American officials with it. He was certified an American citizen.

The San Francisco *Examiner* announced his arrival on April 6 and that it had caused a "flurry of excitement in the . . . Chinese quarter" and "harsh denunciations" from some merchants. The paper reported that Sun would "go into hiding for a time." Since nothing was heard from Sun for three weeks thereafter, the uninformed might have assumed that he was indeed hiding and consulting with his followers in typical revolutionary fashion. In fact, Sun had been detained by the immigration officials and treated in a manner that had already been eloquently described by Chew: "When the steamship was about to set sail, the Chinese were brought to the wharf and transferred to wooden huts, locked and heavily guarded as if they were criminals. The press had no access to them either. The detention might last as long as half a year. . . ." Sun languished in this kind of captivity during those weeks.

Sun was probably detained because of American concern for the safety of a Manchu prince, P'u-lun, who was to pass through San Francisco en route to the St. Louis Exposition, the first such event in which China participated officially. But it is also likely that the strength of the currently powerful Reform party among influential merchants played a part.

Toward the end of April Chew received an appeal from Sun asking for help in securing his release from the detention shed. Though reporters were usually barred, Chew managed to get an interview with Sun. Sun appealed to him as a well-known believer in free speech and a Chinese patriot. Chew's fairness in reporting all the news had won him the friendship of both parties.

Knowing of Sun's ties to the secret societies, Chew met quietly with Wong Duck Sam, the leader of the Chee Kung Tong in San Francisco. Exactly what was said will never be known, but the results appeared dramatically in the *Chung Sai Yat Po* on

April 27, with no explanation. Sun was to enter the city that very day. Members of his party had "retained a lawyer on his behalf" and secured an okay from Washington for his release. "Sun's admirers will 'quench their thirst-thinking'* by seeing him in person."

In the next weeks Chew reported three speeches that Sun made in Chinatown. "At the request of Chee Kung Tong," Sun addressed large audiences on May 5 and May 7. But the third, given on May 16, was the biggest and best attended:

> The speech commenced at 1:00 P.M. and lasted till 3:00 P.M. The theater was so packed that all the seats were occupied and all standing room also filled. The speech was even more provocative than the second one.
>
> A summary follows:
>
> "To strengthen ourselves, the first thing the Chinese people should do is to organize the Han** people and oust the Manchus. In recent years the Chinese overseas nationalists all adhere to this first principle. That is why we sense the overwhelming revolutionary tide. A lot of Han heroes have already joined our revolutionary party. However, a few maintain that if we overthrow the dynasty, we would expose our weaknesses to the powers. They might take the opportunity to divide up China among themselves. But these people do not know that if we refrain from joining the revolutionary party and passively allow ourselves to be slaves of the Manchus, we will be oppressed forever by them, robbed by them. They will lose our China. But if we actively organize ourselves as revolutionaries, assert our human rights, and strengthen our country, the powers would recognize China as a sovereign power. Then we wouldn't be quartered up. We Han people should grasp this opportunity to overthrow the Manchus. . . .

* Literally translated as "fulfill their desire for information."
** The Chinese called themselves the "Han people."

*Chang Chih-tung and Yüan Shih-k'ai have already memorial-
ized the throne about the necessity of a constitution. But they
are not getting anywhere with the diehard Manchus in power.
This would only push further the already overwhelming
revolutionary tide."*

Heady words, those, for young men tired of seeing their
country and fellow citizens treated with contempt both overseas
and on their own soil. For most people in Chinatown in 1904,
Sun may have been asking for too much too soon, yet the size and
enthusiasm of his audiences was in striking contrast to the apathy
of 1896.

Among those who met Sun and were deeply stirred by his
message were the Reverend Huie and his wife, who were visiting
Chew and other San Francisco friends during the spring of 1904.
Huie invited Sun to stay at his mission when he came to New
York. When Sun arrived, however, Huie had to ignore loud noises
about a boycott of Sun's speeches by the Reform party. Nevertheless,
he entertained Sun for several weeks in the late summer of 1904.
Here Sun evolved his famous "Three Principles of the People"
and sketched the first draft of his constitution for China. The Three
Principles are usually translated as "The People's Nationalism,
the People's Democracy and the People's Livelihood," by which
Sun meant "Social Progress."

Huie has left us a vivid portrait of his famous visitor as he
appeared in those difficult days:

> *A fascinating and fluent speaker . . . Dr. Sun could hold
> his audience spellbound for hours at a time, whether they
> numbered by the hundreds and thousands or only a handful.
> He was at his best when in the quiet of the night with a small
> group of followers gathered about the lamplight, as often
> happened in the back-rooms of the little laundries in New
> York City, he spoke to them about the military reverses and
> diplomatic failures of China and expounded his program for*

the liberation and self-rule of the Chinese people. He often appeared weary and worn in body, but always enthusiastic for his cause and never downhearted.[9]

Did Chew's thoughts sometimes go to the travel-worn, rapidly aging, yet ever-hopeful Sun as he crossed the United States on his difficult quest? The Reform party was at the peak of its success. Chew, like most moderates, continued to favor its approach to saving China. Few could have predicted that the unpretentious Sun, who showed such a penchant for addressing the poor and humble, would someday surpass the elegantly robed scholar K'ang, the leader of the Reform party and the darling of rich merchants.

The Rev. Huie Kin (1854–1934), shown here in old age, served the Chinese Presbyterian Church in New York from 1885 to 1925. The hospitable mission run by him and his American wife once sheltered Sun Yat sen for several months in 1904.

(100TH ANNIVERSARY BOOKLET—FIRST PRESBYTERIAN CHURCH, NEW YORK, N.Y.)

CHAPTER 13

THE POLITICS
OF IMMIGRATION

*Economic competition always tends to increase the feeling of
nationalistic prejudice.*

LAWRENCE G. BROWN,
Immigration: Cultural Conflicts and Social Adjustments

*A*MONG the rare journalists who sympathized with the
Chinese in San Francisco at this time was Patrick
Healy. Healy was a disciple of Henry George's "single tax" movement.* Healy's articles sympathetic to the Chinese had appeared
in several magazines. He had been shocked in his investigations by
the violence of the prejudice against the Chinese in all fields of
labor despite the universal conviction that they were honest, reliable

---

* George's theory, much simplified, was that since all wealth is derived
from land, only land should be taxed.

workers. He determined to touch America's conscience and encourage her to render justice to the much-abused Chinese. He looked for a Chinese-American with the background to help him and was introduced to Ng Poon Chew.

Chew, involved at this time in his own plans to fight the stifling provisions of the latest exclusion act, agreed to share with Healy the documentary evidence that he had accumulated on anti-Chinese actions by Americans. Healy and Chew agreed that they would write a book, using only the sobering facts that Chew had assembled. The facts alone, they felt, were powerful enough to tell their story.

At the time of the treaty of 1904 Chew had allowed himself a rare outburst of bitterness:

> . . . we are now stuck with an Agreement, nominally to protect the Chinese in the United States, but in fact all Chinese, whether they are merchants or officials, teachers, students or tourists, are reduced to the status of dogs in America. The dogs must have with them necklaces [their registration] which attest to their legal status before they are allowed to go out [into the streets]. Otherwise they would be arrested as unregistered, unowned wild dogs and would be herded into a detention camp. . . . This is analogous to the present plight of the Chinese in America. The U.S. immigration officers in the interior keep harassing our merchants, officials, missionaries, students and tourists. Their vigilance is not too different from the street dog catchers. . . . Though the treaty was designed to prohibit labor and protect officials, students and merchants, now the U.S. Government is attempting to expel all Chinese.

Spurred on by a comprehension of the extreme situation of the Chinese community in America and by a dynamic mixture of anger and hope, Chew and Healy worked swiftly on their *Statement for Non-Exclusion*. They traced the history of American involvement with the Chinese back to the tea trade conducted by New England merchants in the late eighteenth century, which helped bring China the dubious gift of cheap, plentiful opium. They pointed out that America had usually been the aggressor in Sino-American relations, forcing the Chinese to trade and seeking out the immigrants who labored for the mines and railroads, on the great ranches and in the kitchens and parlors of San Francisco homes. Always the Chinese had come because they were wanted for jobs no one else cared to fill. Sadly, they recorded atrocities against the Chinese going back to the 1850s. They explored how press propaganda had whipped the economic fears of competing labor into hysterical hatred. They enumerated the bitter fruit of this heightened prejudice against the Chinese—from the discriminatory California laws and San Francisco ordinances of mid-century to the exclusion laws and rigid immigration regulations of their own day. As Chew studied the situation, he had become more and more disturbed by the contrast between the treatment of Chinese in the United States and that of other foreign groups. The reason for that difference was all too clear to him and impossible to remedy in the current state of the law:

> In the American political system, the President and legislators are elected by citizens. In America, all other aliens are granted the right to naturalization and hence citizenship and the right to vote. Since the American President, senators and congressmen do not have to court Chinese votes, they can deliberately violate the principles of equality [for the Chinese].

As Chew and Patrick Healy worked on their book, the spirit of newly awakened nationalism was bearing fruit throughout the Chinese world. The reforms instituted by the Manchus, as limited and partial as they were, stimulated a longing for more fundamental reform. And when the giant, backward Russian Empire was defeated by the island kingdom of Japan, the Chinese saw it as a victory of Asia over the West, of constitutional reform over despotism.

The most immediate, practical result for Americans of the new Chinese national pride was a boycott of American goods. The boycott began in the treaty ports where Americans had their main trading centers. The Chinese businessmen there saw their countrymen barred from free entry into the United States, and suffered personally the degrading restrictions when they traveled to America.

By July 1905 Chinese firms in the treaty ports were pressing for a ban on all business dealings with America, including such imports as cotton cloth and kerosene. Schools and colleges discarded American books from their regular course of study. By the end of the month, Getz Brothers, one of the biggest American firms trading with China, was told that the boycott was a total success from the point of view of the Chinese merchants. A *New York Times* editorial explained to American readers the connection between the boycott and American treatment of merchants and other exempt classes. It also spoke of Chinese resentment over the extension of the ban on Chinese labor to our newly won dependencies of Hawaii and the Philippines. "In the context of the Pacific, it makes no sense and threatens the prosperity" of Chinese merchants.

Chinatown in San Francisco responded to the boycott with even more enthusiasm than it had shown for the cause of the Reform party. Placards exhorted all local merchants to observe the boycott and press for the repeal of the exclusion law. Public meetings raised money in support of the boycott.

Americans were stunned by the boycott, especially when it began to pinch Southern cotton growers, Northern textile mills, and Standard Oil with its "oil for the lamps of China." Had America not always been China's friend? they asked somewhat naively.

Though not so eager for land nor so prone to "gunboat diplomacy" as Europe, America had subjected Chinese on American soil, even in some cases diplomats, to such humiliations as to nullify any benefits gained by a lack of territorial greed. One Chinese diplomat in Washington, arrested for lacking a visa or registration, had been tied by his queue to a fence. The loss of honor was unbearable, and he commited suicide.

A month before the boycott had officially begun, American bankers and mill owners visited President Theodore Roosevelt to protest the conditions that were making this anti-American movement possible. Faced with the threat to our China trade, Roosevelt was forced to examine our whole China policy. Lacking the popular support needed to force Congress to amend the law, he informed the worried businessmen he intended to do his best:

> *Our laws and treaties should be so framed as to guarantee to all Chinamen, save of the excepted coolie class, the same right of entry to this country, and the same treatment while here, as is guaranteed to any other nation. By executive action, I am as rapidly as possible putting a stop to the abuses which have grown up during many years in the administration of the law. I can do a great deal, and will do a great deal even without the action of Congress, but I cannot do all that should be done unless some action is taken [by Congress]....*[10]

In this same spring of 1905 Chew went on a cross-country speaking tour to explain to Americans the connection between the Chinese boycott and the rigid American exclusion laws. He even addressed the House of Representatives and was granted an interview with President Theodore Roosevelt. Like most Americans of his generation, Chew was fascinated by the character of Theodore Roosevelt. Roosevelt's strong posture in foreign affairs, his sponsorship of domestic reforms, his honest administration and his executive leadership contrasted strongly with the colorless presidents who followed Lincoln and preceded him.

The interview with the President only reinforced Chew's lifelong admiration of the man. Early in his administration Roosevelt had shocked public opinion by inviting the acknowledged leader of the black community, Booker T. Washington, to lunch at the White House. As the representative of another sometimes despised race, Chew also received a warm welcome from this President who shared with the former Presbyterian minister a concern for the

Circa 1890 a grocer in New York's Chinatown wearing traditional dress provided fresh Chinese vegetables grown nearby and dried delicacies imported from China for his fellow countrymen.
(NEW YORK PUBLIC LIBRARY PICTURE COLLECTION)

"moral tone" of his times. To Chew he pointed out that his executive order calling for fair and courteous treatment of Chinese immigrants and visitors was reportedly bringing improvements, but any major modification of the law had to come from Congress.

Influenced by Chew and the American merchants, Roosevelt issued an executive order to the Immigration Service charging it to stop its abusive treatment of legitimate Chinese merchants and travelers. Meanwhile, Congress conducted an investigation into the causes of the boycott—and concluded only that American immigration practices were the chief cause of Chinese resentment. There the matter rested.

Unfortunately for Roosevelt's good intentions and the hopes nourished in American Chinatowns and Chinese treaty ports by the success of the boycott, America's view of immigration was changing. Chinese immigrants were no longer the main fear of Americans, but the Chinese were to be coincidental losers. For, after 1882, a dramatic change occurred in the size and nature of immigration to the United States. Whereas most of the "old immigrants" had come from northern and western Europe, the "new immigrants" came from eastern and southern Europe. Before this year Italy, the Austro-Hungarian Empire, Russia and the Balkans, together with Turkey and the Near East, had not sent more than 8,000 to 10,000 immigrants a year. But between 1900 and 1914 each of these areas sent as many as ten times that number—and more. There were, from the Austrian Empire 3,100,000, Italy 3,000,000, Russia 2,500,000 and the Balkans and Near East 900,000. Over these fifteen years 9,500,000 people entered the United States. American Protestants suddenly beheld Roman Catholics, Greek Orthodox Catholics, Jews and Mohammedans bringing their customs and modes of worship to the land of the Pilgrim Fathers. And many Americans forgot that they and their forefathers had once been immigrants seeking religious and political liberty and economic betterment. Many did not realize that even in the years of heaviest immigration the foreign-born population of the United States never exceeded 15 percent, a 3 percent rise over the average of other years. Sensing that they were being engulfed by a foreign invasion, many more Americans came to feel about the new immigrants as they had once felt about the Chinese—that they would corrupt and dominate the American way of life.

On the Pacific Coast it was the Japanese immigrants, who had been taking over Chinese jobs, especially in agriculture, who heightened anti-Oriental feelings. Those groups that wanted the exclusion of Chinese took Japanese and Koreans as their targets as well, and they reorganized into Asiatic exclusion leagues.

The "new immigration" also became a target of other groups within America, not just the native Americans and superpatriots who had always opposed immigration. The new immigrants were not dispersing into the countryside, going west to farm or settle new towns, but flooding into the cities. There the immigrants crowded together in slums and came into direct, abrasive contact and competition with Americans for jobs in factories and construction. As a result, organized labor began stridently to oppose all immigration. The immigrants, labor felt, were taking jobs from American workers.

By 1905 immigration had become a central and obsessive concern of the American people. Among those organizations impressed by the importance of the issue was the National Civic Federation, one of many reform groups associated with the Progressive movement. The Progressive movement, which had strongly influenced Theodore Roosevelt, had arisen around the turn of the century to combat the evils spawned by the industrial revolution and the rise of cities. The federation issued invitations to all groups and prominent individuals concerned with immigration to send delegates to a Conference on Immigration to be held at Madison Square Garden Concert Hall in early December 1905.

The Chinese community in San Francisco, the most important in the country, was invited to send a representative to speak in its behalf. By this time the editor of the *Chung Sai Yat Po*, once so fiercely opposed by the establishment in Chinatown, was regarded as among its brightest ornaments. What better Chinese delegate could there be to speak before a distinguished American audience than Ng Poon Chew, the witty, dramatic speaker and editor, coauthor of a major treatise opposing exclusion?

Soon after arriving in New York, Chew was made aware of an intense opposition to his views, even before the conference got around to discussing Asiatic immigration. On Wednesday, December 6, August Belmont II, president of the National Civic Federation, opened the conference before five hundred delegates. He set the keynote—the conference was to be a judicious study of the "relation of alien to domestic labor" as well as the "effect of alien labor upon the progress of the Negro."

Two of the most prominent labor leaders of the day—Terence Powderly of the Knights of Labor and Samuel Gompers of the American Federation of Labor—were among the main speakers. Gompers immediately accused alien laborers of stealing bread from the mouths of American workers. Isidor Straus, an owner of Macy's, the world's biggest department store, responded by pointing out that two of the speakers, he and Gompers—born in England— were immigrants and that the other, Belmont, was the son of an immigrant. While admitting that the crowded situation of modern American cities called for some restriction on immigration, he spoke out for the "fundamental human right to migrate from misery and poverty to hope."

On Thursday Gompers tried to take the floor again with a special attack on Chinese immigration, but he was told to save his remarks on the subject till Friday. Gompers, Chew's most strenuous and determined opponent at the conference, had written a pamphlet, *Meat vs. Rice*, which tried to prove that American workers, family men who needed to eat meat for strength, were no match for the bachelor Chinese, who could work well on rice alone. To bolster the economic argument, Gompers larded it with vicious turn-of-the-century stereotypes of the Chinese.

On Friday morning ex-Senator Anthony Higgins of Delaware chaired the discussion of Asiatic immigration. Though favorable himself to the entry of merchants and students and others, he utterly opposed the admission of laborers "for racial reasons." Chew, the personification of the adaptability of the Chinese that they all claimed was impossible, walked to the platform in his modern dress, short-cut hair, Teddy Roosevelt moustache. The most telling symbol of his American credentials was his exceptional mastery of the English language. The essence of his speech was reported in *The New York Times* the next day:

> I am here to plead the cause of the yellow people, not a yellow cause. Some people have a great fashion of calling things they do not like yellow. You exclude the yellow man. You fear the yellow peril. I edit a white paper turned out by yellow men, and many white men turn out yellow papers.* [Laughter and applause] I do not ask the admission of all the Chinese people, or even of the laboring classes, although of right they ought to come. According to the ideas of civilization of the twentieth century, a nation has no right except that which it can enforce. This doctrine denies us the right of entry here until we have the might to demand equal treatment with other countries.
>
> China will some day be ready for this. She is preparing to be a great nation by learning to kill the largest number of men in a given time, with the least expense to herself. Then, and not until then, will she be looked upon as a power to be reckoned with.
>
> Of course, we have Chinese people of bad character, gamblers and opium eaters. If I were a woman, I would rather my husband, if he insisted on taking something, take opium rather than whisky. Whisky transforms men into brutes. Opium transforms them into living corpses. The American, filled with whisky, comes home and kicks his wife. The Chinaman comes home and his wife kicks him. [Laughter]
>
> You say you are afraid [that] 100,000 Chinamen will contaminate your 80,000,000 people. American workingmen, who fear neither God nor the devil, say they are afraid of the

---

* That is, "yellow journals."

*inoffensive Chinaman. I cannot credit that. I do not ask the
repeal of the Exclusion Act, but its modification. The Exclusion Act forbids the entry of Chinamen into the United States
except five classes, officials, merchants, teachers, students and
travelers, but the restrictions are such that it is impossible for
almost any of these classes to enter. We want better men as
inspectors of immigration, not the pigheaded, oyster-brained
officials you have now.*[11]

A great burst of laughter, cheers and applause arose at the
conclusion of Chew's speech. The *Times* summed it up neatly by
saying that he "made the hit of the day."

Yet the enthusiasm of the crowd in no way deterred the next
three speakers from stereotyped attacks upon the undesirability of
the "coolie." One speaker, Walter MacArthur, a labor leader, went
further, asking that the ban be extended to Japanese and Koreans.
"The Mongolian race is opposed to the Caucasian," he insisted,
using a popular cliché. "They corrupt our men and women. Mr.
Poon Chu [sic] seems able to do more than most other editors. He
can travel across the country to express his opinions when other
editors in California are sticking to their business." This offensive
personal attack upon Chew was highly unpopular with the delegates, who "greeted it with hisses."

After lunch two missionaries praised the good qualities of the
Japanese and Chinese respectively. Perhaps under their influence
the resolutions committee reported a resolution about Chinese
immigration that was a slight improvement over the current law.
It advocated *admitting* all Chinese except "coolies, Chinese skilled
and unskilled labor."

Then Samuel Gompers rose, the personification of the middle-
of-the-road labor leader. With strong irony, he said that it was all
very well for the "reverential and professional gentlemen" to "throw
your gates wide open, but it is a very different proposition for the
American workingman. The American workingman realizes that
his condition is better than that of any other workingman in any

part of the world, but he is not yet satisfied. There is room for improvement and in securing it, the admission of the Chinese would be fatal."

Terence Powderly of the Knights of Labor strongly seconded Gompers's view. The American people, he stated, did not wish to associate with the Chinese. Swayed by Chew's eloquence, the conference had at first recommended a more positive approach to the Chinese immigration question. But, pushed by the anti-Chinese forces, they changed back to the unfortunate wording of "exclusion" with the exempt classes merely "excepted" from the provisions of the law rather than freely admitted.

So Chew had twice journeyed east—to see President Roosevelt and to address the immigration conference with a plea for his people. What had he to show for it? The epitaph for the conference was an editorial in *The New York Times* entitled "The Chinese Labor Puzzle." Chew was "a Chinese humorist upon whose shoulders the mantle of Minister Wu [T'ing-fang, former Chinese minister to the United States and a very popular speaker] has settled." But beyond this brief accolade, the whole editorial dealt with the "yellow peril" in polite terms. Even though the Chinese were unlikely to come here in such numbers as to "engulf" Americans, there was a possibility that they might. After all, they had done so in Mongolia and Manchuria. Far from being inoffensive, as Chew maintained, "the Chinaman's single-mindedness" was what "gives him the upper hand" when he "comes in competition" with another people. "Let us beware of complicating our problems by opening the gates to a flood of yellow brethren."

The conference had still another ironic footnote which Chew could not yet foresee as he rode home on the train, contemplating the wreck of his hopes. His speech had done for Chew what it had not done for the Chinese. He was shortly to emerge as a man much sought after, most desirable for addressing public meetings and speaking before organizations of every stripe, from schools to churches to service clubs to veterans' groups.

CHAPTER 14

DRAGON'S
BREATH

*The old San Francisco, the gayest, lightest-hearted most
pleasure-loving city of the western continent, is dead . . . is
a horde of refugees living among ruins. It may rebuild; it
probably will, but those who have known the peculiar city
by the Golden Gate, have caught its flavor of the Arabian
nights, feel that it can never be the same.*

WILL IRWIN, *The City That Was*

FOR San Francisco the famous convulsion of April 1906
was the dividing line of her whole history. The life of
every citizen, of every event in the city's own story was henceforth
dated before or after that earth-rending shock. It might be better,
it might be worse, but it would never be the same again. The effects
on Chinatown of the great earthquake and fire were just as pro-
found, and perhaps even more so, than on the rest of the city.

The early months of 1906 were unusually busy ones for
Ng Poon Chew. On the one hand, the disappointing results of his
mission to the immigration conference had turned his thoughts

back more strongly to events in China. Despite her weaknesses he felt her to be on the verge of great advances. On the other hand, Chew had not completely given up hope that America would take a more positive view of the Chinese in America. The boycott had persisted into 1906, and the American government was impatient to end it. America seemed eager to extend a hand of friendship to China.

Partly influenced by this changing American view of China, partly swayed by his interview with Roosevelt, Chew decided to expand the case favoring Chinese immigration that he had helped Patrick Healy to write and that he had outlined more briefly in magazine articles and speeches. Night after night he worked at this history of the positive side of Chinese immigration so totally ignored amid the cries of "coolie labor" and "filthy degraded habits," the highly colored stories of opium dens and slave girls. As the nights flew by, the manuscript grew, and with it Chew's confidence that the story would touch the hearts of the American people. By mid-April it was near completion.

Then, at 5:12 A.M. on Wednesday, April 18, 1906, the clocks stopped in San Francisco. Like most other residents of the city, Chew and his family were sleeping. For 65 to 75 seconds—an eternity to the suddenly awakened San Franciscans—the earth writhed and twisted. Then came absolute silence. Everywhere chimneys and roofs collapsed upon sleeping occupants. Houses were shaken to rubble, especially in the low parts of the city—parts of the business district and "south of Market," where cheap hotels and boarding houses had been raised on lands reclaimed by Chinese labor from the bay. It was there that hundreds died, and other unlucky victims were scattered through the city. One critically injured and dying man was to be sorely missed in the next three days—Fire Chief Dennis Sullivan.

The quake and deathly silence were followed by a rush of San Franciscans into the streets, whose contours had suddenly, strangely altered. Some were panicked to find that doors wrenched from their frames would not open. The rush was so spontaneous and unthinking that only when they beheld their neighbors—men, women and children—in nightshirts did the people stop to smile sheepishly, then all to start talking at once.

Bret Harte had noticed fifty years before that San Franciscans claimed "to treat earthquakes as a gigantic practical joke," and that for an hour or two afterward everyone would be promenading up and down the streets. "The slightest shock is sufficient to overthrow the artificial barriers of society."[12]

The severity of this quake could not be laughed off, and no one thought of treating it as a joke. But the "artificial barriers of society" were indeed overthrown and were to remain down for longer than anyone dreamed. Each person noted thankfully his own survival and that of his family and lamented the damage to his house. Then, at 5:26 A.M., the first of a series of severe aftershocks sent everyone back indoors where those whose damage was only partial and those who had escaped relatively unharmed threw on their clothes to find out how the rest of the city had fared.

Chew and his family had also run into the streets, despite the extreme modesty usual among Chinese. The instinct for self-preservation had driven the rest of Chinatown from their beds as well. Many servants, laundrymen and restaurant workers were already up and starting their day. As Chew led his family back into the apartment, the first aftershock wracked the streets.

The members of the family hastened to dress and find out the extent of the damage—Chew to tour Chinatown and discuss future plans with local leaders, Chun Fah to see if all was well at the mission. The older children talked of starting for school, but they had caught the holiday air that was affecting all the survivors on finding that the disaster was not total.

As they left their apartment in the early dawn light, they could smell smoke and see it at several points on the horizon. No one noticed the sinister absence of fire alarms—for the new alarm station near Chinatown was one of the buildings almost leveled by the first quake. In fact the horse-drawn engines were clattering over the cobblestones to every fire in sight within minutes after they were spotted. Engine Company 38 was the first to arrive below Market Street. Quickly the men unrolled their hose to the hydrant. They turned the valve to be greeted first by a feeble trickle—then nothing. Everywhere it was the same; the mains were broken, the reservoirs drained. Even those hydrants that worked at first soon ran dry. San Francisco faced her worst conflagration, almost un-armed, with her best defense useless.

Within three hours of the quake the scope of the threatened disaster was beginning to penetrate the minds and spirits of the watching San Franciscans. Small, isolated fires, some mere cooking fires ignited by choked kitchen flues, began to spread, to leap buildings and even streets. Smoke grew thicker and flames licked at its edges.

Mayor Schmitz organized a Committee of Safety, called together all the police and warned that everyone must keep away from fires and firefighters. Brigadier Gen. Frederick Funston, the ranking military officer in the city, organized the soldiers at Fort Mason and the Presidio and took over the battle against disaster. He declared martial law and announced that looters would be shot on sight. With water almost unavailable, heroic measures, he realized, would be needed to combat the blaze. Only on the waterfront could water be drawn from the bay. There the Marines from Mare Island fought for three days to save the precious piers.

During the long day of April 18, 1906, residents of Chinatown, like other San Franciscans, tried to get accurate news about the spread of the fire. From their vantage point on the side of Nob Hill, they could see all too clearly the terrible destruction of the fire as it raged through the south-of-Market tenements and the central business district. Within the first few hours landmarks and new skyscrapers were ravaged.

As the fire leaped barriers and even the blocks of buildings dynamited to stop its spread, the residents of Chinatown, sensing the hot breath of the dragon coming closer began to flee. Seeing the beginning exodus of refugees, Chun Fah gathered her children together and hurried to Chew's office. He told them that he could

Just behind the two couples at left, Arnold Genthe caught a
group of Chinese girls from the Mission school (friends perhaps
of the Chew sisters) sitting on a bench in fashionable picture hats
as they looked down Clay Street from above Stockton into the
heart of the post-earthquake fire advancing on Chinatown.
(ACHENBACH FOUNDATION FOR GRAPHIC ARTS
FINE ARTS MUSEUM OF SAN FRANCISCO)

not discover that General Funston had any special plans to save Chinatown. Knowing the unpopularity of their quarter, most Chinese were regarding its destruction as inevitable.

As evening approached, armed National Guardsmen stood along Kearney Street near the border of Chinatown to hold back anyone who might want to venture closer to the fire that raged just beyond. Suddenly taking stock of the situation, Chew realized that he had tarried almost too long. All day the fire had been burning westward toward Chinatown from Sansome to Kearney. At 5:00 P.M. the Hall of Justice on Portsmouth Square (formerly Portsmouth Plaza) caught fire.

A demolition squad surveyed the scene. Determined to stop the fire at the natural barrier formed by the square, they decided to blow up a drugstore at the corner of Clay and Kearney. Having run out of dynamite, they used the only explosive they had left— black powder. When the blast detonated, sparks ignited a mattress in an upstairs apartment, and flung it across the street like a flaming torch. The first of Chinatown's houses was ablaze.

The word spread faster than the flames—Chinatown is on fire! Chinatown is doomed! The community had stood its ground for many years against the hostile cries of "Remove it, put it outside the city limits!" Now it was faced with a destroyer it could not withstand. Quietly, on their slippered feet, with poles slung across their shoulders to carry their few belongings, the Chinese joined the exodus to the ferry landing or the refugee camps in the parks. Most astonishing sight of all were the delicate figures of the merchants' wives swaying on their tiny bound feet and three-inch platform soles, clutching the arms of their husbands, blinking at the unfamiliar sun "like fearless Americans."

Turning to Chun Fah, Chew made plans for their escape. The racing fire had cut them off from their apartment; the flames would shortly engulf the newspaper office where the first sheet of the day's paper lay ready to be printed. Chew called to his men to save themselves. There was no time to save anything else. He would meet them in Oakland which was untouched by the disaster; they would try to bring out the paper there as soon as possible. Ng Yee

Yin lingered a moment, looking at his cousin with concern, warning him not to stay too long. Chew promised to follow him as soon as possible, to meet him across the bay. On the other side of the street the flames roared, timbers and brick walls crashed to the ground, and a steadily growing heat began to singe the skin.

Chew told Chun Fah to take the children up Nob Hill and down around the path of the blaze to Golden Gate Park. Their few most precious belongings were piled in ten-year-old Eddie's coaster wagon. He would join them as soon as possible, but he must try to save his papers, especially the almost completed manuscript of his book. Chun Fah gathered the children and began to walk quickly up Sacramento Street. Chew watched them disappear over the crest of the hill, then turned back to his door. But the way was barred by a National Guardsman.

"You can't go back in there," said the young man, then after a moment's hesitation, "sir."

"But my manuscript—if only I could rescue just that," Chew protested.

"I'm sorry, sir, orders of General Funston! See that building across the street. It's going to collapse any minute, and the burning timbers will fly right over here. I got to leave myself; we both do or we'll be trapped."

Chew stood for a moment in stunned silence, looking back at the building that had held his hopes and dreams for six years. It was an ordinary Chinatown building, three stories high, of brick and masonry with a wrought-iron balcony. Its only distinguishing mark was a sign in Chinese characters and English letters—*Chung Sai Yat Po, The Chinese-American Daily Paper.*

"Move on there, move on," called a rough voice. Chew looked around to see a large man brandishing a rifle. Slowly he turned his back on the fire and followed his wife and children up the hill.

On that first devastating day, the fire was only beginning. Over the next three days it would spread desolation across 472 city blocks. But for most people, the later days became a blur, as if the first pain was too intense to allow of more.

For once the Chinese had a pleasant surprise in the lack of

hostility shown toward them by normally touchy white neighbors. Perhaps it was the selfless devotion of so many Chinese servants, who saved both their masters and their masters' treasures. Perhaps it was the sense of common humanity suffering the same blows.

By the time the fire burnt itself out on April 21, as many as two hundred thousand people, among them the Chews, were camping in Golden Gate Park and another fifty thousand in the Presidio. Food had been sent by the carload from all over the country. The U.S. Army and the Red Cross Relief Commission had hurried in to fight disease, feed the starving refugees and build temporary shelters for the hundreds of thousands who had no homes to return to.

As the fires flickered and died, people began to wander among the ruins in hopes of finding some small keepsake, some treasure abandoned in haste on the night of the fire. Little survived—from

In the aftermath of the catastrophic earthquake and fire beginning April 18, 1906, the view of San Francisco from Market Street was littered with piles of rubble and punctuated by the shells of larger buildings like the Fairmount Hotel (right rear).
(NEW YORK PUBLIC LIBRARY PICTURE COLLECTION)

the records of births and deaths in City Hall to precious personal papers like Chew's manuscript and his whole printing plant.

At the earliest opportunity, Chew sent Chun Fah and the children across the bay to stay with friends in Berkeley. Less than a week after that fatal April day Chew had followed them through the miraculously spared ferry building over the water to Oakland. Searching its small Chinatown, he found two things he was looking for—a temporary apartment for his family and Ng Yee Yin. Over a cup of tea the two men discussed the need to bring out the paper as soon as possible. Unlike the regular English-language journals of San Francisco, they could not simply borrow type and a press, and it would take weeks to import new fonts from Japan.

"Well," said Ng Yee Yin, "through years of neglect my brush work is not so beautiful as it was. Still I can write out the paper by hand each day, if you can find a small press to print it. . . ."

The rest of the story became a legend in Chinatown. Chew found "an old hand-operated lithograph press. The patriarch [Ng Yee Yin] sat himself down at the stone with brush in hand and each day wrote the whole paper out by hand, but *backwards*, mind you, because the characters were reversed in stone printing and the paper appeared every day without a break until the plant was again opened. . . ."[13]

A week and a day after the earthquake wrenched San Francisco out of its accustomed ways and turned it into a vast wasteland inhabited by tent dwellers, the first issue of the hand-written *Chung Sai Yat Po* appeared. The date was April 26, 1906, and the tiny office where the press stood was at 1163 Washington Street. Chew was overjoyed to hold the paper once more in his hands. He knew that its rebirth would be a great help to the Chinese in San Francisco just then. The rumor mills, always active in times of disruption, had been busy. If the whispers had any basis in fact, Chinatown faced the biggest crisis in its sixty-odd years of existence. Chew understood that he could help both by tracking down the truth behind the rumors and keeping his countrymen informed about moves for self-defense. On April 29 he was urging his readers not to lose heart:

Since the San Francisco earthquake, the overseas Chinese all agree it is imperative to rebuild Chinatown, but in the meantime they are doubtful if they can do it. Why? Everyone believes that the fire is an excellent excuse to move Chinatown, a plan that the Americans have long contemplated. Every Chinese believes that since they want us to move, we will not be able to rebuild it. We have not tried yet; how do we know that we cannot do it?

The ordinary Chinese were quite determined to rebuild their houses where they had stood. As Chew toured the ruins, talking to leaders and workers, he realized that this quiet determination was the best weapon against all suggestions to transport them elsewhere. Therefore, he was especially incensed on April 30 to learn that the Chinese ambassador to the United States was planning to negotiate the future location of the community. Taking up his pen, Chew prepared an angry retort to such a notion:

a) . . . The formation of Chinatown is a natural concentration and not dictated by treaty right. Our foreign officer simply has no right to ask the U.S. government where to locate the overseas Chinese. It is beyond his authority. . . .

b) The San Francisco government and the U.S. authority have no right to tell the Chinese where to live either. . . . Except in a Sino-American war, the Chinese residing in the United States are protected by the Constitution, which grants freedom of residence. Therefore, we can simply disregard what the San Francisco authority has to say.

Then Chew gave practical suggestions on how best to save Chinatown: Chinese landlords should immediately rebuild on their own land and not sell it to Americans. (This would, of course, discourage Americans who feared for "property values" in a racially mixed neighborhood.) Then Chinese tenants should try to persuade their American landlords to rebuild their buildings and rent to Chinese. The Americans would probably favor this, since they could usually get higher rents from the Chinese, who had less choice of residence. As the number of Chinese returning to Chinatown increased, it would be less and less likely that Americans would want to live there. Chinatown would revert to the Chinese.

Chew was glad to find cheering news in the treatment of the Chinese in San Francisco. All his investigations into the distribution of relief supplies convinced him that "the U.S. Government is very generous towards the Chinese. They were given federal relief like everybody else. Chinese in other cities have also responded by sending us relief material. They are sharing our worries."

Within a few days the merchants began evolving a plan for reconstruction along the lines that Chew had suggested. As counterpoint, the local press continued in the racist vein that had been popular for decades, "Fire has reclaimed to civilization and cleanliness the Chinese ghetto and no Chinatown will be permitted in the borders of the city."[14]

To help smooth his people's return to their historic community, Chew decided it was time for a little of the reforming zeal that had helped lead him into journalism in the first place:

> Prior to the fire, the Americans in San Francisco had already been clamoring for the removal of Chinatown. Whenever we heard about this, we always claimed that their oppression was a consequence of our national weakness. However, we must admit that we are also partly to blame. We could not control our own community and this fact damaged our self-respect. Therefore we should abandon the old ways and adopt the new. Reform could help get rid of some of the causes of persecution.

Among the reforms which Chew suggested were future unity instead of tong fights, the destruction of idols, the closing of opium and gambling dens, the abolishing of foot-binding, and the cutting of the queue.

In April 1906, a lone Chinese surveyed the ruins of Chinatown
before the lens of Arnold Genthe. After the earthquake, Dr. Chew
was a leader in the movement to rebuild Chinatown in the same
location despite the opposition of anti–Chinese politicians and
journalists. (CALIFORNIA HISTORICAL SOCIETY)

Thus did Chew, still a preacher in spirit if not in fact, urge the people of Chinatown to abandon their traditional ways and adopt the customs of the people around them, as he had. Now he was planning an even more radical step to advance the welfare of his family and that of future Chinese who might draw courage from his example.

Six years earlier, when he had come north from Los Angeles to found the *Chung Sai Yat Po*, he had resolved to find a comfortable apartment for his family in an unsegregated neighborhood in San Francisco. After a year of frustration and loneliness, he had been forced to abandon that hope and settle down with Chun Fah and the children in a crowded Chinatown apartment.

With the Chinatown apartment and Chinatown itself destroyed, he intended to find a house of his own in Oakland, whose nonwhite population had been previously confined to a small ghetto near the railroad track. He liked Oakland's neat cottages and gardens; its warm sun appealed to him after the eternal damp of the San Francisco fog. And he refused to be discouraged by the fact that Oakland was just then very upset about the influx of Chinese refugees from the earthquake.

Chew was experienced enough to realize that he could gain nothing by storming the walls of prejudice directly. So he and Chun Fah strolled about the city, looking for a suitable neighborhood but making no direct move to buy a house. When at last they discovered a neat new two-story house for sale at 3765 Shafter Avenue, Chew found a friendly agent who agreed to buy the house in the name of Dr. N. P. Chew. The name, identical with that of an old Philadelphia family, did not alarm the seller, and the deal was quietly signed in the summer of 1906. This is how Chew always described his manner of taking possession of the new house:

> *Having a large family, he thought it would not be wise to take them all into the house at once, as it might alarm the neighbors. He said, "First, my wife and I moved in; then my first daughter arrived; then my second daughter followed my*

first daughter, and my third daughter followed my second daughter, and my fourth daughter followed my third daughter, and my fifth—" Here he lost his breath, but not daughters, and had to stop, amid the roars of the audience.

Soon the neighbors grew to like his family, seeing they were not really vicious and that the police patrol never drove up in front of their door. Now all is harmony on the block. "It wasn't long," he said, "till I smoked my cigar harmoniously with the men in the block, my wife talked over the back fence with the ladies and my children played with the other children in the block, and so far as I have been able to learn no one has ever been contaminated by association with the family."[15]

With his house on a firm foundation, his roots and those of his children sinking deeper into the California soil, Chew dedicated himself even more to improving and broadening the style and scope of the *Chung Sai Yat Po*. During his lifetime it was never to miss another issue. It would record many trials and troubles, many crises for the Chinese in America, but at the same time it seemed as if some of the most virulent anti-Chinese feeling had burned itself out of San Francisco with the fire. Perhaps a new mood had already been in the making when Will Irwin and Arnold Genthe perceived the old Chinatown to be a place of curious and unexpected beauty.

In the immediate future, there was no real improvement in the position of the Chinese in America. The availability of jobs and housing outside Chinatown was a stroke of fortune for the lucky few. Domestic service, the laundry and the restaurant remained the rule. But Chew could believe, in the face of continuing discrimination and oppressive laws, that a better day was dawning. His children, he felt sure, would be in the vanguard of a movement toward greater progress and acceptance.

POLITICIANS
AND
REVOLUTIONARIES

As long as the government refuses to reform, the revolu-
tionary aspirations will mount. They might fail today, but
future uprisings will ultimately topple the government . . .
NG POON CHEW, EDITORIAL, "THE REVOLUTION IN CANTON,"
Chung Sai Yat Po, MAY 4, 1911

ALMOST a year before the earthquake disrupted the lives
of San Francisco's Chinese, there took place half a
world away, in Japan, an event that was ultimately to have a far
more fundamental effect on Chinatown—and on the whole of
Chinese civilization. In the summer of 1905 Dr. Sun Yat-sen had
returned to Japan by way of Europe, buoyed up by his first contacts
with significant numbers of Chinese students overseas. There were
eight thousand Chinese students in Japan, far more than in any
other country. A large welcoming party, several hundred students,
greeted Sun at the dock in Yokohama. Among them was another
hero, fresh from an abortive revolt in China, Huang Hsing.

Huang's failure in this revolt had destroyed his faith both in peaceful reform and in reformers such as K'ang Yu-wei. He had begun to realize that Sun was right—only by changing the hearts of the people could one have a solid basis for changing the government. Huang and Sun were ideally suited to work together because their talents complemented each other. Huang was the soldier, the organizer and general of armies. Sun was the political thinker, the fund-raiser, the spellbinding speaker. Together they agreed to found a new anti-Manchu party.

On August 20 the formal initiation of the new T'ung-meng Hui (Alliance Society) took place at the house of a Japanese friend. Each comrade in the new society swore a solemn oath "to work for the overthrow of the Manchu dynasty, the establishment of the Republic and the solution of the agrarian question. . . ." Sun became president and Huang vice-president of the new brotherhood, in which seventeen of the eighteen provinces of China were represented. From this historic meeting the student movement was to infiltrate universities and military units in China itself. Whatever difficulties lay ahead, Sun reported in his "Reminiscences," "On the day of the organization of the Brotherhood at Tokyo by intellectuals representing the whole of China, I began to have confidence that my revolutionary work might be completed in my lifetime."[16]

Tokyo became the first headquarters of the T'ung-meng Hui. Its official paper, *Min Pao*, or *People's Paper*, was published there. Sun's famous fund-raising tours to overseas Chinese began there. The third of Sun's ten failed attempts to start a revolt in China was launched from Tokyo.

Chew's foreign correspondents kept Chinatown residents informed of these exciting and perplexing developments. The revolts were particularly puzzling because, for the first time, Tzu-hsi seemed genuinely interested in reform. After the Boxer debacle she had even promised her people a real constitution with an elected parliament. But she undercut every reform by retaining the ultimate power for the Manchus. This "sugar-coated constitution," as one Chinese historian called it, fooled the people for a time, but only for a time.

Were the Chinese in far-off America fooled by the superficial reforms of Tzu-hsi? The Pao-huang Hui remained strong—most Chinatown residents felt that Tzu-hsi was an old woman who could not last forever. When Kuang-hsü reclaimed his throne at her death, all would be well.

In his position as head of Chinatown's biggest newspaper, Chew had come to know the traveling leaders of both revolutionary and reform parties. He was also on good terms with local Chinese diplomats. Despite his assistance to Sun in 1904, Chew still favored the reformers in 1906. He hoped that the existing government would be able to modernize itself and make China a strong, respected nation. When the Manchu government offered Chew a position as adviser to the Chinese consul in San Francisco, he was glad to accept it for the help he could give his people in the wake of the disaster of 1906.

Chew's diplomatic skills were put to a different kind of test in fitting into the small-town American atmosphere of Oakland. He and his family passed the test with flying colors, becoming true neighbors on the block. Mansie, Effie, Rose, Eddie and Caroline walked to school without incident and played with the children without self-consciousness. Eddie turned out to be a natural athlete whose speed and timing matched those of any of the boys on the ball fields.

Chew's ties to the American world were soon drawn closer in still another way in that eventful year of 1906. The prestigious Hillside Club of Berkeley asked for his version of the Chinese immigration problem. He gave one of his most dramatic and amusing speeches to the socially prominent club members, and they loved it. A reporter who happened to be present wrote up the speech, dubbing the editor "the Chinese Mark Twain," a title often applied to him afterward.

From the point of view of the local press, Chew had been duly "discovered," and his speeches were often quoted in San Francisco newspapers from that time on. Given his success in the American world, Chew might easily have developed the split in spirit which so often troubles leaders of minorities who are themselves highly educated and easily assimilated but speak for a group that is not. Whatever anguish of soul Chew may have experienced from living in two worlds, he never forsook his basic loyalty—to serve his people's best interests through the spoken and written word. For example, in September 1906, with most of the city still in ruins, the San Francisco school board decided to enforce a section of the state education law giving local boards the option of setting up separate schools for different races. "When such schools are established, Indian, Chinese or Mongolian children must not be admitted to any other schools."

This measure was inspired more by the rising tide of anti-Japanese feeling than by the remaining feeling against the Chinese. Japanese immigration had been growing just as Chinese immigration was declining. Moreover, the Japanese brought their wives and consequently had more children. With its militant stance, the Japanese government had sent a strong protest to President Theodore Roosevelt.

Ng Poon Chew made use of his new-found public platform to denounce the school-board decision. While addressing the Unitarian Club in suburban Alameda, he scoffed at the possibility that ninety-three Japanese boys and girls and a mere handful of Chinese students "would taint the purity of the American boy and girlhood." On the contrary, teachers and pupils declared the Chinese to be "perfect in deportment."

In the long run, it was a fear of Japan which caused Theodore Roosevelt to take the unusual step of intervening in a local school-board decision because of the international repercussions. Local resentment was strong when he insisted that the board rescind its order segregating Japanese students in public schools. Ironically, the order against Chinese children attending mixed schools was allowed to stand. Roosevelt then proceeded to solve the Japanese labor problem by writing a gentleman's agreement into the treaty of 1907, calling for Japan herself to stem the flow of laborers.

Far from protesting the school-board action, the Chinese

西曆一千九百零六年正月三十號

光緒三十二年正月初七日禮拜二

中西日報

CHUNG SAI YAT PO
CHINESE DAILY PAPER
New Years Edition

Published at 804 Sacramento St.   San Francisco, Cal., Tuesday, January 30, 1906.   Ng Poon Chew, Managing Editor.

中國將來世界萬歲

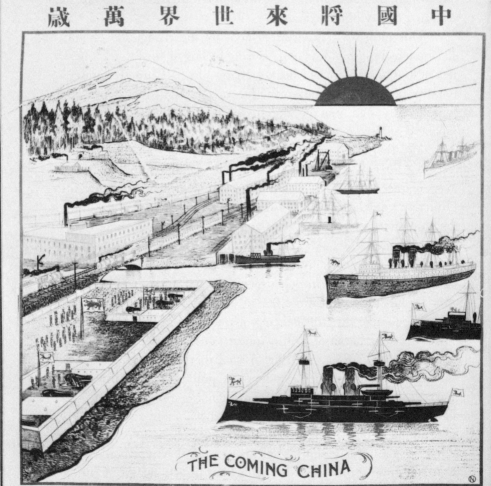

THE COMING CHINA

government evidently considered it a lost cause. Within a year after it started, the Chinese officials suppressed the boycott as well. Partly, they were yielding to American pressure; partly, they feared that the anti-American movement would also lead to anti-Manchu actions.

In dismay Chew watched the immigration officers revert to their former practice of harassing immigrants. He decided to try once again to reach Americans with a plea for justice. The result, spelled out in fifteen cogently written and compressed pages, was *The Treatment of the Exempt Classes of Chinese in America.* China, Chew explained, had reluctantly agreed to the prohibition against Chinese laborers, but the treatment of the exempt classes was not "settled." It remained "a fruitful source of irritation between America and China. If it was not "settled," it would continue to hinder the development of commercial relations between the two great countries.

> *During twenty-five years the Chinese exclusion policy has steadily increased in stringency, as Senator [George F.] Hoar said on the floor of Congress, the United States enforced the exclusion laws first with water, then with vinegar, and then with red pepper, and at last with vitriol. The Exclusion Law has been carried out with such vigor that it has almost become an extermination law. The Chinese population in the United States has been reduced from 150,000 in 1880 to 65,000 at the present time.*

Beyond the Chinese boycott there was evidence of a backlash developing against American immigration policy among the students

In a cover for the Chinese New Year's edition of Dr. Chew's newspaper, the Chung Sai Yat Po, *for January 30, 1906, called "The Coming China," the artist envisioned the industrialized, independent China that both reformers and revolutionaries of the early twentieth century were working to achieve.*
(BANCROFT LIBRARY, UNIVERSITY OF CALIFORNIA)

and merchants who had been so discourteously treated. After the Educational Mission ended, students tended to avoid America and speak ill of her. The great merchants who had once paid "one third of the customs duties at the port of San Francisco, have gone back to China or do business in other countries." American exports to China had dropped 50 percent between 1906 and 1907.

Chew's eloquent plea went largely unheeded, despite the support of such prominent American leaders as President Roosevelt and William Howard Taft, secretary of war, who was elected President in November. However, one great advance was made in American relations with China in 1908. The United States decided to remit to China that part of the Boxer indemnities that had not been needed to rebuild American schools, hospitals and property damaged in that conflict. The money was to be used to educate Chinese students in America. For the first time since 1881, a sizable number of Chinese would enter American colleges and universities.

These students, traveling and arriving as a group, were usually able to avoid the indignities heaped all too often upon other Chinese travelers. American social service organizations like the YMCA and YWCA welcomed the students and attempted to smooth their adjustment in American colleges and universities. A Chinese Student Association was set up, and for the first time in almost thirty years, Americans were given small contacts with Chinese of the most educated class.

With such snaillike progress toward Chinese civil rights in America, Chew's eyes naturally focused, like the rest of Chinatown, on the exciting train of events that marked the final years of the Manchu dynasty. Hardly had Chew finished hailing the election of Taft than alarming reports began to reach him from Peking. The Emperor Kuang-hsü died on November 14, and the next day his aunt, the true ruler, Tzu-hsi, aged and ailing, also died. The suspicious circumstances of the emperor's death gave rise to a rumor that Tzu-hsi and Gen. Yüan Shih-k'ai had conspired to poison him. To the end Tzu-hsi imposed her will on the shaky

Ch'ing dynasty; she named P'u-i, the three-year-old nephew of Kuang-hsü, as emperor, and as regent his father Prince Chün (known also by his personal name Tsai-feng).

The news of the death of the two figures who had dominated Chinese political life for so long, one actively and one passively, spread consternation through Chinatown. The Pao-huang Hui had based its whole program on Kuang-hsü's surviving the old dowager. Could they rally around a three year old? Sun Yat-sen, meanwhile, had not visited America since 1904. And every revolt his T'ung-meng Hui had attempted in China had failed.

As he had done so often in the past, Chew summed up perfectly in an editorial on the death of the emperor the mood of the community, saddened and apprehensive. "Encroached by strong neighbors, we are at a trying moment. Ideally we should have a grown-up and competent successor who could handle the situation properly." Because of these fears, Chew officially expressed relief when Peking remained quiet after the succession of P'u-i. The Chinese people, he explained, unlike the French at the time of their revolution, were not ready for a republic.

Yet the articles Chew's reporters began sending in after the death of Kuang-hsü permit a different interpretation of Chew's hopes for the future of his country. As early as November 12, before the emperor's death was reported, an interesting brief "news" article appeared, called "Chinese Youth":

> The future of China is hopeful. The pent-up national-istic sentiments in Chinese youth will overthrow the Ch'ing dynasty. The reform zeal of youth will also overwhelm the conservative Manchus. Although the three uprisings last year failed, yet their eventual victory is inevitable. Chinese students in America, after discarding their slave mentality, will be a potent force.

This article was a sign of a great change in sentiment that began to spread in Chinatown and in China itself after the royal deaths of 1908. Each armed revolt led by Huang Hsing and financed by Sun's indefatigable fund-raising tours would fall like a pebble tossed into the vast, indifferent sea of Chinese life. Yet the ripples sent out by that pebble would finally reach the remotest corners of the kingdom, carrying the message, "Down with the Manchus! China to the Chinese!"

Prince Chün, the regent, played into the hands of the revolutionaries by weakening the promised reforms and keeping the power in the hands of conservative Manchu nobles. He fired Yüan Shih-k'ai because Yüan had been an enemy of his brother. Yüan's fall shocked the world. Whatever may have been Yüan's defects of character, he had built up the only modern military force in China.

The changes and upheavals in the Chinese government gave a great impetus to Chew's speaking career. When addressing Americans, he stressed the continuous progress of China during the last thirty years. He reassured his audiences that the fall of Yüan would not alter the timetable that was destined to bring a completely constitutional monarchy to China by 1917.

Another favorite theme of Chew's speeches was America's opportunity in the transformation of China. A reporter for the San Francisco *Chronicle* caught vividly Chew's impact on his audience in "an address which teemed with dramatic illustrations, relieved with humorous touches which, delivered with the quaint manner of the speaker, brought an abundance of applause from his listeners." In speeches such as this Chew would begin by touching on recent political events in China but then settle down to develop his main subject: China must adopt Western ways yet not lose the best of her own civilization, which was, in certain respects, superior to that of the West.

Yüan Shih-kai, reviewing the smartly uniformed and well-disciplined troops that formed the basis of his power (the only such troops in China at the time), was father of the New Army and Governor-General of Chihli (Peking Province) from 1901–1908. (NEW YORK PUBLIC LIBRARY PICTURE COLLECTION)

Chew gave the people of the West credit for being good Christians as individuals, yet the nations of Europe were always ready to fly at each other's throats. "Am I blind or am I short-sighted that I am unable to discern the working out of these lofty sentiments in the national life of the people of Christendom?" And when it came to the Western powers conferring the benefits of their civilization on simpler nations, these benefits usually took the form of "fire water and firearms."

America was less guilty than Europe of imperialist ambitions, but she had her blind spots. The most damaging to minorities in her midst was her blatant racism:

> *You think you are high above others in all that makes up the man. You call the people with black diamond complexion niggers; you nickname the men from sunny Italy Dagoes; you style the plucky representatives from the Island Empire Japs. You sneer at the proud products of a forty-five-century civilization as Chinks. When you regard yourselves as superior and all the people of darker skin as inferior, you forget the superiority of a people is not an inherent character but the result of a force working inwardly toward the uplift of a people. And if that force is brought to bear upon any race or people, it will produce the same result.*[17]

America must not, in her pride, Chew warned, make the mistake that England made in failing to support the Taiping in 1860. Had England done so, China would have chased out the Manchus fifty years before and become one of the most progressive, instead of one of the most regressive, nations on earth. What America could do was to help educate the Chinese leaders of tomorrow "for the management of our national affairs, social, political, industrial, commercial and educational."

While Chew was hailing the shades of the Taiping leader Hung Hsiu-ch'üan, the modern revolutionaries under Sun Yat-sen seemed in disarray. Banished first from Japan, then from Indochina by Manchu pressure, Sun left early in 1909 on another fund-raising tour, reaching America in November 1909. He noted a change in the attitude of American Chinese: "When our comrades had carried on a protracted revolutionary propaganda in America for several years, members of the 'Hung Men' [Chee Kung Tong] societies at last realized they were old nationalist revolutionaries.[18]

Chew was happy to greet his friend, Sun Yat-sen, and he reported Sun's speeches enthusiastically. But Chew was not yet ready to support the T'ung-meng Hui openly. His paper had tried to avoid identification with any one party. So much stronger had Sun's American party become that he was able to start his own revolutionary paper in San Francisco, *Young China.*

While Sun was touring America, a great opportunity came Chew's way. He was asked to return to China as part of a delegation from the Associated Chambers of Commerce of the Pacific Coast. This group, wishing to promote better trade relations with China, wanted the well-known editor and lecturer to serve as an interpreter in Canton. They felt sure he could help them even in explaining the "touchy subject of exclusion" to skeptical and resentful Cantonese merchants.

By taking this trip Chew would be able to answer for himself the questions about the new China that had been troubling him. By chance Sun Yat-sen was passing through San Francisco in that same spring of 1910. The failure of another revolutionary attempt was calling him back to the Pacific. Chew discussed with Sun at length the temper of the Chinese people and how he might learn more about the progress of the revolutionary spirit among them. Sun advised him to speak to Chinese in all walks of life, from peasants in the villages to students in the universities.

Before Chew left his own rapidly growing brood of Chinese youth, he wanted to take a positive step toward advancing Chinese rights in the United States. His house was full of hope and excitement of its own. His oldest daughter Mansie was preparing to enter the University of California in nearby Berkeley—a daring step for a Chinese girl at that time. Soon his other children would follow the trail she was blazing. For their sakes and that of other young people he knew, such as the sons and daughters of his old mentor Soo Hoo Nam Art, he helped organize the Chinese League of Justice of America. Under its auspices he encouraged two young men, C. K. Toy and Fong Sing, to publish the first regular Chinese monthly magazine in the English language—*The Chinese Defender.* The magazine made its debut in May 1910.

Meanwhile, Sun Yat-sen had sailed for Japan. His penniless

followers, depressed by a bungled attempt to capture governmental headquarters in Canton, were in immediate need of a strong infusion of the hope and the money that only Sun was capable of supplying. Huang Hsing and other followers met Sun in Yokohama in June 1910. A letter written by a Japanese friend, Nagatomo, describes their reunion:

> *When the time finally came for Huang to leave, he said to Sun: "Oh yes, money. Do you have money?" Sun answered, "Yes, I have," and showed him the whole trunk filled with money . . . from the overseas Chinese.*
>
> *Huang Hsing took the trunk without even estimating the amount of money in it and prepared to leave. Then, as if suddenly remembering something, he said, "Oh yes, I had better leave you some, in case you should need it." Without even pausing to count them, he gave several rolls of bills to Sun and left. He left for his own country the same day. . . .*
>
> *. . . I was watching all this . . . and was greatly impressed. Both the giver and the receiver of the money seemed completely indifferent to the amount. Throughout their lives these two leaders shared a feeling that cannot simply be described as "comradeship," and their attitude toward money was always just like this.*[19]

For the next year both Sun and Chew were part of a swift-moving chain of events. After leaving Japan, Sun went to keep a rendezvous with his followers on the borders of China itself. He found them greatly depressed, almost ready to give up in despair. Once again he was able to cheer them on.

By February 1911 Sun was back in America, but this time the newspapers formed a chorus as they followed his trail from coast to coast. The hearts and pocketbooks of Chinese-Americans were opened to him as never before. The news that Huang Hsing had failed in a massive assault on the Canton government headquarters in April merely kindled this fervor. The seventy-two leaders executed by Ch'ing authorities became the Seventy-two Martyrs whose blood was needed to water the tree of liberty. Huang Hsing barely escaped with his life. But Sun went on collecting money and announced in May in San Francisco that he was combining the T'ung-meng Hui with the Chee Kung Tong. Now the money raised by the society flowed directly into the coffers of the revolution. Through the summer and fall of 1911 Sun continued to canvass the Chinatowns of America, speaking, planning, hoping.

Meanwhile, Chew had set out in September 1910 on his trip to China. It took him from his native village in the south to the government halls in Peking, and everywhere he was overwhelmed by the size and beauty of the land that had borne him. He spoke to farmers, to merchants, to officials and politicians of every party and creed. His understanding of and sympathy for his people grew stronger and deeper.

When Chew returned in May 1911, Sun was at his most active in San Francisco, and the aftermath of the Canton uprising was ringing like a death knell through the quarter. Yet for the first time the ringing anti-Manchu phrases of Sun echo openly through the editorials of Chew. "According to humane principles, we have to start a revolution. Only a revolution can help save Kwangtung." "No corrupt government in the world can expect to survive. Why? Because it would obstruct justice and hence the progress of the people. Even though the Ch'ing government hangs on today, who of right mind can argue that it is a good government."

By September even the elders in Chinatown were preaching the need for the modernization of China. Along the Yangtze valley, riots swept through the province of Szechwan in protest against foreign financing of Chinese railroads.

Meanwhile, Sun Yat-sen was traveling indefatigably from third-class hotel to fourth-class lodging house and speaking earnestly, eloquently, unendingly in quiet back rooms where piles of unironed shirts lay waiting for dawn. It was probably in late September, while passing through some Western state, that Sun received a coded telegram from Huang Hsing. Since he had expected no message of importance, he had packed his deciphering code in his trunk and sent it ahead to Denver. Almost two weeks elapsed before he reached Denver, on the evening of October 10.

Sun sat down with the code book and worked out the message —funds were needed because the Wuchang* revolutionaries were preparing to rise. Since it was too late in the evening to get money and Sun was especially weary after an all-day journey, he planned to wire that he would seek out the funds as soon as possible and suggest that the rising be postponed till the money could be found. At eleven he arose refreshed and headed for a nearby restaurant, buying a newspaper en route. As he unfolded the paper, the headlines fairly shouted at him: "Wuchang Occupied by Revolutionaries!"

Alone, unrecognized, without means to reach his men, Sun stared at the dancing black letters. Was the dream of a lifetime coming to sudden, astonishing fruition?

---

* One of three cities comprising the modern industrial capital of Wuhan in China's heartland at the junction of the Yangtze and Han rivers. The other two cities are Hanyang and Hankow.

CHAPTER 16

TWO
REPUBLICS

*In the last two decades they [the revolutionaries] have ac-
complished the impossible; they have risen again and again
in their quest to overthrow the Ch'ing government. They
have changed the heart of the people and the opinion of
society. . . . But what is the "primal force" that triggered off
the cause and effect of the Chinese Revolution? Who is
the man who comes and goes alone spreading the seeds of
the Revolution? He is the one and only (medical) Dr. Sun
Yat-sen. . . .*

NG POON CHEW, EDITORIAL, "THE REVOLUTION IN CANTON,"
Chung Sai Yat Po, MAY 4, 1911

*I*N October 1911, most of the 71,000 Chinese in the United
States were living in relative peace behind the storefronts
and tenements of the nation's Chinatowns. The attrition encouraged
by the exclusion laws had resulted in the drop from 89,000 in 1900.
Moreover, the population of Chinatown in San Francisco had
dropped from 15,000 to 10,000 after the earthquake as many
Chinese sought residence in towns that provided their children with
unsegregated schooling.

One evening, just as Chew was about to return to his suburban
retreat, he saw coming over the wires the incredible news that the

followers of Sun Yat-sen had successfully risen against the Manchus at Wuchang. Chew rushed into the pressroom and told the printers to stop the press. Sitting down at his desk, he grasped his brush and quickly wrote out the story of the century:

> *Peking 10/10—The city of Wuchang in Hupei is now occupied by the revolutionaries. In the few days prior to the incident, the soldiers and guards defending the city were killed by the revolutionaries. The governor narrowly escaped. There are five foreign gunboats patrolling the Yangtze to protect the foreigners in Hankow.*

Thus did Ng Poon Chew inform Chinatown that a new order was in the making in the world's most ancient kingdom. As an editor with access to the telegraph wires, Chew actually knew about the revolution before Sun heard of it. This date, known in China as the "Double Ten," was ever after to be celebrated by the governments of China as a national Day of Independence.

As Chew composed his first story about the revolution, he thought back to the great journey that had so changed his view of his country, its future and his own part in that future.

In September 1910 Chew had joined the delegation of Americans aboard a Pacific Mail Steamship Liner seeking better trade relations with China. The comfortable cabin and elegant public rooms which Chew frequented on the journey were in striking contrast to the crowded steerage where he had eaten and slept on his trip to America thirty years before. Both Chinese and American businessmen on board were generally in agreement that the Manchu princes had made surprising strides in the direction of reform. Chew was a middle-aged man with five children who had prospered in his work. He was not a young student and natural revolutionary. So his views paralleled those of the successful businessmen on board:

> *When I started for China I had a great deal of sympathy with the existing Chinese government, in spite of the fact*

that my relations with Dr. Sun Yat-sen and other present leaders of the revolutionary movement were rather close. I took the ground that as long as the Manchu government would progress toward reform, giving up its powers to a parliament and retaining the Emperor merely as a figurehead, we might await the conclusion of peaceful means.[20]

Chew first visited Canton, where he was very busy with his mission of interpreting for the American delegates from the Chambers of Commerce of the Pacific Coast. Friendly relations were established between the business leaders of the two nations, and everyone was left with a euphoric sense of accomplishment. Here, indeed, was the new and awakened China which so many American travelers had been writing and talking about back home.

After completing his work with the delegation, Chew started back into the interior to visit the village "where I first saw the light of day." One striking evidence of change was in the way he traveled to his native village compared with his outgoing trip thirty years before. Instead of the ancient junk with its painted eyes on the bow, he boarded a modern comfortable river steamer bound for Kung Yick.

This completely new city had been built as the terminus of a brand-new railroad, constructed by a returned sojourner named Chin Gee Hee. Chin, who had been a construction worker and then an engineer on the Central Pacific and Great Northern Railroads, had completed the first link of his projected railroad, the fifty-four miles from Kung Yick to the town of Towshan in 1909. He had easily raised money for his project among other returned sojourners.

At Kung Yick, Chew transferred from his modern steamer to an equally modern steam train with American-built cars and locomotive, which was soon "whistling and puffing along with customary train speed." Three hours later Chew left the train at the station near his village to be greeted "with open arms, with gladness" by a troop of relatives.

They did not kill the fatted calf, but they did kill the fatted hen and tender pig. Apparently I was a total stranger, for I could not recognize a single face though I remembered the names of a large number. So I had to know them not by sight but by faith.[21]

On the short walk to the village, Chew passed the old Taoist shrine he had once been destined to serve and found it in "a very sorry condition and almost deserted." Unlike the dilapidated temple, the village looked more prosperous than he remembered it. Money sent back by sojourners had helped repair and brighten the houses with red-tiled roofs and blue-tiled façades. As an even bigger surprise, the village school boys marched out to meet him in their smart blue uniforms with gold-braided caps and epaulets. How different were these lively youngsters from the scholars of his youth who tried to avoid "any physical exertion, for such actions were unbecoming the dignity and genteel manner of the scholar."

Chew learned from his family that sports and exercise were part of the curriculum of all modern schools. Even girls were being sent to school so that China might face the future with "a noble and educated womanhood" to guide her. "Their advancement is going on in leaps and bounds. It is only a question of a short time when they will be mistresses of the social situation and no more will the sterner sex be their lords and masters, but will only be mere men and nothing more."

Chew's appearance inspired a major change in the customs of the village. First the idols were brought out and burned; then all the men wanted Chew to cut off their queues. "I had a strenuous time while I was there for I not only had to do the work of a preacher, but also perform the duties of a barber." By the time he had finished snipping, over a hundred queues lay in a pile at his side. "An old village elder, over seventy years old, who had but a few hairs left on his head, wanted to part with it too. With one clip of the scissors I had it removed. Afterwards I felt rather sorry for the poor old man for it was his only personal property in the great wide world."

Seeing all these changes in science and education, did Chew become convinced that the Manchus were doing the best possible job in modernizing and strengthening China? Such was not at all the case. He finally realized that he and the Chinese long resident in America generally had a nostalgic view of their homeland. They imagined it eternally stable under a benevolent emperor, who would make the necessary changes to strengthen China without disturbing the placid surface of Chinese life.

Chew himself had not had such faith in the emperor but had still believed that a constitutional monarchy was in the making. Now, instead of an easy transition to a parliamentary government, Chew sensed a different spirit stirring, especially when he left his village and traveled from city to city on a northward course. Wherever Chew went, the whispers of revolution followed him. Even among peasants and merchants, there was a growing, if passive, acceptance of the need to get rid of the Manchus.

In Peking Chew received the final shock to his views about the possible reform of the monarchy:

> *I saw the conditions in Peking, how the same crowd filled the offices and the same graft methods were in vogue, and that the Manchu were not making any real reforms . . . it required not only influence but actual cash . . . to get the ear of a Manchu prince.*[22]

Many returned students had therefore refused in disgust to seek government jobs which might have used their talents to best advantage.

With the disillusionment bred by the corruption of Peking fresh in his mind, Chew pushed north as far as the Mongolian border, then returned south by rail to Hankow on the Yangtze, forming with Hanyang and Wuchang the industrial heart of the nation, now known as Wuhan. In this frame of mind, Chew found the atmosphere of Wuhan electrifying. It was a hotbed of revolution. In other cities there were whispers, but in Wuhan students and workers alike discussed revolution openly in teahouses. Here especially Chew received the impression of a whole city, indeed a whole country, breathlessly awaiting a leader to organize the underlying sentiment of the people.

His mind assailed with new and dizzying ideas, Chew continued southward. He had originally thought about starting a newspaper in Canton "with American notions, energy and so on." But when he consulted with Wu T'ing-fang, former Chinese ambassador to the United States and a well-known progressive, Chew realized that the time was not ripe for such a project.

> *I talked much with people in all the different cities of the empire I visited and they spoke of nothing but revolution. Wu T'ing-fang did not take me wholly into his confidence, but when I mentioned what I had heard he said he too had heard about it and that he feared it was coming sooner than anybody expected.*[23]

Sun was in America by early 1911, Huang Hsing in the South Seas preparing for a spring attack on the magistrate's office in Canton, using a plan similar to, but better organized than, the one that had failed so miserably a year before. As far as Chew could find out, the revolution was scheduled to come in about two years. "The idea was to have made a thorough propaganda among the army and navy and finally turn the whole government upside down without the sacrifice of a single life."

Propelled by his sense of the rising hope among his people and the decadent government that stood in the way of that hope, Chew finally realized what he had gradually been drifting toward: "I became as hot a revolutionary as could be found in any part of the empire." Acknowledging this truth about himself, Chew knew it was time to go home to rouse the Chinese in America to support the revolution wholeheartedly. At this very moment Sun Yat-sen was in San Francisco working toward that same end. Chew booked passage for an April sailing and arrived home around May 1.

News of the failure of Huang Hsing's attack on the magistrate's office in Canton arrived in San Francisco at about the same time as Ng Poon Chew. But for Chew, doubt and hesitation were over. On May 4, 1911, he wrote in the *Chung Sai Yat Po*:

> *It was a pity that the news of the planned uprising leaked and the person who masterminded the uprising was caught. The rank and file had to execute the plan prematurely. They did not intend to start so soon. But as soon as they started, they were as sweeping in their movements as Hung and Yang [Taiping leaders]. . . . But success or failure is unpredictable.*

Chew was now certain that the revolution would ultimately succeed. Day after day he wrote editorials praising the courage of the revolutionaries, their high ideals, their good deeds. In a speech delivered to Chinese students shortly after his return, Chew issued a stirring call to arms to the younger generation:

> *During the last few years here, there and everywhere, wherever Chinese are found, we hear this sentiment, "China for the Chinese." It is very good as far as it goes. But if we turn the wording around, it would be better still. Yes, turn it around like this, "The Chinese for China." That is, think for China, aim for China, work for China, live for China, die for China. That is what the Chinese students should strive for. . . .*[24]

Meanwhile Chew had established contact with Sun, who was living and working quietly in San Francisco's Chinatown. "When I saw Sun Yat-sen in San Francisco I told him I would cooperate with him to the fullest extent of my ability." Two strong streams flowing from the same source had come together at last—the Chinese in America who had left to seek a fortune across the seas and the revolutionary remnant who had passed among them with so little apparent effect for so many years. There is no recorded account of this meeting, but we know that Sun asked Chew for the same thing he asked of every Chinese he met—Give me the money, and I will make the revolution through my students and soldiers in China.

When the official notification came out in June that Chee Kung Tong and the T'ung-meng Hui had formed a "grand alliance," Chew printed up ten thousand notices at his own expense. These were mailed out by Chee Kung Tong to their contacts from coast to coast. The same notice appeared in the *Chung Sai Yat Po*, on the walls of Chinatown and even in an interview with the press. It stated, in part, "The elders and brothers of this 'tong' welcome the admission of the new good righteous brothers. We will forget our differences hoping that one day we will accomplish the magnificent task of restoring the Han and annihilating the tyrannical, corrupt system. . . ."

Sun left San Francisco to travel to other cities. At Wuhan, with neither Sun nor the military leader Huang on the scene, the riots over the nationalizing of the railroads and building them with foreign loans had been flaring up and spreading since August. The merchants of Szechwan, who would lose their railroad rights by this act of the Manchu government, at last inclined toward the revolution. By early October the Wuhan revolutionaries were waiting for Huang Hsing to come lead them. And in Hong Kong Huang was waiting for Sun to read the coded telegram and send him the money.

Receiving no word from Huang, the leaders of the rising in Wuhan postponed the starting date from October 6 to October 16. But on October 9 some party members who were checking over a supply of weapons at the Russian concession in Hankow by accident set off an explosive. Immediately, the police were attracted to the spot. Arrests followed, and a list of party members fell into government hands. Fearing that all the revolutionaries in Wuhan would be picked up, Hsiung Ping-k'un, a sergeant in the engineers, led a bloody assault on the government ammunition dump, which fell after fierce fighting.

Learning of this defeat, Governor Jui-ch'eng feared the revolutionaries had risen in force and fled. After him the commanding general Chang Piao retreated with those soldiers who had not deserted to the insurgents. Thus by accident, by luck, by the changed heart of the army and by the cowardice of the Manchus did the Chinese revolution begin. Wuhan had truly fallen to the revolutionaries.

Huang Hsing hurried to join his army, arriving in Wuhan on October 28. Sun, verifying the astonishing headlines, decided that his greatest contribution to the revolution would be in the diplomatic field and in raising money. He set his course for home by way of England, but having sent all his money to Huang, he did not even have the price of a ticket. According to an account published after the deaths of both men, Sun slipped back into San Francisco and appealed to Chew. Chew collected $700 from his friends, which enabled Sun to continue on to Europe. All the men who participated in this gesture, including Chew and Sun, must have been dazzled by the vision of China's future which suddenly rose before their eyes. As a pledge of his faith in the future of their country, Sun presented Chew with $70 in military money printed by the revolutionaries, "saying that upon the successful consummation of the revolution, each dollar would be exchangeable for $100 U.S."

As Sun embarked for Europe, the revolution was racing from province to province. In the *Chung Sai Yat Po*, Chew wrote, "The revolutionary waves have been mounting and are about to reach the apogee. Every new revolutionary experience reinforces and intensifies the next. Now the people are imbued with a revolutionary fervor unknown to them before." One after another, cities and whole provinces declared themselves independent of the Manchu rulers; the reformers joined hands with the revolutionaries and accepted posts in the newly forming government.

Only in the provinces around Peking did the Manchus still retain power. The inexperienced regent, Tsai-feng, was forced to call Gen. Yüan Shih-k'ai, the old fox of Chinese politics, out of retirement. Taking command of the army again, Yüan prepared to signal to the revolutionaries that he was ready to negotiate. Here Yüan had a great advantage over the revolutionaries, for they were divided into many factions, agreeing only that the Manchus must go. Yüan knew very clearly what he wanted—the most power he could obtain.

Meanwhile, Sun, having reached Europe, tried to divert a large loan intended for the Manchus to the republic in the making. The bankers did not say no. They indicated that a regularly established government would be looked on with favor. It was while staying with his friend Dr. Cantlie in London that Sun received a telegram from his followers asking him to return and become provisional president of the republic.

While Yüan was conspiring to thwart all the revolutionary factions, while Sun was passing through Europe toward China, euphoria was sweeping over the Chinese people, not alone in China, but in every part of the world. Typical was the scene in New York's Chinatown on October 23, 1911. Most of the residents lined the narrow curve of Mott, Pell and Doyers streets, which enclosed the local Chinese colony, while down the middle of the cobblestone pavement marched young boys with toy guns to rhythmic cheers. One carried a newly sewn Republican flag with a white sun shining upon a blue square against a red field. Sun's Young China Association, which had only two hundred members, entertained two thousand people at a rally in the Chinese Rescue Mission, and two of Sun's American aides, Wong Wan Su and Jue Chock Man, addressed them in the name of their absent leader.

Chew was in an especially good position to take the pulse of the Chinese. Money began to pour in to his office: all together he raised close to $500,000 for Sun's cause, some from as far away as Boston. One day a poor laborer came into the office, still wearing the traditional costume and queue, with a small sack in his hands. "Here," he said to Chew. "I am too old to go back there to fight, but I willingly give all my money to help the cause." In the sack was his life's savings—$1,500. So the old and the middle-aged gave money while the young students boarded steamers heading back to

China. "We can do no more than die for our country," they would tell Chew's reporter at the pier. For some, loyalty to country now superseded loyalty to family: for fear that filial piety would be invoked to stop them from going, they left without saying good-bye.

Sun, who evoked this new patriotism in the young by exemplifying it in his own life, arrived in Shanghai on December 25. Greeted by his jubilant supporters, he came ashore with a sureness of step, an upward thrust of the head, which bespoke a man who had achieved all he desired in life. On December 29 Sun was chosen provisional president of the Chinese Republic by the parliament in Nanking. On New Year's Day, 1912, he was inaugurated, taking a Western-style oath of office. He officially proclaimed the Republic and substituted the Western calendar for the traditional Chinese one.

Meanwhile, the negotiations between the liberated south and the Manchu north went on. Chew, like many of Sun's supporters, felt that the revolutionary leader would not stand in the way of peace with the north. On a two-month transcontinental speaking tour, stopping at such major cities as St. Louis and Chicago, Chew told a reporter from the New York *Sun*:

> So far as Dr. Sun Yat-sen is concerned, I can say with absolute assurance that he is not looking for the presidency of the Chinese Republic. He stands willing at any time to give up the office to the best man that can be found. . . .
>
> Yüan Shih-k'ai is facing a complicated situation. I believe he is more in sympathy with his fellow countrymen than with the Manchus. . . . I think he will come to an agreement with the revolutionists.[25]

Less than ten days after Chew visited New York on February 12, 1912, the Manchu emperor abdicated, Sun Yat-sen resigned and Yüan Shih-k'ai officially accepted the presidency. In the first honeymoon year of the Republic, despite doubts about Yüan, Chew could share the hope of Chinese everywhere that a strong democratic

Sun Yat-sen at the height of his success was inaugurated provisional president of the new Chinese Republic on January 1, 1912, after seventeen lonely wandering years as propagandist, fundraiser and organizer for the Revolutionary Party.

China would replace the shaky structure of the Chinese Empire in its declining days. A reporter for *Sunset* magazine found him in his modern, businesslike office one spring day, where a bowl of lilies and the flag of the Republic supplied a deft touch of beauty.

Discussing with the reporter the success of the *Chung Sai Yat*

Po, Chew noted that seven hundred papers were appearing regularly in China, many using the technical methods worked out by his paper. "The growth of the radical spirit in China has been marked by the growth of the press." In a ringing voice Chew spoke of the "Spirit of '76" which had infused the new republic. Though there had been only fifty thousand rebels, the whole people was in sympathy. Chew ended the interview with the appeal which had become his constant refrain, "The republicans want the United States to be the first nation to recognize the new republic."

Chew's enthusiasm for the new republic was almost as great as that of the young, but he had a mature man's appreciation of the many difficulties it faced. Even if Yüan Shih-k'ai were as dedicated a patriot as Sun Yat-sen, he faced an immense task in transforming the four-thousand-year-old Chinese Empire into a modern republic. And Yüan had two basic defects. He did not comprehend republican institutions; and he was greedy for power.

Because of his power, the politically dubious Yüan Shih-kai (third from left with the American Legation staff), though distrusted by the revolutionaries of 1911, seemed the logical choice for President of the Republic when the child Emperor P'u-i abdicated on February 12, 1912.

In the summer of 1912 the heroes of the T'ung-meng Hui organized a regular political party for the forthcoming parliamentary elections—the Kuomintang, led by Sun, Huang and a promising young leader named Sung Chiao-jen. Chew, like most American Chinese, felt that the Kuomintang could counter any autocratic moves by Yüan. The Kuomintang won a large number of seats in the February 1913 elections. Then in March Sung Chiao-jen was assassinated in a railroad station, and suspicions were raised that

Dr. Ng Poon Chew seated at his desk in his book-lined office shortly after the success of the 1911 Revolution in China.
(CHINESE HISTORICAL SOCIETY OF AMERICA)

this was a plot by Yüan. Events in China continued to be disquieting.

Compared with the difficult birth of democracy in China, Chew could not help appreciating more strongly the blessings of his adopted land. Chew still had faith that his children, native-born Americans, would come to enjoy fully the civil rights denied to him. Mansie was busy with her music and university classes; Effie was preparing to enter Miss Barnard's Kindergarten Training School in Berkeley. Eddie and Rose in high school and Caroline in grade school were busy and happy. Eddie had become one of the most popular boys at Oakland High and played on the Plymouth Center basketball team.

Chew himself was pleased when, in early 1913, he was named vice-consul for China in San Francisco. Then, invited to speak at commencement at the University of Pittsburgh in June, an unexpected honor was conferred on Ng Poon Chew. The peasant boy from Kwangtung was awarded the honorary degree of doctor of letters.

CHAPTER 17

MAKING
THE WORLD SAFE
FOR DEMOCRACY

Dr. Ng Poon Chew . . . said he believed that China contemplated with the same satisfaction the embroilment of the great powers in Europe that a lonely traveler would contemplate one wolf fighting four other wolves who had been just about to attack him.

San Francisco Chronicle, NOVEMBER 27, 1914

J UNE 27, 1914, was a bright sunny day in Corvallis, Oregon, the county seat of Benton County. Though its population was only seven thousand, the quiet, tree-shaded streets were unusually busy on that day. By car, by wagon, on horseback, on foot, by bicycle, individuals and whole families were converging on a Chautauqua tent, erected on the grounds of the State Agricultural College.

In 1900 there had already been four hundred local communities offering Chautauqua weeks in imitation of the original institute at Chautauqua, New York. Each year since then the number had multiplied. The Chautauqua offered the average middle-class citizen in small towns and cities from coast to coast a uniquely American blend of entertainment, uplift and education at a price he could afford. For $2.50 any man, woman or child could attend any or all programs at the Corvallis Chautauqua, which ran morning, afternoon and evening for a week. Gone were the long, serious lectures of the Victorian era. The Chautauqua program promised its audience: "The lectures on this program are full of life. Some of the ablest platform orators in America will speak to you. . . . Their messages will be full of meat—served with humor sauce."[26]

To no lecturer on the varied program did those words of an anonymous advertising man apply better than to the one who was to speak that afternoon. Dr. Ng Poon Chew, the "Oriental Mark Twain," would tell them about "The New Republic of China," enlivened with his "rare logic, bubbling humor and keen satire." By the summer of 1914 Dr. Chew had been a regular on the Chautauqua circuit and its winter counterpart, the Lyceum Lectures, for several years.

Explaining the troubles of the young republic required all the resources he could command. The dictatorial ambitions of Yüan Shih-k'ai were no longer a secret; the Kuomintang leaders, including Sun and Huang, had been driven into exile or underground, their party outlawed. The defeat of the Kuomintang and the ease with which Yüan had been able to buy off most of the remaining representatives to the parliament had helped discredit foreign ideas of democracy in China. The caretaker of the new republic seemed the man most likely to strangle her in her cradle.

Faced with this depressing situation, as a lover of the Republic Dr. Chew could only insist that the strength of China had been sapped by the corruption and inefficiency of the Manchus; time and modern methods would finally save her. "China's great problem is to reconstruct out of ancient customs and ideas a modern self-reliant republic."

Even more important than Dr. Chew's attempt to explain

Chinese history and civilization to his audience was his role in furthering one of the main purposes of the Chautauqua movement: "The Chautauqua is tearing down the barriers of intolerance and bigotry; it is warring against superstition and fanaticism, ignorance and illiteracy, demagogism and factious zeal."[27]

At a time when most black people were trapped in rural serfdom in the South, the Hann Jubilee Singers, in impeccable evening dress, presented not only the expected spirituals but grand-opera selections as well. While "Chinese cheap labor" was still the cry of most American workingmen, Dr. Ng Poon Chew, scholar and journalist, appeared before them as a highly educated man, a polished and amusing speaker and often the first true Chinese that any of them had ever seen. The historian Clifford Drury heard Dr. Chew, like so many thousands of Americans, as a boy in Iowa:

> As I remember him, he was rather short of stature, spoke good English, and made a fine impression as a lecturer on the Chautauqua circuit. He was the first Chinese I had ever seen —it must have been about 1907 when I was ten years old—and he made a deep impression on me.[28]

The physical grind of the Chautauqua circuit was considerable. Six Chautauquas were arranged in nearby cities so that each lecturer or entertainer could perform at all six within the week. Dr. Chew was away from home almost all summer and had frequent winter lecture tours on the Lyceum circuit as well. While he was gone, Chun Fah kept the home in her warm and quiet way. Rose had joined Mansie at the University of California and was proving herself, as expected, a brilliant student. The youngest, Caroline, was full of surprises. She scandalized everyone by asking for dancing lessons, something totally outside the Chinese conception of what a respectable young woman should do. Even the Chews were not modern enough to encourage their daughter to become a member of the "Pear Orchard," or acting fraternity.

In the beautiful summer of 1914 the darkening shadows over

Europe seemed far from America. Americans still largely gloried in their freedom from "entangling alliances" with the Europe they had left for greater freedom and opportunity. Though far less provincial than before the Spanish-American War, Americans had as yet played only minor roles in the drama of international politics. The assassination of an Austrian archduke, Ferdinand, in Serbia on June 28, 1914, led to a series of charges and countercharges between the Great Powers, which heightened European tension but had little impact on most Americans.

Then, in August, as a climax of the diplomatic conflict, Germany struck at France through Belgium; Britain came to the defense of Belgium, and Russia backed Serbia against Germany and Austria. The peace that Europe had known since 1871 was shattered. But to many Americans besides Dr. Chew, the war first seemed a case of thieves falling out and attacking one another. He was rather glad to see the Great Powers occupied by something besides gobbling up pieces of Chinese territory.

As the conflict widened, Dr. Chew, like many other Americans, but for somewhat different reasons, found his sympathies engaged by the events of World War I. Japan had immediately entered the war on the side of the Allies and helped herself to the German possession of Kiaochow in Shantung on the Chinese coast. Chinese around the world were outraged, but they could do little to stop their aggressive neighbor.

In December 1914, Yüan caused a different kind of alarm by performing the sacred rites of the emperor at the winter solstice. Then in January 1915, with the European powers busy on the battlefields, the Japanese ambassador knocked on Yüan's door at midnight, a great affront to his dignity. The ambassador presented the head of the Chinese government with Twenty-one Demands so outrageous that if China had acceded to them she would have become a Japanese protectorate. Alone among the world's powers, the United States protested, but she was too preoccupied with German submarine warfare to take action.

Chinese patriotism had not been so deeply stirred by any

event since the revolution as it was by the Twenty-one Demands. Yüan probably handled them as well as any man could have. He resisted the more extreme demands, which would have given Japan control over most of China's internal affairs. But he was forced to accede to Japanese control in Shantung and to give Japan a foothold in Manchuria as well as letting her manage China's largest iron works.

While the unpopularity of the Twenty-one Demands was spilling over onto the ill-fated Yüan, his followers unwisely continued to manufacture sentiment for turning the republic back into an empire with Yüan as emperor. As they stage-managed a national referendum on January 1, 1916, which favored the enthronement of Yüan, they ignored that same passive resistance that had destroyed the Manchus. Dr. Chew, for example, who had accepted Yüan as a necessary evil to strengthen the country at a difficult moment, regarded Yüan's claim to the throne as constituting an "unpardonable sin" which would "cause a national decline."

Suddenly, revolt flared in Yunnan in December 1915. The enthronement was postponed. Rival generals were encouraged by the Japanese to turn against Yüan. The revolt spread, nourished by the anti-Yüan sentiment of the people and the reawakened revolutionaries. By March, with several provinces declaring their independence, Yüan announced that he was abandoning his claim to the throne. In June he died, partly of his disappointed hopes.

The Nationalists rejoiced as the moderate Li Yuan-hung became president and recalled the parliament. Sun's supporters in America celebrated the fall of the usurper. Dr. Chew adopted a new theme in his lectures. China needed a strong president like former President Roosevelt, still his hero. A "fighting spirit" like his would unite China and bring her through the agonies of dissension that threatened her.

Unfortunately for China's loyal sons, the fall of Yüan ushered in a period of anarchy more terrible than the oppressions of either Yüan or the Manchus. The uprooting of the Confucian civil service, the lack of any central moral power to serve as a counterweight, the availability of modern weapons and the rise of absentee landlordism allowed amoral warlords to divide China into separate dictatorships.

In the cataclysms of the years from 1916 to 1928, China was further split into north and south. In each section, the competing warlords fought among themselves for control. Some warlords observed the forms of parliamentary government and some did not, but the warlord wielding the biggest stick always held the real power. In the north the prize was Peking and control of the nominal government there, which was more or less recognized by the Great Powers. During those dark years the pressure of foreign powers increased the miseries and divisions within China.

In the south Sun Yat-sen set up a democratic parliament in Canton. But he, too, lacking the strong army necessary to power, was forced to negotiate and compromise constantly with warlords. And there, as in the north, the peasants paid and suffered most.

These events naturally depressed Dr. Chew, but in his lectures he pointed out that the readjustment after such a violent change as the revolution of 1911 was bound to be slow. At the same time, like many Chinese patriots, he was becoming disillusioned by the weakness of Sun, who was clearly destined never to be the strong president that China needed to recover the leadership of Asia. Above all, since the Twenty-one Demands, Dr. Chew shared with the majority of thinking Chinese a deep suspicion of Japanese intentions. Prophetically, he feared that China might suffer the fate of Korea—which had been conquered by Japan.

At the same time, Dr. Chew was becoming preoccupied with World War I, which was closing in on the American people. As representative of the Chinese who were settling down in America with their families, he had to interpret the coming conflict as it would affect them and their native-born children. To Chinese parents the American manners of this new generation of Chinese children were often bewildering. Growing up in tough urban neighborhoods, some of these children had learned to defend themselves like Americans instead of turning the other cheek like the older generation of Chinese.

Despite this healthy instinct for self-defense, the Chinese

children who were growing up in the back rooms of laundries and restaurants and curio shops were usually the hardworking, well-behaved young people who lent a new image to the Chinese in America. The newer, cleaner Chinatown in San Francisco was home to many of these families. Others grew up in relative isolation in smaller communities where the services of a Chinese laundry or grocery were acceptable, or in the East where the number of families was much smaller. They flourished side by side with the bachelor society, which still required the solace of gambling dens and bordellos. The stout-hearted Miss Cameron continued her rescues, though in diminishing numbers, as tong warfare and the importation of slave girls declined.

The existence of this second, and even third, generation of Chinese-Americans had given impetus to attempts to form an Equal Rights League in the 1890s. By 1904 an organization developed out of these attempts that was to be longer-lived and more deeply rooted. In that year the Native Sons of the Golden State first joined together that small minority of Chinese-Americans who had been born and grown to maturity on American soil.

The group was headed by Walter U. Lum, Joseph K. Lum and Ng Gunn. As it spread to other states, it became the Chinese-American Citizens Alliance. The need for these young men to exercise eternal vigilance was well demonstrated in 1913. State senator Joseph Caminetti introduced a measure in the California legislature petitioning Congress to pass a constitutional amendment disfranchising citizens of Chinese ancestry. Such an amendment would have eliminated the protections of the Fourteenth Amendment, that "all persons born or naturalized in the United States and subject to the jurisdiction thereof, are citizens of the United States and of the state wherein they reside." The CACA lobbied successfully against the bill, and it never passed the legislature.

Dr. Chew aided in this effort, and he kept his readers informed of the progress of the young group. In October 1915 the Department of Labor adopted another harassing regulation which would have denied citizens of Chinese ancestry the right to verification of their citizenship before leaving this country. This regulation would have left their fate on returning in the dubious hands of immigration officers. Fortunately, the CACA was once again successful in its efforts, and the rule was rescinded.

By 1917 the more perceptive Americans sensed the coming of war. In January, Germany, starving under the Allied blockade, announced unrestricted submarine warfare against all merchant ships sailing in enemy waters, regardless of the flag they flew. America's indignation, and her sympathy with the Allies, grew as the Germans sank ships. She even pressured the nominal Chinese government in Peking to break off diplomatic relations with Germany. China yielded, in part because she wanted to be able to keep an eye on her neighbor Japan at the peace table.

All through March the idealistic Wilson, elected on the slogan "He kept us out of war," agonized over the need to defend American "freedom of the seas" and stand by the Western democracies, who were faltering in the third year of stalemate on the western front. And with a new democratic government in power in Russia after the revolution there, he could truly say the Allies were fighting "to make the world safe for democracy."

The entry of the United States into the war in April found Americans far from wholehearted in their devotion to the war effort. Public opinion had to be mobilized by propaganda, and in the process people of German ancestry and socialists and pacifists suffered from intolerance.

To many new immigrants, however, World War I offered the first opportunity to prove their patriotism. Though a few Chinese had attempted to organize a brigade in the Spanish-American War, that conflict had ended too quickly and involved too few men to give them a chance to serve. But World War I offered such a chance to all new Americans. There were 2,810,000 draftees and 2,000,000 reserves during the war.

Chinese-Americans were swept along on the current of patriotism. In New York City new Americans of all backgrounds were heavily represented. The enlistees and draftees from these first- and second-generation families made such divisions as the Seventy-seventh, recruited in New York, true melting pots.

In California Edward C. Chew was as caught up in the war spirit as his friends. Though only halfway through his engineering course at the university, he enlisted and took an exam for officer's training school. He was selected, finished the course and became the first Chinese-American to receive a commission. In still another competition entered by seven hundred newly commissioned second lieutenants, Edward Chew was one of nineteen chosen for special training at Camp Eustis, Virginia.

Lt. Edward Chapin Chew, son of Dr. Ng Poon Chew, was commissioned a lieutenant after officers' training in World War I, thus becoming the first American of Chinese descent to be an officer in the U.S. Army. (CHEW FAMILY PHOTO)

While Edward was busy preparing for military service, Dr. Chew enlisted the *Chung Sai Yat Po* in the war effort on the homefront. He helped promote the sale of Liberty Loans, by which the billions needed for the first modern war were raised. Partly as a result of his efforts Chinatown exceeded the quota in each Liberty Loan drive.

The rewards of such Chinese-American patriotism were often tinged with irony, as is shown by a story which appeared in *The New York Times* on October 23, 1918. Tie Sing, born fifty years before in Carson City, was classified as a Chinese alien because he was unable to prove his place of birth. For this reason, he could not bring over his wife and child from China. He was a cook for the Geological Survey, and therefore defined as a laborer by immigration law. Nevertheless, he gave all his savings to the second Liberty Loan. The *Times* appealed for anyone who might verify Tie's birth in Carson City to step forward and help him prove his citizenship.

Though at first only token American forces reached Europe, by March 1918 three hundred thousand had landed in France. By summer the Seventy-seventh, or Metropolitan Division, was in action, and with it was Color Sgt. Sing Kee, who had enlisted in New York. Kee and his division were involved in repelling the last German offensive in the late spring and summer.

In the trying August days on the Vesle, when the 308th Infantry was being relieved at Mont Notre Dame, a Chinese named Sing Kee was operating a message centre in that village, under heavy fire. The Germans were bombarding and gassing the centre at the rate of thirty shells a minute. Sing Kee's companions were wounded one by one. Sing Kee was gassed. But he would not leave his post, and for twenty-four hours under these conditions, he ran his message centre alone. He received the Distinguished Service Cross in recognition of his courage and endurance.[29]

Sing Kee became the first Chinese-American to receive so high an honor for bravery in battle; he also won the French *Croix de Guerre* for the same action.

China itself entered the war in the summer of 1917. Dr. Chew hailed her action, recalling German atrocities at the time of the Boxer rebellion and German involvement in an abortive attempt to restore the Manchus to the throne in the same summer of 1917. China's actual participation in the war was small, consisting of the dispatch of labor battalions to France to replace a work force crippled by conscription.

On November 11, 1918, an exhausted Germany, beset by a workers' revolt against Kaiser Wilhelm, signed the armistice. The other Central Powers—Austria, Turkey, Bulgaria—had already capitulated. The guns fell silent.

Across America everyone danced in the streets. The Chinese communities of America celebrated the end of the war in time-honored tradition by setting off fireworks. They felt a brave new world was in the making. They had served their country in time of war and expected to be welcomed as equal partners in the American experiment.

Evidently, Dr. Chew cherished a hope that his son would go to China to build railroads, for he was so quoted in the spring of 1919. Edward, however, had different ideas. As soon as he was demobilized, he told his father he did not wish to leave his native land. It must have given Ng Poon Chew a bittersweet pang to learn that his son's homeland was not his own. But then he had educated his children to become Americans and that was what they felt themselves to be. Caroline, the youngest, had entered prestigious Mills College, her strange passion for the dance still unsatisfied. Rose was working on a master's degree in social work at the same school. Mansie was serving as her father's English secretary, and teaching music. Effie, like Edward, had designs upon the white world. Having graduated from the Kindergarten Training School, she intended to apply for a job in the Oakland public school system.

The new, if very quiet, spirit of self-assertion originating among the college-educated Chinese-Americans affected Edward C. Chew especially. He had two years of engineering college and his army experience behind him, so he returned to Berkeley to finish college. Taking his degree in 1921, he began to apply for jobs. Door after door was shut in his face, ever so politely if a prospective employer knew his father, less tactfully if he did not. But Edward was persistent. First he had to get the job; then he would prove that a Chinese-American could work as well an anyone else. Discouraging weeks and months passed by. At last, Pacific Gas and Electric Company in San Francisco, after some hesitation by the personnel manager, agreed to take him on as a draftsman. Edward had no doubts of his ability to do the job. He had always worked well, been popular, become a part of the team in the white world. His optimism was justified. Within three days, he was "one of the boys."[30]

Edward and his friends of the second generation were ready to grope their way toward the biggest step in American life—the transition from immigrant to citizen. All around them were millions of second-generation children of the great waves of European immigration who had reached America between 1890 and the war. Each of them was seeking that same dignity and respect, that same sense of belonging to their new land. They were ready for America, but was America ready for them?

HOPE
DEFERRED

*Anti-Asian sentiment is hitting a new high. China is pres-
ently embroiled in internal strife; asking her to protect
overseas Chinese is a waste of breath. We have to be on our
own and our only hope rests with the over 10,000 American-
born Chinese who have the right to vote.*

NG POON CHEW, EDITORIAL,
"THOSE WITH THE VOTE SHOULD PAY ATTENTION,"
Chung Sai Yat Po, MAY 6, 1924

BY 1920, almost forty years of exclusion had reduced the
Chinese population of the United States to its lowest
point—61,000 men, women and children. The lopsided imbalance
of men to women was still an incredible seven males to every
female, yet it was twice as good as the ratio of fourteen to one in
1910. A slow, steady increase in the number of wives brought over
by their husbands had formed the basis for a new community of
Chinese families.

The Chinatown of the 1920s had become a recognized tourist
attraction. Superficially, Chinatown had been given exotic touches

such as pagoda telephone booths and carved façades of buildings painted in traditional Chinese colors. But the older, more authentically Chinese atmosphere was fading before a dwindling population, the growth of the second generation and the rise of modern education and customs in China itself. Gone were most of the queues, the Chinese blouses and pantaloons, the street peddlers with their bamboo baskets of fish or vegetables slung from poles and their picturesque cries. Dupont Street, with its dignified new name of Grant Avenue, was lined with glossy modern art and curio shops where college-educated clerks addressed the tourist in impeccable, if inflected, English.

Old San Franciscans sighed in inconsistent nostalgia for the "good old days," for the dirty, crowded slum which they had once anathematized as "the pest-hole of Western civilization." In part, no doubt, it was nostalgia for that vanishing, much lamented institution of the California rich—the Chinese houseboy. The second generation of American-born Chinese had quickly absorbed the American attitude to domestic service, and most of them would have none of it, except as a temporary means of working their way through college.

In 1920 this modernizing trend with its cleanup of Chinatown had not totally removed the earlier aura of "sin" that made visiting Chinatown a naughty adventure, like seeing the Latin Quarter in Paris. Tour guides hated to give up this colorful image of Chinatown.

However, the idea of the Chinese as hardworking and law-abiding made considerable progress in the 1920s, despite a brief violent outbreak of tong warfare in the middle of the decade. Americans had long since caught up to and surpassed the highbinders by generating bootleggers and racketeers such as Al Capone and Dion O'Bannion.

Dr. Chew and the *Chung Sai Yat Po* could take a great deal of credit for the increasing Americanization of the Chinese, while providing them with information they could find nowhere else. A typical issue recorded action against American merchants in

Foochow, harassment of Chinese by Mexicans in Tijuana, raids on gambling dens, captures of illegal immigrants to America and the larger issues of the Chinese or American political situation as it affected the Chinese. In his editorials Dr. Chew urged his people to educate themselves and their children and to make intelligent use of their vote if citizens. In this way they would advance both the interests of the Chinese community and their own assimilation into American society.

Dr. Chew was an especially effective link between his people and the white world because his tours into the heartland of America on the Chautauqua and Lyceum circuits continued. The Chautauqua movement reached its apex in 1924, when 40,000,000 Americans attended its sessions in 10,000 communities from coast to coast.

In his career as a lecturer Dr. Chew crossed the United States eighty-six times, touching all forty-eight states. Whether it was the sophisticated China Club of Seattle and the Cosmopolitan Club of Stanford or the mountain boys and girls in Miss Berry's charitable school in Rome, Georgia, Dr. Chew undoubtedly met and influenced more Americans in more places than any Chinese before the era of mass media. For example, between October 14 and 30, 1920, the Dixie Lyceum Bureau scheduled Dr. Chew to speak in one-night stands at Albany, Abilene, Nocona, Paris, Hillsboro, McGregor, Bryan, Austin, Lockhart and New Braunfels in Texas and Hot Springs and Scarry in Arkansas. On November 1 he joined the Georgia circuit under the Alkahest Bureau of Atlanta.

The weeks on the road, summer and winter, were wearing. But Dr. Chew was convinced of the importance of improving the climate of American opinion about the Chinese. Only in this way could the young people of his children's generation enjoy the opportunities America seemed to promise.

And that promise was difficult to realize. Edward Chew barely could get a draftsman's job despite the boom of the Roaring Twenties. Effie, by persistence, had become the first Chinese woman in the California public school system. Rose, armed with a cum laude degree from Mills in social work, was employed by the Chinese YWCA. Caroline was working on a master's degree in music—and planning to take dance lessons when she was finished.

If the Chews, with their connections, had such difficulty finding jobs outside the Chinese world, the situation was even more critical for Chinese young people from less well-known families. The United States in the twenties was in the grip of an intense reaction against the "foreign adventure" of World War I, which had pulled the country for the first time from its traditional isolation. The resurgence of old animosities in Europe and the failure of Wilson's grand idealism to achieve lasting peace confirmed the feelings of most Americans that this country should avoid "entangling alliances" with the crafty foxes of the Old World. The turn to Bolshevism taken by the Russian revolution, and the anarchy of China in the warlord era added to the distrust of foreign ideas and foreign ways felt by the average American.

This antiforeign attitude was behind the institutionalized discrimination in jobs, housing, social and country clubs that was becoming such a striking aspect of American life. This discrimination was directed not only at racial minorities like the Chinese, but also at religious minorities like the Jews and Roman Catholics and ethnic minorities like the Poles, Italians and Irish.

The problem was most acute for the racial minorities who had no hope of "passing" in the white world. Most Chinese college graduates were driven by this intolerance to apply their education to the small number of business and professional openings in Chinatown. The turning back to Chinatown, more from necessity than desire, led to the phenomenon of college-educated clerks in Chinatown bazaars. A few of them managed to secure lower-level white-collar jobs in white-owned companies where they were generally stranded for years with minimal raises and no promotions.

The young Chinese who remained in Chinatown and became well established there began to contest the dominance of the older generation of China-born merchants in the Six Companies. New organizations like the Chinese-American Citizens Alliance and the

Cathay Post of the American Legion also bid for influence. Dr. Chew knew of the ideas and aspirations of these forward-looking groups. The hope of the second generation was that by paralleling the organizations and ideas of the white society, by being peaceful and law-abiding and by working very hard, they would eventually win acceptance from other Americans.

For some of the young college-educated Chinese-Americans the wait was too long. Even in the years of the warlords opportunities existed for engineers, medical personnel and teachers in China. Among those who elected to return to China in 1919 were two daughters of Soo Hoo Nam Art who had gone to the University of California with Mansie and Rose Chew. One intended to study at Canton Christian College, the other at the School of Physical Culture in the London mission in Hong Kong.

For those like the Chews who elected to remain in America, there was one consolation. The violent acts of lynching and looting had largely disappeared. Otherwise it might have seemed to the Chinese in America that their future led ever downward. For the antiforeign sentiment of so many Americans culminated in Congress's enacting more laws to restrict immigration.

As soon as the war ended, immigration from Europe picked up with surprising speed, and so did the resistance of the anti-immigration forces. In 1921, Congress passed a law restricting immigration to 350,000 persons a year and allowed 3 percent of the number of people from each nation resident in the United States in 1910 to enter. For the first time, national origin was made the basis of immigration, and the quota system discriminated against immigrants from southern and eastern Europe.

Soon the anti-immigration forces found the 1921 immigration act too weak. By 1924 Congress was debating passage of the National Origins Act. This time the quota was set at 2 percent of the number of Americans of that national background resident in this country in 1890, when the percentage of northern Europeans was much higher.

Asians were not even included in the quota; they were simply to be totally excluded except when traveling on temporary visas as tourists, students or teachers. This total prohibition was also directed at the Japanese, Koreans and Hindus, who had followed the Chinese as farm laborers in California. It did not, however, apply to Filipinos, who immigrated from an American protectorate and became the next group to tend the fields and orchards.

The imminent passage of the new immigration bill registered a strong shock among overseas Chinese. The bill was passed in May and scheduled to go into effect on July 1, 1924. By a special cruelty, even the China-born wives of American citizens were not to be allowed entry into the United States. Faced with this total ban, which would condemn them to virtual celibacy for life, many Chinese hurried home to the hills of Toi Shan, Hiangshan and the other districts around Canton. They arranged to bring their wives and their children back to the unwelcoming land which was nonetheless their home. Sing Kee, the daring, bemedaled sergeant of World War I, had become a successful merchant in New York's Chinatown. He hurried back to his native village to bring his wife home. Because of the great demand for passage at that time, he was barely able to reach the United States with his wife before the doors closed for good. The New York *World* commented on the irony of a war hero whose wife would have been automatically barred from entering the country if she had arrived a few days later.

Dr. Chew was in the vanguard of those leading the hopeless fight against the total ban on Chinese immigrants. He urged those few Chinese who could vote to weigh carefully whom they would favor for President in the 1924 election. Calvin Coolidge, the Republican, would probably be better than the Democrat, whoever he might be, since the Democrats were closer to labor unions, which still opposed the Chinese.

For the information of his readers, Dr. Chew quoted the words of a sympathetic lawyer, long associated with the Chinese, who suggested that "more troublesome" laws had been passed before. "They pass laws, but they seldom execute them." The lawyer suggested that the Chinese wire Secretary of Commerce Herbert

Hoover, who was distinguished for his humanitarian views and knowledge of international affairs. The Chinese should suggest to Hoover that he review for the Congress the history of the Chinese in America, how "they have contributed to developing the West and helped make it what it is today. They have done a lot for the country. If they should pass this law discriminating against the Chinese they would suffer the pangs of their conscience for being ungrateful. . . . If you stay united and persist in your resistance, you could still win." In a brief footnote Dr. Chew gave his reaction to the lawyer's optimistic statement: "This proposal might be feasible but it is too late."

In addition to waging the battle on the immigration front, Dr. Chew had to explain the convulsions of the warlord period in China to his two audiences. When he addressed his Chinese readers through the pages of the *Chung Sai Yat Po*, he tended to take a realistic and pessimistic view of the confusing events in China. But when he spoke to American audiences, he stressed Chinese accomplishments over Chinese problems.

Indeed, a new spirit of national self-assertion was beginning to rise in China, but its fruits would be slow to mature. This spirit was born among the students in Chinese universities when Chinese interests were sacrificed to those of a stronger Japan at the Versailles peace table. The result was the May Fourth movement of 1919, when students rallied in the streets of Peking against the terms of the treaty. Sustained by popular feeling, they picketed government offices and inspired strikes in other cities and a boycott of Japanese goods.

Allied with industrial workers and older intellectuals in the cities of foreign concessions, the students turned against some of the Western ideas which they had earlier embraced. The failure of Western democracies to exhibit Christian virtues in their treatment of China disillusioned many students with Christianity and missionaries, even though they might have been educated by the missionaries. Democracy had been discredited by the fumblings of the Republic since the time of Yüan as well as by the Allies' recognition of the undemocratic Peking government and the continuance of unequal treaties.

While the United States and the European powers ignored Sun's Canton republic, the new Soviet state gave him aid and recognition. This strengthened the influence of Marxist ideas on Chinese intellectuals.

The question of Sun's relations with the Communists is still subject to controversy today, for both the Chinese Communists and the Nationalists claim to be his heirs. He probably never intended to let the Communists take away his leadership of the Kuomintang. But when friends were few, he was glad to send Chinese to Moscow to learn how to build a revolutionary army. The most notable graduate of this program, a far-from-Communist young man named Chiang Kai-shek, established the Whampoa Military Academy. The academy became the foundation of the Chinese Republican Army.

Chew himself had begun to doubt Sun's ability to become the George Washington of China when he failed to wrest control of the new republic from Yüan. Chew did not share the view of many Americans that the southern republicans were "communist agitators," but he found Sun's programs impractical. His disillusionment with Sun Yat-sen continued right up to March 1925, when Sun died on a trip to Peking trying to negotiate greater unity between north and south.

Dr. Chew gave credit to Sun's early work in bringing about the revolution. "His will and persistence were really admirable and he was a great hero. During the years of revolutionary failures, he was noble and strong. His deeds had all become legends." However, Dr. Chew shook his head sadly over Sun's later maneuvers to gain support from local warlords on the one hand and Russian advisers on the other. Chew's reporters in Kwangtung had written about the desolation left by the warlords' marauding soldiers.

Soon after Sun's death Chew began to sense the growing strength of Chinese nationalism in the student movement. In 1925 the students' enthusiasm was feeding into two movements that were temporarily allied—the Kuomintang and the Communist party. Most Americans lumped them together as "reds," but Chew was more farseeing. In 1925 when students and workers rioted in the streets against foreigners because a worker was beaten to death in a Japanese-owned factory, Chew explained:

> *China indeed sees red, but the red is different from the red which the West believes she sees. The red is not from the red banner which floats over Moscow, flouting its arrogant defiance to all the civilized world, but rather the red blood of indignation and resentment and anger. This red cannot be dispelled by the sword, but only by reason and justice in international dealings, and by the restoration to China of her rights as an independent sovereign nation.*[31]

During the next year Dr. Chew watched Chiang Kai-shek emerge as the dominant leader of the moderate wing of the Kuomintang, expel the Communists from posts in his party and begin his spectacular march northward in the footsteps of the Taiping rebels. The Communists remained active in the left wing of the Kuomintang, including a young organizer of peasant "soviets" in Hunan named Mao Tse-tung.

Meanwhile, inside the Kuomintang, the conservative and moderate merchants and the intellectuals with ties to the West began to fear the power and disruption of the Communists. In March 1927 they were alarmed by attacks on foreigners in Nanking which brought on the British gunboats. Then, in April, Chiang suddenly turned on the unsuspecting Communists in Shanghai and shot several hundred of their leaders. The purge spread to Canton and the peasant soviets in the fall. Eventually the remaining Communists, driven from the eastern cities entirely, established themselves in the mountainous province of Kiangsi under Mao Tse-tung. The victorious Chiang reached Peking on June 8, 1928, after very little fighting.

To Dr. Chew and the majority of overseas Chinese, as well

as to most Chinese patriots except those of the left, Chiang seemed to be what they had been waiting for.

> *The present situation in China offers a very bright prospect for a peaceful solution of the country's internal affairs, and the future is extremely hopeful. The Chinese people consider the Civil War has ended and that from now on a period of reconstruction will begin in which the program of the Nationalist movement can be realized.*

Removal of the warlords had been the first priority of the Nationalists. Now that this had been accomplished, the young well-educated leaders of Chiang's government would begin the struggle against "all the other infringements of Chinese sovereignty."

> *These include the cancellation of extraterritorial rights now enjoyed by foreigners in China; the return of foreign concessions; the elimination of foreign guards and soldiers stationed in different parts of China, and the abolition of all special rights and privileges accorded to foreigners living in China and not enjoyed by the Chinese people themselves.*[32]

As the Nationalists rode to victory at Peking, America basked in the "Coolidge prosperity," the high point of the Roaring Twenties. When Coolidge did not "choose to run" in 1928, the Republicans nominated Secretary of Commerce Hoover, who was easily elected over Democrat Al Smith in the fall. Hoover had long been a friend to the Chinese, but in an America devoted to normalcy and material progress, there was little interest in softening exclusion laws against Asians. The *Chung Sai Yat Po* and the Citizens Alliance continued to lobby for the immigration of wives of citizens. Finally, in the depression year of 1930, Congress agreed to admit wives of Americans citizens of Chinese background provided they had been married before May 26, 1924. The government evidently expected the rest of the Chinese in America to live like monks, especially since many states had enacted laws forbidding marriages between races.

The young American-educated Chinese of the 1920s suffered constant frustration if they desired to assimilate. They dressed like their white companions and spoke English better than Chinese. In school they learned "The Star-Spangled Banner," the Pledge of Allegiance to the flag and devoured the details of American history and geography, "determined to absorb the knowledge that would one day make them responsible citizens of their adopted land."[33]

Indeed, to that older generation of which Chew was becoming a part, it sometimes seemed as if the younger generation were a different breed, all American and not at all Chinese. They were largely ignorant of their traditional language and culture despite a reluctant exposure to Chinese school for some. Chew had always been the apostle of Americanization, and he remained so to the end of his life. But he was also a loyal son of Han, and he knew his own culture deeply, as his English-speaking children did not.

When Dr. Chew looked back toward China, he could see the ancient traditions breaking down there as well. Troubled by a sense of loss, he felt poignantly the equivocal nature of the victory he had fought for all his life: "The second generation have almost forsaken the ideas and ideals of their fathers—they are as American as Americans and more so."

One could trace the change in little ways—in the increasingly American first names in newspaper accounts or in church donation lists, in a world of tennis matches and basketball tournaments exactly paralleling those of white society. As one missionary lamented, the young Chinese-Americans were "restless, as are our American young people."

The results of this rapid Americanization were ironic, for America was not ready to welcome immigrant sons and daughters even if they were white. Not surprisingly, the disappointed young Chinese-Americans began to absorb in somewhat different form their parents' cynicism about American justice. Even they, with their American citizenship, were detained at the border on returning from a trip abroad or were swept up in a dragnet search for illegal immigrants, and their civil rights trampled underfoot. In 1923 when taking a train to El Paso which passed briefly over the Mexican border, Chew himself was detained and questioned by American immigration officials in such a rough, humiliating way that the president of the Sheldon Hotel, Joe Goodell, wrote a letter apologizing for the "unpleasant incident which you experienced with our Federal *mis*representatives while here."

The cynicism that the Chinese developed because of the harassment of travelers and the continuing desire of many Chinese to reach America led them to a unique solution which has unfortunate consequences for many Chinese-Americans to this day. They sought to outwit their persecutors by indulging in a form of smuggling called the "slot racket," and it has left a shadow of illegality hanging over many of their lives. The slot racket did not involve jumping ship or slipping over the border in a truck, though this ruse was used as well. These Chinese simply walked in after withstanding the weeks and months of examination on Angel Island. They presented themselves to the immigration officers as sons of native-born American citizens of Chinese descent. To do this they memorized pages of details about the houses and villages of their presumed father which immigration officers asked for in the attempt to catch up the "paper sons" and separate them from the real ones. Unfortunately, the vagaries of human memory under such inquisition are so unpredictable that sometimes real sons were rejected and paper sons accepted. Once in the country the paper sons naturally lay low in Chinatown, and their labor was sometimes exploited by those who brought them over.

How was it possible for the slot racket to work? It was all because of the earthquake and fire. When the old City Hall was destroyed by that catastrophe, the vital statistics of San Franciscans to that date were destroyed, those of the Chinese among them. Since it was impossible to prove which of the Chinese were or were not American-born, many claimed American birth. Thereafter, when a Chinese returned from a visit to his family in China, he recorded the birth of a son. If he claimed more sons than he actually had, he could sell a "slot" to any young man of the right age wishing to emigrate.

A Chinese scholar has tried to explain the reactions of the average Chinese in America to the slot racket and smuggling:

> *If some patriotic Chinese were asked to pass their moral judgment upon the problem of smuggling, they would probably answer that in the last century, the Chinese did not want to see foreigners in China just as the Americans did not want to see Chinese coolies in the United States, but the foreigners went to China nevertheless, under protection of warships and troops. . . . In the same way, if China were strong, the Chinese would come to the United States from the front door and under no disguise, as every American does when he enters China. From the viewpoint of the patriotic Chinese, therefore, smuggling is to be condemned as undignified.*[34]

Unfortunately for people like Dr. Chew, who worked for "more honorable ways of effecting the same purpose," success seemed far away. By the middle twenties, even before the victorious march of Chiang to Peking, he was beginning to show the strain of his years on the lecture circuit. He was forced to cut down on his travels. In any case the Lyceum and Chautauqua circuits themselves were slowly dying. Radio and movies, the automobile, the increasing sophistication of audiences and the adoption of lecture series by other groups were combining to kill the movement. In fact, Dr. Chew made his debut on commercial radio in 1923, when the infant medium was but three years old, and surprised his listeners by his command of this means of reaching vast audiences.

In 1926 Dr. Chew passed his Great Birthday (age sixty), the age at which the Chinese are thought to be old enough to have obtained wisdom. He could look back upon his long campaign to Americanize his people and to bring Americans the truth about

China and feel that something, even much, had been accomplished. He could applaud the dimming of the hatchet-man–slave-girl image of the Chinese. He could cheer, with a growing optimism, the new young government of Chiang. What he could not foresee was how the split between the triumphant Kuomintang and the tiny out-lawed Communist party, as well as the Japanese invasion, would result in a fierce twenty-five-year battle for control of the country he loved.

CHAPTER 19

FULL
OF YEARS
AND HONORS

Race, nationality do not count; what counts is the noble character of Dr. Chew.
EDITORIAL, "IN MEMORY OF DR. NG POON CHEW."
Chung Sai Yat Po, MARCH 17, 1931

O<small>N</small> March 12, 1931, employees of the *Chung Sai Yat Po* in San Francisco had a pleasant surprise. Dr. Ng Poon Chew, their founder and editor, was driven to the Sacramento Street office by his eldest daughter, Mansie, for a regular editorial meeting. During the past year, Dr. Chew had been forced to spend a good deal of time at his Oakland home because of failing health. His doctor, diagnosing the trouble as an overtaxed heart, had ordered him to rest.

Dr. Chew seemed in good spirits that afternoon. He joked with his employees in the jovial way that had once brought smiles of delight to audiences the length and breadth of the United States. He still wore a walrus moustache in honor of his hero Theodore Roosevelt, but both hair and moustache were almost white. Seeing him so like his old self, Mansie had signaled to an office boy to go to the restaurant across the street and bring him some of the Kwangtung dishes he loved.

When the food arrived, Dr. Chew ate sparingly, as his doctor had ordered, but with good appetite. Ng Yee Yin and Ng See Yee, still active, and other old employees sat around him, telling him that they expected him to return to work soon, for his health had obviously benefited from the rest. He shook his head, a little sadly, told them to work hard for his sake and quoted a favorite maxim, "The newspaper is the people's tongue." Then, smiling again, he told them he would celebrate his sixty-fifth birthday at a family dinner the following night. He invited them to come to Oakland after the paper was put to bed and join him for tea, fruit and cakes.

As he walked back to his car, evening had fallen over China- town. The streets were quiet except for a few workers hurrying home to their evening rice. Most of them recognized the face and figure of one of their beloved elder statesmen, the "Nestor" of Chinatown as American journalists were fond of calling him after the oldest and wisest of Ulysses' comrades.

In 1931 the luxurious Chinese restaurants with their neon signs where politicians and movie stars dined on Peking duck had not yet come into being. In that Depression year some knowing Americans had discovered the good food to be enjoyed despite the dingy fronts and indifferent service of the family restaurants where the Chinese ate their tasty suppers. But many more Americans could eat out only at the soup kitchens supplied by local charities. Chinatown and Chinese-Americans had not escaped the widening economic crisis. Vacant stores had appeared in the compact net- work of streets that defined Chinatown. On the soup lines elderly Chinese men, who could barely speak English after having worked in America for thirty or forty years, patiently waited their turn for the day's only meal.

Dr. Chew was saddened and deeply concerned over these problems. He wondered at the mystifying turns of the wheel of fortune which had converted him from a poor peasant boy into a man of substance. Though the Depression had shrunk his holdings, he would not leave his family destitute. His success over the years had allowed him to buy a controlling interest in the *Chung Sai Yat Po*; he had been asked to become a director of the China Mail Steam Company and Marcot Copper Company. He thought of China with her vast territory, her multiplying population and her many miseries. Would the new government of Chiang bring her stability and strength? And if the Chinese giant, stumbling toward the future, had reason for hope, surely rich, powerful America would be able to solve her problems.

It was close to the Chews' usual supper hour of 6:00 P.M. the next day when Ng Poon Chew sat down at the table. All his children were gathered about him, the very symbol of his and Chun Fah's success in the task that traditional Chinese regarded as one of life's central purposes—the proper raising of one's children. Mansie, in addition to teaching music, had taken a greater interest in running the *Chung Sai Yat Po* as her father's health declined. Effie had been for over ten years a teacher at the Lincoln Public School in Oakland. Rose had become associate director of the San Francisco International Institute, which helped immigrants adopt to life in the San Francisco area. Eddie had risen to the position of planning engineer with Pacific Gas and Electric and headed a department of twenty men, all white. With him were his wife and young son, Eddie, Jr. Caroline had been for several years a secretary at the Chinese YWCA in San Francisco. Though no one talked about it, everyone understood she was taking dancing lessons after work.

Dr. Chew bowed his head to say grace. His voice, which had begun to sound frail, rose strong and clear with the ministerial resonance of old as he said, "Lord, bless this bread to our use and we to thy service." As the members of the family raised their heads from the snowy tablecloth, they noticed their husband and father wrinkle his brow, as if puzzled by something. "I have a little pain," he said. His hands, which had been joined in prayer, fell apart and he turned the palms up on the table with the fingers spread, as if appealing to heaven. Then he fell forward, his face suddenly drained of color and expression. Nothing moved. No one spoke. Then someone, Mansie perhaps, started up in shock and cried, "Father, are you ill?" Still Dr. Chew did not move. The voice that had amused and thrilled so many thousands of Americans was silent. Dr. Chew had "died a good death," peacefully, without suffering.

From coast to coast, newspapers noted the passing of the man who had worked so hard and so long to make his countrymen better known and better understood by Americans. In a lead article on his life and death, *The New York Times* stressed his importance: "By his death both Chinese and English literature lost a contributor recognized as an authority on events in China. For the last thirty years his chief object had been the dissemination of American ideas among the Chinese in the United States."

The San Francisco *Chronicle*, which had recorded so many of his words, mourned the passing of "Dr. Ng Poon Chew, Chinese editor, lecturer and essayist, beloved in Chinatown for his quiet dignity and altruism. . . . His outlook on China's attitude during the World War and later his articles on Chinese exclusion . . . gained for him a high place in the esteem of leaders in all walks of life throughout the country."

Most of all, the *Chung Sai Yat Po*, which had become Dr. Chew's legacy to his people, expressed a sense of what the Chinese had lost: "His voice is still echoing in our ear at this moment yet he has already left us. We can only work harder so as not to disappoint Dr. Chew." Looking back over thirty years to the founding of the paper, the editor explained what Chew had accomplished. "This was the first Chinese newspaper [daily] outside China. . . . The papers in mainland China were under censorship and their editorials were insignificant. Since this paper was published overseas and enjoyed freedom of speech, therefore all the revolutionaries were acquainted with Dr. Chew."

On March 16, 1931, the Chew family and a large crowd of

In his late years Dr. Ng Poon Chew was acclaimed by Chinese and Americans alike for his wisdom and kindliness; years of one-night stands as a lecturer had ruined his health, forcing him to retire by the end of the twenties; he died in 1931.
(CHEW FAMILY PHOTO)

"old friends of the family, of the clan and from our village" joined American friends and admirers in all walks of life at the First Presbyterian Church of Oakland. The funeral service, completely Western in form, had been arranged by the Lakeshore Masonic Lodge of Oakland, of which Dr. Chew had been the first Chinese member, becoming a thirty-second-degree Mason during his lifetime.

The Reverend K. Y. Tse of the Chinese Presbyterian Church in San Francisco read the simple, solemn words of the funeral service, offering comfort to the mourners that Dr. Chew lived beyond the view of earthbound eyes. Dr. Stanley Armstrong Hunter, pastor of St. John's Presbyterian Church in Berkeley, delivered the main eulogy. "Dr. Chew and I have been friends for some decades. . . . Race, nationality do not count; what counts is the noble character of Dr. Chew. Among the 400,000,000 Chinese, I just cannot forget him."

At the Chews' house, 3765 Shafter Avenue, Oakland, there was a void that was never to be filled. To this day, the unmarried surviving daughter of Dr. Chew, Mansie, lives there, but the phone is still listed in the Oakland directory under the name of Dr. Ng Poon Chew. On March 17, the day after the funeral, the *Chung Sai Yat Po* carried an epitaph for its founder. It summed up especially well the main purposes of his life and his influence on those around him.

The founders of this paper "worked toward national and racial equality. They worked for the overseas Chinese. [They opposed] the autocratic Ch'ing government and sympathized with the Revolution. . . . Why did we help Sun? It was not that we loved him but because what he did was consonant with the pronounced purpose of this newspaper, that is, to fight for national freedom." After the revolution, Dr. Chew, "totally devoid of the drive for power and personal ambitions . . . fought only for freedom and equality. This is Dr. Chew's undying spirit."

The editorial writer looked back on the chaotic years of Chinese history through which Dr. Chew had passed in his lifetime. He recalled the anarchy of the warlord years when the heroes of the revolution had fought, each for his own version of the truth, over the prone and bleeding body of his wounded country. Even the most high-minded like Sun Yat-sen had been to some extent corrupted by the fierce power struggle.

Those who massacred indiscriminately and committed a number of immoral acts to get in power may be honored for a while but they will not stand the test of history. They will decay like grass and wood. Only Dr. Chew abstained from self-seeking and grew old "leisurely." He would not plunge into the whirlpool of political corruption, but never lost his will to fight for freedom and equality. Autocracy, whether under the Ch'ing or the Republic, he opposed adamantly. Inequality, he fought indefatigably, regardless of country or people. At the height of anti-Chinese activity in the United States, Dr. Chew engaged the anti-Chinese leaders in numerous debates. He also promoted Chinese culture among the Americans, increasing their respect for us. This growing respect is a tangible result of Dr. Chew's lifelong struggle. Dr. Chew was a great man. Among the celebrated few, there were some who sacrificed their honor for name and power but Dr. Chew sacrificed his name for his honor. Those who benefited from his life and deeds will sing praise to his name. Though he is gone, yet this paper embodies his spirit. Today we mourn his departure, but at the same time we know that his undying spirit will always be with us.

Despite the quiet way in which he had impressed himself on his contemporaries, Dr. Chew's "undying spirit" remained memorable among those who had known him or heard him speak. Twenty years after his death, he was the only Chinese included in Rockwell Hunt's book, *California's Stately Hall of Fame*. Even more significant, when the San Francisco *Examiner* called for nominations to a Gallery of Great Americans in 1965, Dr. Chew was again the only Chinese included.

By his death Dr. Chew was spared both greater sorrow and greater joy than he had ever known from the causes to which he had devoted his life. On September 18, 1931, the Japanese began their aggression against Chinese territory in Manchuria, using as an excuse the mysterious blowing up of a section of Japanese-controlled railroad near Mukden. This incident was only the first of many initiated by Japan to gain gradual control over her vast but less developed neighbor. For China was the cornerstone of the new order that Japan wished to construct in Asia, the Greater East Asia Co-prosperity sphere.

By the middle thirties China was becoming more concerned with the increasing encroachments of Japan than with the battle between Communist and Nationalist. Chinese patriotism was responding to the challenge with protests and boycotts organized by students and intellectuals in the cities. When the Japanese had turned Manchuria into a puppet government controlled from Tokyo in 1931–32, the countries of Europe were weak and divided, preoccupied with the effects of worldwide depression. Through the League of Nations, they had responded feebly to the first important challenge to their usefulness. They had issued no sanctions against Japan for her aggression. Though America, which did not belong to the League, offered to support stronger measures, she was unwilling to oppose Japan alone. As one famous historian put it, "In a very real sense, therefore, the second of the world wars began on that September night in 1931. The shots then fired were the opening of the global conflict. From Mukden the path led to Ethiopia, Munich, the invasion of Poland and Pearl Harbor."[35] Eventually, all the major countries of the world, including the United States, were to be drawn into the conflict launched that day. But China was to suffer the longest agony. It endured for over eighteen years, lasting beyond the conclusion of the world war until a new but repressive government took over the task of making China strong and united.

Dr. Chew also missed by twelve years the fulfillment of his greatest dream, a fulfillment which, ironically, was made possible because of the titanic struggle launched by the Japanese aggression against China. By 1943 the United States was totally involved in World War II. As Japan swept across Southeast Asia—Burma, Indochina, Netherlands East Indies, Philippines, Malaya and the Pacific islands—she brought propaganda as well as soldiers, for Japan wished to conquer the peoples ideologically as well as physically. Cleverly, the Japanese posed as the friend of all Asians against the colonial and extraterritorial ambitions of the European powers and the United States.

From China throughout Southeast Asia to India, still unconquered, the Japanese words struck a sympathetic chord. Asians could well remember how they had been exploited by the European powers. They remembered the British sahibs who had barred even upper-class Indians from their clubs and swept ordinary folk off the pavement as they walked. The better-informed knew how the European countries had drained Asian countries of their resources and pocketed their tax revenues. Even the United States, which was less open about its colonial ambitions, had barred Asians from her shores as inferior, ineligible for citizenship.

In 1943 the United States and her Allies were fighting hard to stem the tide of Japanese victories. At the same time, China, the chief Pacific ally, was prostrate from six years of fighting. Chiang, loath to send his exhausted troops into battle against the Japanese, wanted more American aid. He reminded Americans that they did not treat his people as equal to the nationals of other countries.

To make his plea for aid and equal status more effective, Chiang sent his most astute and charming ambassador to the United States in the spring of 1943—Madame Chiang. She toured the country, speaking from coast to coast and evoking wild enthusiasm for our Chinese allies. She even became the first woman to address a joint session of Congress. After her visit the foes of exclusion were joined by a majority of Americans. The ground swell reached Congress. In early December 1943, first the House and then the Senate voted on a bill to repeal the sixty-one-year-old exclusion law, bring Chinese under the quota provisions of the National Origins Act of 1924 and provide for the naturalization of all resident Chinese. In both houses the measure passed by a voice vote, and on December 17 President Franklin D. Roosevelt signed it into law. The barrier of total exclusion had been smashed.

When Dr. Chew died, mourned by friends of both races, he was a rare example of a Chinese-American who had succeeded in bridging the gap between two such different worlds. In the forty and more years since then, an increasing number of Chinese-Americans have continued in the tradition he established. If one excludes the remnants of the bachelor laborers, the Chinese, with the Japanese, have the highest percentage of college-educated members of any American group. They have breached the walls of Chinatown, moved into a variety of city and suburban neighborhoods and branched out into all kinds of white-collar and professional jobs. As creative artists and intellectual pioneers, they have contributed greatly to the cultural and technological development of their adopted land—I. M. Pei in architecture, Dong Kingman in painting, James Wong Howe in cinematography, Ming Cho Lee in stage design, Nobel winners Chen Ning Yang and Tsung-dao Lee in physics, Gerald Tsai in finance, and many others.

With the increasing acculturation of the Chinese in America, one might have predicted the disappearance of Chinatowns except for the two largest, in San Francisco and in New York. Indeed, writing in 1960, Rose Hum Lee, a leading American sociologist of Chinese ancestry, believed that in a decade most Chinatowns would vanish. And Dr. Chew, had he been alive, would probably have agreed with her. Yet in 1970 there were 435,062 Chinese in the United States, almost six times the number here when Dr. Chew died in 1931. And Chinatowns once again were bulging at the seams and spilling over into the quarters of neighboring groups, like the Italian section and the old Jewish Lower East Side in New York.

The action leading to this surprising result was the new immigration law of 1965. Under its provisions, for the first time since the Exclusion Law of 1882 the Chinese could emigrate to the United States in the exact same numbers as any other nationality. Up to 20,000 a year from any one country could come under a complicated preference scheme which involved giving priority to parents, wives, children and other relatives of citizens and to certain trades and professions in demand in America. Going into effect in 1968, this law significantly altered the nationalities of immigrants to the United States. For example, Filipinos and Italians replaced Canadians and British with the largest number of immigrants. The number of Chinese rose from 2,628 in 1965 to 16,274 in 1970.

This rapid growth in the number of Chinese reaching the United States coincided with the rise in ethnic consciousness of racial and national groups in America, following the civil rights movement of the 1960s. Many assimilated young Chinese, knowing little of their heritage, began to return to their roots; they also became interested in helping the new arrivals in Chinatown, who were having the problems of adjustment and acceptance that beset all immigrants. It was as if the wheel had come full circle, except that this time the new Chinese immigrants were met by Chinese who were American in all except that final, total acceptance by white society.

Problems and promise fill Chinatown today with ferment. Just as Chinese-American citizens have greater opportunities than ever, the new immigrants are caught again in the cycle of poverty with its by-products of juvenile delinquency, exploited labor and frustrated aspirations. And even for the most educated and as-similated, the problem of continued American racism brings obstacles. In high schools and colleges today, Chinese and other Asian Americans struggle to resolve the dilemma which troubles other nationalities in the unmelted "melting pot" as well—how to retain their individual heritage and their American citizenship without diminishing either.

Perhaps the story of Dr. Chew, a pioneer Chinese adventurer in this field, provides clues. Many of the themes that Dr. Chew sounded in his speeches touched upon those very concerns that trouble all Americans, and not just those of Chinese descent, in the insecure and self-conscious 1970s:

> *This is a fact which cannot be gainsaid, that you [Westerners] have a deeper knowledge into the mysteries of the force of nature, that you have a stronger control over the elements and to make them serve your end than we ever dream to have. Yet the moral feature of the Western civilization is, in my mind, inferior to the Oriental one. You develop your material civilization at the expense of the moral one.*

And we, on the other hand, emphasize the moral civilization at the expense of the material accumulations. You have far more than your forefathers had; You have more luxuries; you have more comforts; but has your real happiness increased in keeping with the increase of material accumulations? Are you enjoying more true joy and happiness than your fathers on the inhospitable coast of New England? I doubt it. For the possession of material accumulation does not necessarily imply the possession of happiness or the serenity of life. People in this country think more of the accumulation of the means of living than reflect upon the character and value of the life lived.[36]

Part I

1. *Daily Alta*, San Francisco, *California* August 29, 1850.
2. William Shaw, *Golden Dreams and Waking Realities* (London, 1851), p. 34.
3. John K. Fairbank, *The United States and China* (Cambridge, Mass., 1972), p. 18.
4. J. D. Borthwick, *Three Years in California* (Edinburgh, 1857), p. 261.
5. All quotations taken from letters of Presbyterian missionaries to the Chinese are reprinted from the Correspondence of the Board of Foreign Missions, courtesy of the Presbyterian Historical Society, Philadelphia, Pa.
6. *The People* v. *George W. Hall* (Sacramento, Calif., 1854).
7. *The Murder of M. V. B. Griswold by Five Chinese Assassins* (Jackson, Calif., 1858).
8. Stanford M. Lyman, "Secret Societies," *The Asian in the West* (Reno, 1970), p. 44.
9. Leon Comber, *Chinese Secret Societies in Malaya* (Locust Valley, N.Y., 1959), p. 272.
10. Guillermo Prieto, *San Francisco in the Seventies* (San Francisco, 1938), p. 31.
11. Albert D. Richardson, *Beyond the Mississippi* (Hartford, 1869), pp. 438–440.
12. Crocker MSS., quoted in Wesley B. Griswold, *A Work of Giants* (New York, 1962).
13. Robert L. Fulton, *Epic of the Overland* (San Francisco, 1924), p. 34.
14. Griswold, op. cit., p. 161.
15. San Francisco *Examiner*, May 12, 1869.
16. Robert W. Howard, *The Great Iron Trail* (New York, 1962), p. 336.
17. J. H. Beadle, *The Undeveloped West or Five Years in the Territories* (Philadelphia, 1873), p. 165.
18. Otis Gibson, *The Chinese in America* (Cincinnati, 1877), p. 388.
19. *The Chinese Massacre at Rock Springs, Wyoming Territory, Sept. 2, 1885* (Boston, 1886), p. 85.
20. Willard B. Farwell, *The Chinese at Home and Abroad* (San Francisco, 1885), p. 5.

21. *Chae Chan Ping* v. *United States,* Supreme Court of the United States, No. 1446 (October 1888), p. 8.

22. Jacob Riis, *How the Other Half Lives* (New York, 1957), p. 76.

Part II

1. Ng Poon Chew, unpublished speech, Chew MSS.

2. Ira M. Condit, *The Chinaman as We See Him* (Chicago, 1900), p. 209.

3. "Autobiography of Dr. Sun Yat-sen," trans. by Leonard S. Hsu, *China Tomorrow,* quoted in Lyon Sharman, *Sun Yat-sen, His Life and Its Meaning* (Stanford, 1968), p. 44.

4. Sun Yat-sen, *Kidnapped in London* (Bristol, 1897), p. 55.

5. Letter from Ira G. Lee to the author, Nov. 4, 1975.

6. L. Eve Armentrout, "Reform and Revolutionary Parties among Overseas Chinese in the Americas" (Ph.D. diss., University of California, Davis, 1975–76).

7. Arnold Genthe and Will Irwin, *Pictures of Old Chinatown,* (New York, 1908), pp. 7–8.

8. *Chung Sai Yat Po,* Feb. 28, 1900. All translations from the *CSYP* are by Joseph C. K. Ng.

9. Huie Kin, *Reminiscences* (Peiping, 1932), p. 71.

10. Theodore Roosevelt, *State Papers,* vol. 4, p. 498.

11. Dec. 9, 1905, p. 2.

12. Bret Harte, *San Francisco in 1866* (San Francisco, 1951), p. 3.

13. Henry Evans, *Curious Lore of San Francisco's Chinatown* (San Francisco, 1955), p. 30.

14. Pierre Beringer, "The Destruction of San Francisco," *Overland Monthly,* May 1906, p. 396.

15. Jessie Juliet Knox, "A Chinese Horace Greeley," *Oakland Tribune Magazine,* Dec. 3, 1922, quoted in *Bulletin, Chinese Historical Society of America,* April 1971, p. 3.

16. Sun Yat-sen, "My Reminiscences," *Strand Magazine,* March 1912, p. 305–306.

17. "America's Opportunity in the Transformation of China," unpublished speech, Chew MSS.

18. Sun Yat-sen, *Memoirs of a Chinese Revolutionary* (New York, 1927), p. 192.

19. Kayano Nagamoto, quoted in Chun-tu Hsüeh, *Huang Hsing and the Chinese Revolution* (Stanford, 1961), pp. 82–83.

20. New York *Sun,* Feb. 3, 1912, p. 16.

21. Ng Poon Chew, unpublished speech describing Chew's return to China, Chew MSS.
22. New York *Sun*.
23. New York *Sun*.
24. Ng Poon Chew, unpublished speech to Chinese students, Chew MSS.
25. New York *Sun*.
26. Chautauqua Program, Corvallis, Oregon, June 26–July 1, 1914, Chew MSS.
27. Chautauqua Program.
28. Letter from Dr. Clifford M. Drury to the author, June 11, 1973.
29. "Cosmopolitan Heroes," *The New York Times*, May 4, 1919, II:1.
30. Albert W. Palmer, *Orientals in American Life* (New York, 1934), p. 36.
31. Ng Poon Chew, Review of Putnam Weale's *Why China Sees Red*, San Francisco *Chronicle*, June 17, 1928.
32. Ng Poon Chew, "Dr. Chew Is Hopeful for Improved Status in China," San Francisco *Chronicle*, June 17, 1928.
33. Grace W. Wang, "A Speech on Second-Generation Chinese in the U.S.A.," *Chinese Digest*, Aug. 7, 1936, p. 6.
34. Wu Ching-chao, "Chinatowns: A Study of Symbiosis and Assimilation" (Ph.D. diss., University of Chicago, 1928), p. 139.
35. Kenneth Scott Latourette, *A Short History of the Far East* (New York, 1947), p. 576.
36. Ng Poon Chew, "America's Golden Opportunity in China's Transformation," unpublished speech, Chew MSS.

SINCE Dr. Chew left no autobiography, and no major biographical study of his life has ever been attempted, the main sources of his life are the collection of unpublished speeches, clippings and letters in the possession of Miss Mansie Chew, his daughter; conversations with Miss Chew, her brother Mr. Edward Chapin Chew and others of their friends and contemporaries who had known their father; contemporary newspaper and magazine articles about Dr. Chew; records of his speeches in contemporary periodicals; his own published writings in English; mentions of him in the reminiscences of other prominent men and women of his time; and of course the files of his own Chinese-language daily, the *Chung Sai Yat Po*, as translated by my able research assistant, Mr. Joseph C. K. Ng. The files of the Presbyterian Historical Society in Philadelphia yielded the Correspondence of the Board of Foreign Missions, where we catch our earliest glimpses of Ng Poon Chew as a young immigrant worker, a school and college student and a young minister.

The chief works by and about Dr. Chew are:

Chew family MSS., letters, clippings and unpublished speeches (in possession of Miss Mansie Condit Chew, Oakland Calif.).

Chew, Ng Poon. "The Chinaman in America," *Independent*, Apr. 3, 1902.

Chew, Ng Poon. "The Chinese in Los Angeles." *Land of Sunshine*, (later *Out West*), Los Angeles, October 1894.

Chew, Ng Poon. *The Treatment of the Exempt Classes of Chinese in the United States*, pamphlet, San Francisco, 1908.

Healy, Patrick J., and Chew, Ng Poon. *A Statement for Non-Exclusion*. San Francisco, 1905.

Hunt, Rockwell D. "Ng Poon Chew" in *California's Stately Hall of Fame*. Stockton, Calif., 1950.

Knox, Jessie Juliet, "A Chinese Horace Greeley," *Oakland Tribune Magazine*, Dec. 3, 1922, quoted in *Bulletin: Chinese Historical Society of America*, April 1971.

Laughlin, J. H. "What America Has Meant to One Immigrant." *The Continent*, Jan. 28, 1915.

"Ng Poon Chew." *Dictionary of American Biography*. Vol. VII.

"Ng Poon Chew." *The Examiner's Gallery of Great Americans*. San Francisco *Examiner*, July 4, 1965.

"Ng Poon Chew." *Sunset,* May 1912.
"Ng Poon Chew." *Who's Who in America.* 1922–31.
Stellman, L. J., "Edward Chapin Chew—Interesting Westerners." *Sunset,* April 1919.

BIBLIOGRAPHIES

Cowan, R. E., and Dunlop, B. *Bibliography of the Chinese Question.* San Francisco, 1909.
Hansen, Gladys. *The Chinese in California.* San Francisco, 1970.
Yuk Ow. *A Selected List of Published and Unpublished Materials Written by California Chinese and Brief Biographies of the Authors,* unpublished manuscript, Bancroft Library, 1960.

PERIODICALS

Chinese Defender, San Francisco, August 1910–October 1911.
Chinese Digest, San Francisco, 1935–40.
Chinese Repository, Canton, 1831–50.
Chung Sai Yat Po, San Francisco, 1900–1931.
Daily Alta California, San Francisco, 1849–1878.
Harper's Weekly, New York, 1856–1910.
The New York Times, scattered, 1851–1931.
The Oriental, or *Tung Ngai San Luk.* Ed. by William Speer and Lee Kan, San Francisco, vol. I, nos. 2, 5, and 6, vol. II, no. 8, 1855–56.
Overland Monthly, scattered, 1868–1910.
San Francisco *Chronicle,* 1906–1931.
San Francisco *Examiner,* 1866–1878.

PAMPHLETS AND DOCUMENTS

Baldwin, Mrs. S. L. *Must the Chinese Go? An Examination of the Chinese Question.* Boston, 1886.
Brooks, B. S. *Appendix to the Chinese Question,* San Francisco, 1877.
Chae Chan Ping v. *U.S.* Supreme Court of the United States, No. 1446, October 1888.
The Chinese Massacre at Rock Springs, Wyoming Territory, Sept. 2, 1885. Boston, 1886.
Correspondence Concerning the Chinese Immigration Treaties. U.S. Government document, Washington, D.C., 1904.
Culin, Stuart. *China in America: A Study of the Social Life of the Chinese in the Eastern Cities of the United States.* Philadelphia, 1887.

Draft of a Proposed Treaty between China and the U.S. Relating to the Exclusion of Laborers. U.S. Government, Washington, D.C., 1904.

Fiftieth Anniversary (1853–1903) Chinese Presbyterian Mission. San Francisco, 1903.

Gulick, Sidney L. *A Comprehensive Immigration Policy and Program,* 1916.

"The Invalidity of the Queue Ordinance of the City and County of San Francisco," *Ho Ah Kow v. Matthew Nunan.* U.S. Circuit Court. San Francisco, 1879.

Journal of the Fourth Session of the Legislature of the State of California, Jan.–May, 1853. San Francisco, 1853.

Lai Chin Chuen. *Remarks of the Chinese Merchants upon Gov. Bigler's Message.* Trans. by W. Speer in *Oriental,* San Francisco, 1855.

Liang Cheng, Chentung. *Note from the Chinese Minister to the Secretary of State on Chinese Exclusion and the Anti-American Boycott.* U.S. Government, Washington, D.C., 1905.

Memorial of the Six Chinese Companies, An Address to the Senate and House of Representatives of the United States. San Francisco, 1877.

Michie, Alexander, *The Political Obstacles to Missionary Success in China.* Hong Kong, 1901.

The Murder of M. V. B. Griswold by Five Chinese Assassins. Jackson, California, 1858.

Report of the Joint Special Committee to Investigate Chinese Immigration. Senate Report No. 689, 44th Congress, Second Session, 1877.

Report of a Meeting to Protest against the Chinese Outrages, Held in Steinway Hall, Mon. April 5, 1886. New York, 1886.

Report of the Special Committee of the Board of Supervisors of San Francisco on the Condition of the Chinese Quarter and the Chinese in San Francisco. Jan. 7, 1885, in Willard B. Farwell, *The Chinese at Home and Abroad,* San Francisco, 1885.

Robbins, Mrs. E. V. *Ten Years among the Chinese in California, 1873–1883.* San Francisco, Nov. 1, 1883.

Speer, William. *An Humble Plea Addressed to the Legislature of California in Behalf of the Immigrants from the Empire of China to This State.* San Francisco, Calif., 1856.

Talmage, J. V. N. *The Anti-Missionary Movement in South China.* Hong Kong, 1871.

BIOGRAPHIES, REMINISCENCES, TRAVEL BOOKS AND GUIDEBOOKS

Abeel, David. *Journal of a Residence in China.* New York, 1836.

Beadle, J. H. *The Undeveloped West, or Five Years in the Territories.* Philadelphia, 1873.

Beck, Louis J. *New York's Chinatown*. New York, 1898.

Benard de Russailh, Albert. *Last Adventure—San Francisco in 1851*. Trans. by Clarkson Crane. San Francisco, 1931.

Borthwick, J. D. *Three Years in California*. Edinburgh, 1857.

Bowles, Samuel. *Our New West, Records of Travel*. Hartford, 1869.

Brace, Charles Loring. *The New West*. New York, 1869.

Brewer, William H. *Up and Down California in 1860–64*. Ed. by Francis P. Farquahar. Berkeley, 1966.

Bridgman, E. J. G. *The Life and Labors of Elijah Coleman Bridgman*. New York 1864.

Bruff, J. Goldsborough. *The Journals, Drawings and Other Papers, April 2, 1849–July 20, 1851*. Ed. by Georgia Willis Read and Ruth Gaines. New York, 1944.

Buck, Franklin. *A Yankee Trader in the Gold Rush*. Compiled by Katherine A. White. Boston, 1930.

Burgess, Gelett. *Bayside Bohemia*. San Francisco, 1954.

Burnett, Peter H. *Recollections of an Old Pioneer*. New York, 1880.

Cantlie, James, and Jones, C. Sheridan. *Sun Yat Sen and the Awakening of China*. New York, 1912.

Chiang, Monlin. *Tides from the West*. New Haven, 1947.

Clappe, Louise. *The Shirley Letters from the California Mines*. New York, 1949.

Condit, Ira M. *The Chinaman as We See Him*. Chicago, 1900.

Conwell, Russell H. *Why and How the Chinese Emigrate*. Boston, 1871.

DeWitt, Frederic M. *An Illustrated and Descriptive Souvenir and Guide to San Francisco*. 1897.

Evans, Henry. *Curious Lore of San Francisco's Chinatown*. San Francisco, 1955.

Fang, John T. C. *Chinatown Handy Guide*. San Francisco, 1959.

Forbes, Robert Bennet. *Personal Reminiscences*. Boston, 1878.

Genthe, Arnold, and Irwin, Will. *Pictures of Old Chinatown*. New York, 1908.

Gerstäcker, Friedrich. *California Gold Mines*. Oakland, 1946.

Greeley, Horace. *An Overland Journey from New York to San Francisco in the Summer of 1859*. New York, 1860.

Haldane, Charlotte. *The Last Great Empress of China*. Indianapolis, 1965.

Harte, Bret. *San Francisco in 1866*. San Francisco, 1951.

Helper, Hinton R. *The Land of Gold, Reality versus Fiction*. Baltimore, 1855.

Hoffman, Hemmann. *Californien, Nevada and Mexico*. Basel, 1879.

Holinski, Alexandre. *La Californie et les Routes Interocéaniques*. Bruxelles, 1853.

Howe, O. T. *Argonauts of '49.* Cambridge, 1923.

Huie, Kin, *Reminiscences.* Peiping, 1932.

Hunter, William C. *Bits of Old China.* Shanghai, 1911.

———. *The Fan Kwae at Canton before Treaty Days, 1825–1844.* Shanghai, 1911.

Jackson, Helen H. *Bits of Travel at Home.* Cambridge, 1878.

Kimball, Charles P. *The San Francisco City Directory.* 1850.

Kipling, Rudyard. *Kipling in San Francisco,* from *American Notes.* San Francisco, 1926.

Knox, Jessie Juliet. *In the House of the Tiger.* Cincinnati, 1911.

Langworthy, Franklin. *Narratives and Scenery of the Plains, Mountains and Mines.* Princeton, 1932.

Lecount and Strong. *San Francisco City Directory.* 1854.

Lee Yan Phou. *When I Was a Boy in China.* Boston, 1887.

Leslie, Mrs. Frank. *California, A Pleasure Trip from Gothan to the Golden Gate.* New York, 1877.

Lewis, Oscar. *This Was San Francisco.* New York, 1962.

Lloyd, B. E. *Lights and Shades in San Francisco.* San Francisco, 1876.

Lo Jung-pang. *Kang Yu-wei, A Biography and Symposium.* Association for Asian Studies, Monograph no. 23. Tucson, 1967.

Loines, Elma (ed.). *The China Trade Post Bag of the Seth Low Family of Salem and New York.* Manchester, Maine, 1953.

Lowe, Pardee. *Father and Glorious Descendant.* Boston, 1943.

Lowrie, Walter (ed.). *Memoirs.* New York, 1849.

Lui, Garding. *Inside Los Angeles Chinatown.* Los Angeles, 1948.

Marryat, Frank. *Mountains and Molehills.* New York, 1855.

Meriwether, Lee. *A Tramp at Home.* New York, 1889.

Morrison, Eliza. *Memoirs of the Life and Labours of Robert Morrison, D.D.* 2 vols. London, 1839.

Neville, Amelia Ransome. *The Fantastic City.* Boston, 1932.

Newmark, Harris. *Sixty Years in Southern California.* Boston, 1930.

Nordhoff, Charles. *California For Health, Pleasure and Residence, A Book for Travelers and Settlers.* New York, 1878.

Norris, Frank. *Frank Norris of The Wave.* San Francisco, 1931.

Payne, Robert. *Chiang Kai-shek.* New York, 1969.

Peters, Charles. *Autobiography.* San Francisco, 1915.

Phelps, William Lyon. *Autobiography with Letters.* New York, 1939.

Pond, W. C. *Gospel Pioneering . . . 1833–1920.* New York, 1921.

Prieto, Guillermo. *San Francisco in the Seventies.* San Francisco, 1938.

Purdy, Helen Throop. *San Francisco As It Was, As It Is, and How to See It.* San Francisco, 1912.

Richardson, Albert D. *Beyond the Mississippi.* Hartford, 1869.

Sharman, Lyon. *Sun Yat-sen, His Life and Its Meaning*. Stanford, 1968.

Shaw, William. *Golden Dreams and Waking Realities*. London, 1851.

Sun Yat-sen. *Kidnapped in London*. Bristol, 1897.

———. *Memoirs of a Chinese Revolutionary*. New York, 1927.

Taylor, Bayard. *Eldorado*. New York, 1870.

Tiffany, Osmond, Jr. *The Canton Chinese*. Boston, 1849.

Van Norden, Warner M. *Who's Who of the Chinese in New York*. New York, 1918.

Williams, Albert. *A Pioneer Pastorate and Times*. San Francisco, 1879.

Wilson, Carol Green. *Chinatown Quest, The Life Adventures of Donaldina Cameron*. Stanford, 1931.

Wong, Jade Snow. *Fifth Chinese Daughter*. New York, 1950.

Wood, William Wightman. *Sketches of China*. Philadelphia, 1830.

Yung Wing. *My Life in China and America*. New York, 1909.

HISTORY AND SOCIOLOGY

Armentrout, L. Eve. "Reform and Revolutionary Parties among Overseas Chinese in the Americas." Ph.D. dissertation, University of California, Davis, 1975–76.

Bancroft, Hubert Howe. *History of California*. Vol. 7, 1891.

Barth, Gunther. *Bitter Strength, A History of the Chinese in the United States, 1850–1870*. Cambridge, Mass., 1964.

Bean, Walton, *California, An Interpretive History*. New York, 1968.

Beebe, Lucius, and Clegg, Charles. *San Francisco's Golden Era*. Berkeley, 1960.

Bodde, Dirk. *China's Gifts to the West*. Washington, D.C., 1942.

Bronson, William. *The Earth Shook, The Sky Burned*. New York, 1971.

Brown, Lawrence G. *Immigration: Cultural Conflicts and Social Adjustments*. New York, 1969.

Cain, Ella M. *Story of Bodie*. San Francisco, 1956.

Capron, Elisha Smith. *History of California*. Boston, 1854.

Carter, Marjorie M. *The Chinese in the United States and the Chinese Christian Churches*. New York, 1955.

Cattell, Stuart H. *Health, Welfare and Social Organization in Chinatown, New York City*. New York, 1962.

Caughey, John W. *Gold Is the Cornerstone*. Berkeley, 1948.

Chang Hsin-pao. *Commissioner Lin and the Opium War*, Cambridge, Mass., 1964.

Chen Ta. *Emigrant Communities in South China*. New York, 1940.

Cheng David Te-ch'ao. *Acculturation of the Chinese in the United States, A Philadelphia Study*. Foochow, 1948.

Chinn, Thomas W. (ed.). *A History of the Chinese in California, A Syllabus*. San Francisco, 1969.

Chiu Ping. *Chinese Labor in California*. Madison, Wis., 1963.

Cleland, Robert Glass. *California in Our Time, 1900–1940*. New York, 1947.

———. *A History of California, American Period*. New York, 1922.

Cohen, Paul A. *China and Christianity, The Missionary Movement and the Growth of Chinese Antiforeignism*. Cambridge, Mass., 1963.

Coleman, Terry. *Going to America*. New York, 1972.

Comber, Leon. *Chinese Secret Societies in Malaya*. Locust Valley, N.Y., 1959.

Coolidge, Mary Roberts. *Chinese Immigration*. New York, 1909.

Danton, George H. *The Culture Contacts of the United States and China, 1784–1844*. New York, 1931.

Davis, Sir John F. *The Chinese*. New York, 1836.

Dillon, Richard. *The Hatchet Men*. New York, 1962.

Dobie, Charles C. *San Francisco's Chinatown*. New York, 1936.

Dressler, Albert. *California Chinese Chatter*. San Francisco, 1927.

Drury, Clifford M. *San Francisco YMCA, 100 Years by the Golden Gate, 1853–1953*. Glendale, Calif., 1963.

Eaves, Lucille. *A History of California Labor Legislation*. Berkeley, 1910.

Edwards, E. H. *Fire and Sword in Shansi*. New York, n.d.

Elegant, Robert S. *The Dragon's Seed*. New York, 1959.

Fairbank, John K. *The United States and China*. Cambridge, Mass., 1972.

Fleming, Peter. *The Siege at Peking*. New York, 1959.

Freedman, Maurice. *Lineage Organization in Southeastern China*. Monographs on Social Anthropology, no. 18. London, 1958.

———. *Chinese Lineage and Society*. Monographs on Social Anthropology, no. 33. New York, 1966.

Fulton, Robert L. *Epic of the Overland*. San Francisco, 1924.

Gibson, Otis. *The Chinese in America*. Cincinnati, 1877.

Glick, Carl. *Double Ten, Captain O'Banion's Story of the Chinese Revolution*. New York, 1945.

Goss, Helen Rocca. *Life and Death of a Quicksilver Mine*. Los Angeles, 1958.

Gregory, J. S. *Great Britain and the Taipings*. New York, 1969.

Griswold, Wesley B. *A Work of Giants*. New York, 1962.

Heyer, Virginia. *Patterns of Social Organization in New York's Chinatown*, Ph.D. thesis, Columbia, 1954.

Higham, John. *Strangers in the Land*. New Brunswick, N.J., 1955.

Hittell, John S. *A History of the City of San Francisco*. San Francisco, 1878.

Howard, Robert W. *The Great Iron Trail*. New York, 1962.

Hoy, William. *The Chinese Six Companies*. San Francisco, 1942.

Hsu, Francis L. K. *Americans and Chinese*. New York, 1972.

————. *The Challenge of the American Dream*. Belmont, Calif., 1971.

Hsü, Immanuel C. Y. *Rise of Modern China*. New York, 1970.

Hsüeh Chun-tu. *Huang Hsing and the Chinese Revolution*. Stanford, 1961.

Hummel, Arthur W. *Eminent Chinese of the Ching Period*. 2 vols. Washington, D.C., 1943–44.

Isaacs, Harold. *Scratches on Our Mind*. New York, 1958.

————. *The Tragedy of the Chinese Revolution*. Stanford, 1961.

Jacobs, Paul, and Landau, Saul. *To Serve the Devil*. Vol. II *Colonials and Sojourners*. New York, 1971.

Jansen, Marius B. *The Japanese and Sun Yat-sen*. Stanford, 1970.

Konvitz, Milton R. *The Alien and Asiatic in American Law*. Ithaca, N.Y., 1946.

————. *Civil Rights in Immigration*. Ithaca, N.Y., 1953.

Kung, S. W. *Chinese in American Life*. Seattle, 1962.

La Fargue, Thomas E. *China's First Hundred*. Pullman, Wash., 1942.

Lang, Olga. *Chinese Family and Society*. New York, 1968.

Latourette, Kenneth Scott. *A History of Christian Missions in China*. London, 1929.

————. *A Short History of the Far East*. New York, 1947.

Lee, Rose Hum. *The Chinese in the United States of America*. Hong Kong, 1960.

Leong Gor Yun. *Chinatown Inside Out*. New York, 1936.

Lewis, Oscar. *The Big Four*. New York, 1966.

————. *San Francisco: Mission to Metropolis*. Berkeley, 1966.

————. *San Francisco Since 1872*. San Francisco, 1946.

Li Chien-nung. *The Political History of China, 1840–1928*. Trans. and ed. by S. Y. Teng and Jeremy Ingalls. Stanford, 1967.

Lieberman, Jethro K. *Are Americans Extinct?* New York, 1968.

The Life, Influence and the Role of the Chinese in the United States, 1776–1960, Proceedings/Papers of the National Conference held at the University of San Francisco, July 10, 11, 12, 1975. Sponsored by the Chinese Historical Society of America. San Francisco, 1976.

Lin Yu-tang. *History of the Press and Public Opinion in China*. New York, 1968.

Lyman, Stanford M. *The Asian in the West*. Reno, 1970.

————. *The Structure of Chinese Society in Nineteenth-Century America*. Ph.D. thesis, Berkeley, 1961.

McClellan, Robert. *The Heathen Chinee, A Study of American Attitudes toward China, 1890–1905*. Columbus, 1971.

McKenzie, Roderick D. *Oriental Exclusion.* New York, 1927.

McLeod, Alexander. *Pigtails and Gold Dust.* Caldwell, Idaho, 1947.

MacNair, H. F. *The Chinese Abroad.* Shanghai, 1924.

McWilliams, Carey. *Factory in the Fields, The Story of Migratory Farm Labor in California.* Boston, 1939.

Marden, Charles F., and Meyer, Gladys. *Minorities in American Society.* New York, 1968.

Margo, Elisabeth. *Taming the Forty-Niner.* New York, 1955.

Martin, W. A. P. *A Cycle of Cathay.* New York, 1897.

Mears, Eliot Grinnell. *Resident Orientals on the American Pacific Coast.* Chicago, 1928.

Miller, Stewart Creighton. *The Unwelcome Immigrant, The American Image of the Chinese, 1785–1882.* Berkeley, 1969.

Nee, Victor, and Nee, Brett de Bary. *Longtime Californ.* New York, 1973.

Olmstead, Roger, and Wollenberg, Charles (eds.). *Neither Separate nor Equal, Race and Racism in California.* San Francisco, 1971.

Palmer, Albert W. *Orientals in American Life.* New York, 1934.

Park, Robert E. *The Immigrant Press and Its Control.* New York, 1922.

Park, Robert E., and Miller, Herbert A. *Old World Traits Transplanted.* New York, 1969.

Paul, Rodman W. *California Gold.* Cambridge, Mass., 1947.

Phillips, Catherine Coffin. *Portsmouth Plaza, the Cradle of San Francisco.* San Francisco, 1932.

Purviance, Wilham Fenn. *Ah Sin and His Brethren in American Literature.* Peking, 1933.

Riis, Jacob. *How the Other Half Lives.* New York, 1957.

Rolle, Andrew F. *California, A History.* New York, 1963.

Sabin, Edwin L. *Building the Pacific Railway.* New York, 1919.

Sandmeyer, Elmer Clarence. *The Anti-Chinese Movement in California.* Urbana, Ill., 1939.

Schlegel, Gustave. *Thian Ti Hwui, The Hung League or Heaven-Earth League.* Batavia, 1866.

Seward, George. *Chinese Immigration in Its Social and Economic Aspects.* New York, 1881.

Siu, Paul C. P. *The Chinese Laundryman: A Study in Social Isolation.* Ph.D. thesis, University of Chicago, 1953.

Smith, William Carlson. *Americans in the Making.* New York, 1939.

———. *Americans in Process; A Study of Our Citizens of Oriental Ancestry.* Ann Arbor, 1937.

Social Science Institute, Fisk University, *Orientals and Their Cultural Adjustment.* Nashville, 1946.

Soulé, Frank. *Annals of San Francisco.* San Francisco, 1854.

Speer, William. *The Oldest and the Newest Empire.* Cincinnati, 1870.

Starr, Kevin. *Americans and the California Dream, 1850–1915.* New York, 1973.

Stewart, George R. *Committee of Vigilance, Revolution in San Francisco.* Boston, 1964.

Sung, Betty Lee. *Mountain of Gold.* New York, 1967.

Swasey, W. F. *The Early Days and Men of California.* Oakland, 1891.

Swisher, Earl. *China's Management of the American Barbarians, A Study of Sino-American Relations, 1841–1861.* New Haven, Conn., 1953.

———. *Chinese Representation in the United States.* Boulder, Colo., 1967.

Tan, Chester C. *The Boxer Catastrophe.* New York, 1971.

———. *Chinese Political Thought in the Twentieth Century.* Garden City, 1971.

Thompson, Warren S. *Growth and Changes in California's Population.* Los Angeles, 1955.

Tow, Julius Su. *The Real Chinese in America.* New York, 1923.

Townsend, L. T. *The Chinese Problem.* Boston, 1876.

Tung, William L. *The Chinese in America, 1820–1973.* Dobbs Ferry, N.Y., 1974.

Valentine, Alan. *Vigilante Justice.* New York, 1956.

Wakeman, Frederic, Jr. *Strangers at the Gate, Social Disorder in South China, 1839–1861.* Berkeley, 1966.

Waley, Arthur. *The Opium War through Chinese Eyes.* Stanford, 1968.

Wang, Y. C. *Chinese Intellectuals and the West.* Chapel Hill, N.C., 1966.

Wicker, Edward A. *The Presbyterian Church in California, 1849–1927.* New York, 1927.

Williams, Frederick W. *Anson Burlingame and the First Chinese Mission to Foreign Powers.* New York, 1912.

Williams, Stephen. *The Chinese in the California Mines, 1848–1860.* Unpublished thesis, Stanford, 1930.

Wollenberg, Charles (ed.). *Ethnic Conflict in California History.* Los Angeles, 1970.

Wu Cheng-Tsu. *"Chink!": A Documentary History of Anti-Chinese Prejudice in America.* New York, 1972.

Wu Ching-Chao. *Chinatowns: A Study of Symbiosis and Assimilation.* Unpublished dissertation, Chicago, 1928.

Wu Ting-fang. *America through the Spectacles of an Oriental Diplomat.* New York, 1914.

Young, Donald. *American Minority Peoples, A Study in Racial and Cultural Conflicts in the United States.* New York, 1932.

ARTICLES

"American Wife of a Chinese Missionary." *Literary Digest*, June 1, 1907.
"Annual Report of the Board of Foreign Missions of the Presbyterian Church in the U.S.A.," in *Proceedings of the General Assembly, 1889–1901.* New York.
Chin Gim. "The Chinese in America." *Foreign Missions*, October 1886.
"Chin Tan Sun." *Current Literature*, September 1900.
"Chinese Boycott." *Asia, Journal of the American Asiatic Association*, July 1905.
"Chinese in California." *Littell's Living Age*, July 1852.
C.J.W.K. "Dinner with the Chinese." *Hutchings California* Magazine, vol. 1, 1856–57.
Clemens, S. "Disgraceful Persecution of a Boy," from *Mark Twain on the Damned Human Race*, ed. by Janet Smith. New York, 1962.
Condit, I. M. "Interesting Anniversary," in *Foreign Missions*. New York, November 1884.
Culin, Stewart. "Customs of the Chinese in America." *Journal of American Folklore*, July–September 1890.
———. "The I Hing or Patriotic Rising, A Secret Society among the Chinese in America." *Journal of American Folklore*, February–March 1890.
Daniels, Roger. "Westerners from the East, Oriental Immigrants Reappraised." *Pacific Historical Review*, 1966.
DuFault, David. "Chinese in the Mining Camps of California." *Historical Society of Southern California Quarterly*, June 1959.
Falla, M. de. "Lantern in the Sky." *Historical Society of Southern California Quarterly*, March–April 1960.
Fong, Walter N. "Chinese Labor Unions in America." *The Chautauquan*, July 1896.
"From the Orient Direct." *Atlantic Monthly*, November 1869.
Healy, Patrick J. "A Shoemaker's Contribution to the Chinese Discussion." *Overland Monthly*, April 1886.
Holder, Charles F. "Chinese Press in America." *Scientific American*, Oct. 11, 1902.
Holt, Hamilton. "The Life Story of a Chinaman," in *Life Stories of Undistinguished Americans*. New York, 1906.
Karlin, Jules Alexander. "The Anti-Chinese Outbreaks in Seattle, 1885–86." *Pacific Northwest Quarterly*, April 1948.
Kuo Ping Chio. "Canton and Salem, The Impact of Chinese Culture upon New England during the Post-Revolutionary Era." *The New England Quarterly*, 1930.

Lee Chew. "Biography of a Chinaman." *Independent*, Feb. 19, 1903.

Lee, Rose Hum. "Social Institutions of a Rocky Mountain Chinatown," from *Social Forces*, October 1948.

Loomis, A. W. "Chinese Women in California." *Overland Monthly*, April 1869.

———. "Holiday in the Chinese Quarter." *Overland Monthly*, Feb. 1869.

———. "How Our Chinamen Are Employed." *Overland Monthly*, March 1869.

———. "Medical Art in the Chinese Quarter." *Overland Monthly*, June 1869.

Louis, Kit King. "Problems of Second Generation Chinese." *Sociology and Social Research*, January–February 1932.

———. "Program for Second Generation Chinese." *Sociology and Social Research*, May–June 1932.

Lyman, Stanford M. "Marriage and the Family among Chinese Immigrants to America, 1850–1960." *Phylon*, Winter 1968.

Lynch, George. "Two Westernized Orientals." *Outlook*, March 1901.

Miller, Joaquin. "The Chinese and the Exclusion Act." *North American Review*, December 1901.

Miner, Luella. "Chinese Students and the Exclusion Law." *Independent*, Apr. 24, 1902.

"Morrison Education Society Annual Reports." *Chinese Repository*. Macao, Hong Kong, 1841–1850.

O'Meara, James. "Chinese in Early Days." *Overland Monthly*, May 1884.

Ourada, Patricia K. "The Chinese in Colorado." *Colorado Magazine*, October 1952.

Pang, Sunyowe. "The Chinese in America." *Forum*, January 1902.

Paul, Rodman W. "The Origin of the Chinese Issue in California." *Mississippi Valley Historical Review*, September 1938.

Renner, George T. "Chinese Influence in the Development of the Western U.S." *Annals of the American Academy of Political and Social Science*, November 1930.

Ridout, Lionel U. "The Church, the Chinese and the Negroes in California, 1849–1893." *Historical Magazine of the Protestant Episcopal Church*, June 1959.

Robinson, Ednah. "Chinese Journalism in America." *Current Literature*, March 1902.

Seager, Robert, II. "Some Denominational Reactions to Chinese Immigration to California, 1856–1892." *Pacific Historical Review*, February 1959.

Sexton, Alexander. "The Army of Canton in the High Sierra." *Pacific Historical Review*, May 1966.

Sienkiewicz, Henryk. "The Chinese in California." *California Historical Society Quarterly*, December 1955.

Spier, Robert F. G. "Food Habits of Nineteenth-Century California Chinese." *California Historical Society Quarterly*, March 1958.

Stahler, Michael L. "William Speer, Champion of California's Chinese." *Journal of Presbyterian History*, Summer 1970.

Stimson, Marshall. "A Los Angeles Jeremiah, Homer Lea, Military Genius and Prophet." *Quarterly of Historical Society of Southern California*, March 1942.

Wheat, Carl I. (ed.) "California's Bantam Cock; The Journals of Charles E. de Long." *California Historical Society Quarterly*, September and December 1929.

Wortman, Roy. "Denver's Anti-Chinese Riot, 1880." *Colorado* magazine, Fall 1965.

MANUSCRIPTS AND DOCUMENTS

In the California Historical Society: The papers of Frederick A. Bee, Wellington C. Burnett, Reginald del Valle, Henry H. Ellis, William B. Fox, Eric Baker Hulbert, A. W. Loomis, Frederick W. MacCondray, reminiscences of William Buell Meek, scrapbook of Amelia Ransome Neville, journal to R. F. Putnam from William K. Spencer, letter of William Walker, Jr. Also declaration of intention for citizenship of Chan Yong, and marriage certificate of Ah Sum.

Correspondence of the Board of Foreign Missions of the Presbyterian Church, from the Chinese Missions, 1846–1888. Presbyterian Historical Society. Philadelphia, Pa., 1911–1923.

Dare, Richard Koch. *The Economic and Social Adjustment of the San Francisco Chinese for the Past Fifty Years, 1915–1965.* Unpublished manuscript, 1965.

Lee, Betty Jean. *The Life History of Ock Wing Lee.* Unpublished dissertation, Vassar College, May 12, 1971.

Letters to author from L. Eve Armentrout, Mr. Edward C. Chew, Miss Mansie C. Chew, Mr. Hilary Crawford, Dr. Clifford M. Drury, Mr. Ira G. Lee, and Mrs. William Z. L. Sung.

Speer, William. *The Founding of the Mission to the Chinese on the Pacific Coast*, San Francisco, n.d.